871.04　　　　　　　　179178
Sec
Sch
　　　Schoolfield.
　　　Janus Secundus.

**The Lorette Wilmot Library
Nazareth College of Rochester, N. Y.**

TWAYNE'S WORLD AUTHORS SERIES

A Survey of the World's Literature

NETHERLANDS

Egbert Krispyn, University of Georgia

EDITOR

Janus Secundus

TWAS 536

JANUS SECUNDUS

JANUS SECUNDUS

By GEORGE SCHOOLFIELD

Yale University

TWAYNE PUBLISHERS
A DIVISION OF G. K. HALL & CO., BOSTON

Copyright © 1980 by G. K. Hall & Co.

Published in 1980 by Twayne Publishers,
A Division of G. K. Hall & Co.
All Rights Reserved

Printed on permanent/durable acid-free paper and bound
in the United States of America

First Printing

The frontispiece is a copy of a portrait done by Jan van Scorel, which hangs in the Gemeentemuseum, the Hague.

Library of Congress Cataloging in Publication Data

Schoolfield, George
Janus Secundus.

(Twayne's world authors series ; TWAS 536 ; Netherlands)
Bibliography: p. 167–69
Includes index.
1. Secundus, Joannes Nicolai, 1511–1536.
2. Poets, Latin—Biography.
PA8580.Z5S3   871'.04   79-22767
ISBN 0-8057-6378-3

Contents

About the Author
Preface
Acknowledgments
Chronology
1. The Life, the Early and Occasional Verse, and the *Itineraries* — 13
2. The Elegies — 72
3. The *Basia* — 101
4. The Other Poetry — 118
5. Conclusion: Speculations and Surmises — 141
Notes and References — 149
Selected Bibliography — 167
Index — 170

About the Author

George Schoolfield received his doctorate at Princeton, served at Harvard, the University of Buffalo, Duke, the University of Cincinnati, and the University of Pennsylvania, and was appointed professor of German and Scandinavian at Yale in 1969. He has held Fulbright fellowships (1952–53, 1967–68, 1972), a Guggenheim (1955–56), and fellowships from the German Federal Republic (1964), Sweden (1975), and the Republic of Finland (1976); in 1978, he was named a fellow at the Institute for Advanced Studies in the Humanities at the University of Edinburgh. Among his publications are *The Figure of the Musician in German Literature* (1957), *The German Lyric of the Baroque* (1961), Fredrik Böök's *Hans Christian Andersen* (tr., 1961), Hagar Olsson's *The Woodcarver and Death* (tr., 1965), *Rilke's Last Year* (1969), *Swedo-Finnish Short Stories* (1974), A.M. Nagler's *The Medieval Religious Stage* (tr., 1976), and Henning Fenger's *Kierkegaard, The Myths and Their Origins* (tr., 1980); with Donald H. Crosby, he edited *Studies in the German Drama: A Festschrift in Honor of Walter Silz* (1974).

Preface

Although it is agreed that Janus Secundus was among the most gifted of the sixteenth century's Neo-Latin poets, and, thanks to his *Basia,* the humanistic lyricist best known to the broad reading public of later times, a monograph has never been devoted directly to his life and works: F. A. Wright's volume of 1930 was comprised, in the main, of translations;[1] Crane's dissertation of 1931, *Johannes Secundus, His Life, Work and Influence on English Literature,* puts its emphasis on the title's third subtopic.[2] (After Crane's study appeared, a wavelet of interest—mostly in the form of articles—arose, cresting with the admirable prose rendering of the *Basia,* the epithalamium, the odes, and the elegies published by Maurice Rat in 1938.[3]) The present little guidebook does not bring any "new material" concerning the poet's life; only a handful of the letters of Janus has come down to us, and his brothers did such an excellent job of collecting his works—abetted, at the opening of the seventeenth century, by the zeal of Daniel Heinsius and Petrus Scriverius—that there is scant hope of "hitherto unknown poems" turning up. What the manual does do, however, is to make use of the detailed research, carried out in the main by Dutch and Belgian scholars, which illuminates the corners of the poet's existence; investigations of this kind available to Crane were not employed by him—even as Adalbert Schroeter, in his long Secundus-essay (1909),[4] had remained unaware of secondary literature published outside Germany's boundaries.

The *Basia* have been the object of what critical attention Janus has received; likewise, the *Basia*—together with the epithalamium—have attracted gentlemen (and ladies) in search of what they thought would be elegant pornography. The remainder of what Janus wrote—the elegies, the odes, the poetic epistles, the epigrams, the funerary poems, the *silvae,* the travel descriptions in prose—has been given far less attention, save by Georg Ellinger.[5] The most recent translator of the poetry of northern humanism, Harry C. Schnur, takes his examples from the *Basia* alone; Fred J. Nichols again devotes his main attention to the famous cycle,[6] and rightly so: the *Basia* are the most dazzling of the poems of Janus. Yet the author has tried to accord the other poetry its due, in particular the elegies;[7] furthermore, he must confess a weakness for Janus' *Itineraries*. He trusts that the description of the poet's works will provide necessary insights into the stylistic and structural peculiarities of the verse; a section devoted exclusively to an analysis of Janus' style would have been difficult going for the reader whose knowledge of Latin is slight. Also, since a systematic account of the influence of the poetry on English, French, German, and Netherlandic literature is readily found in the pages of Crane, Laumonier, Ellinger, and Vorrink,[8] a chapter on this material has not been included here.[9]

All quotations from the Latin have been translated by the author, unless otherwise noted; flying in the face of providence, he decided to try to render the pieces of Janus' verse into equivalents of the distichs, hendecasyllabics, and "Horatian meters" which Janus used. For reasons of space, the Latin originals have been given only where necessary for linguistic illustration; Latin book titles, however, have been left untranslated, save where their meaning is not apparent from the context. The text employed has been that of the edition of 1821 [10] (called BB in the references), made by Pieter Bosscha with the aid of notes compiled in the previous century by Peter Burmann; [11] the *Opera* published by Herman van Borculo in 1541,[12] through the efforts of Janus' brothers, and the *Opera omnia* [13] edited by Scriverius, in the augmented edition of 1631, have also been consulted. As for the poet's first name, it has been decided to use the Netherlandic-Latin mixture, Janus, rather than the Latin Joannes or the popular Teutonization Johannes, which many of us know from the title of Goethe's poem "An den Geist des Johannes Secundus." After all, Janus has rightly been called (by J. P. Guepin) "de beroemdste nederlandse dichter," and he is rightly included in a series devoted to Netherlandic letters. The English forms of place-names have been used wherever possible—for example, Mechlin instead of Mechelen or Malines. Netherlandic humanists have been called by their Latin names, Spaniards by their Spanish ones—in both cases, in an effort to employ the more familiar form.

GEORGE SCHOOLFIELD

Yale University

Acknowledgments

Dougall Crane wrote that the poetry of Janus Secundus is "for the young and unsophisticated." As an undergraduate, trying to add some excitement to his Latin studies, the present author became an admirer of Janus Secundus; he must thank Professor Egbert Krispyn, the editor of the Netherlandic section of the Twayne World Author Series, for giving him the chance to transform his enthusiasm, decades later, into words and chapters. (Professor Krispyn has won an additional laurel by his monumental patience.) Gratitude must also be expressed to Mrs. Okey Richardson, former interlibrary loan librarian at the University of Pennsylvania, Mrs. Steven Ozment, interlibrary loan librarian at Yale, and Dr. A. W. Willemsen of the Koninklijke Bibliotheek at The Hague, for their aid in obtaining necessary materials, and, as well, to the author's former colleagues at the University of Pennsylvania, Dr. Rudolf Hirsch and Professors Guy T. Hollyday and Heinz Moenkemeyer. Mrs. Waltraut Lehmann of the Department of Germanic Languages and Literatures at Yale has shown not just great skill, but also great intelligence, in typing the manuscript. Thanks of a special sort must go to Gloria D. Schoolfield for her fortitude when the composition of the manuscript was rudely interrupted.

Chronology

1511	November 14: Janus Secundus born at The Hague.
1522–28	Studies at the Collegium Trilingue in Louvain (?).
1528	Family moves to Mechlin.
1529	Contributes to his brothers' translation of Lucian.
1530	Contributes to Joannes Dantiscus' *De nostrum temporum calamitatibus silva*.
1531	Composition of the Julia-elegies (?).
1531	Summer: Visit to Middelburg on Walcheren.
1532	March: To Bourges, by way of Paris, with his brother, Hadrianus Marius.
1532–33	Studies law at Bourges with Andreas Alciatus.
1532	August 9: Father, Nicolaus Everardi, dies at Mechlin.
1533	March: Return to Mechlin.
1533	May 28: Departure for Spain.
1533–34	Accompanies his brother, Nicolaus Grudius, secretary to Charles V, through Spain.
1534	May: Appointed secretary to Cardinal Tavera, Archbishop of Toledo; first signs of illness.
1534	Summer: Palencia.
1534–35	Autumn and winter: Madrid.
1535	February–May: Plans to accompany Charles V on his expedition against Tunis but falls ill.
1535	Late spring or summer: Leaves Spain.
1535	Spends two months in Poitiers with Cornelius Musius.
1536	Appointed secretary to Georges van Egmond, Bishop of Utrecht and pro-abbot of the Benedictine abbey at St. Amand.
1536	Summer: Receives news that he has been appointed secretary to Charles V.
1536	September: Leaves Mechlin for Brussels.
1536	September 24: Dies at St. Amand and is buried there.
1536	*Basia* published at Leiden; *Naenia in mortem . . . Thomae Mori* published at Louvain.
1541	*Opera*, collected by Nicolaus Grudius and Hadrianus Marius, published at Utrecht.

CHAPTER 1

The Life, the Early and Occasional Verse, and the Itineraries

I *The Family*

THE list of more or less selfmade men among the humanists is not limited to those who won fame in literature; the law and public administration had a crying need for men able to think clearly and to write good Latin, and Nicolaus Everardi (or Nicolaas Everaerts or Klaas Evertszoon) was one of these. Thus Janus Secundus had his obscure beginnings,[1] but at one remove: the hard work had been done by Nicolaus Everardi himself, who managed to transmit to his children a sense of duty, and of responsibility to a family tradition which he had created, as it were, all at once. The father of Nicolaus Everardi had been a sailor—a sea captain?—at Middelburg on Walcheren in Zeeland; he saw to it that Nicolaus, born in 1462, got a first-rate education —a praiseworthy ambition which comprises about all we know of the "nauta." His grandson Nicolaus Grudius, an elder brother of Janus, gives us (in a poem)[2] the additional information that the first name of the sailor's wife was the Horatian-sounding Glycera, a translation of the Dutch Zoetze and by no means a hint that the paternal grandmother had had classically minded parents. The history of the son of Zoetze and the sailor may be quickly told; but the reader should not forget the amount of toil it must have entailed. Nicolaus Everardi became doctor of laws at Louvain in 1493, served on the faculty there, and eventually, in 1504, was elected Rector magnificus. In 1505 Philip the Fair appointed him as a member of the Grand Council at Mechlin (in present-day Belgium); from there he went to The Hague, having earned for himself the Presidency of the Council of Holland. This was in 1509, two years before the birth of Janus; in 1528 he was sent back to Mechlin, where he served until his death, on August 9, 1532, as President of the Grand Council of the Netherlands.[3] He was a man of the greatest fairness, probity, and justness; in his honesty, he was (as Janus says of him in the long obituary poem which is the first number in his *Funera*, BB, II, 97–109) his own worst enemy, unwilling to take bribes, or to be threatened or cajoled. But it is precisely for this reason (Janus ends the poem with the father's charge to the son) that he is able to pass on the greatest treasure of all to his progeny, an unsullied name. Luckily for the stern old gentleman, Charles V knew how to reward virtue better than Henry VIII did; Nicolaus Everardi was made a Knight of the Golden Fleece by his master, and the move back to Mechlin may have been arranged by Charles to make up for the tribulations suffered during the years in The Hague. Very likely, Nicolaus Everardi was delighted to return to Brabant and to Mechlin, of which his wife was a native and where several of his children had been born.

Nicolaus Everardi's career had had another side, to be sure, *procul negotiis*. Good humanist that he was, he cultivated the literary giants of his time and place, carrying on an epistolary friendship with none other than Erasmus; they had met, no doubt, during Erasmus' first sojourn in Louvain (1502–04). Six letters from the archhumanist to the jurist are extant,[4] all of them falling into the late and happy Mechlin years, being dated from 1520 to 1525; among other news, they bring Erasmus' worries about German religious turbulence to the attention of his friend, living in Belgian serenity: "With what hateful things Luther burdens both learning [*bonas litteras*] and Christianity!" Apart from the friendship with Erasmus, the worthy official showed his quasi-literary side in his two books on legal topics, the *Topicorum seu de locis legalibus liber* and the *Consilia sive responsa juris*. It was with reference to these classics, which were reprinted during the next century, that Janus made a bold prediction in the *Funera*: his father would wander in the Elysian fields as an equal of Solon and Lycurgus, Numa and Ancus. (Janus strains a little in his effort to find appropriate parallels.) Earlier, Janus had devoted a remarkably dull epigram to the *Topica* of his still living father (I, 61), claiming immortality for the work in no uncertain terms. Janus was not immune to the humanistic disease of hyperbolic praise; the epigram is thirty-two lines long. However, he is able to come up with a small but saving poetic grace: in the catalog of comparisons by which he tries to show how long his father's fame will endure, he includes a memorable vignette. The paternal reputation will last: "As long as there're schoolboys to groan beneath the harsh rule of their tutors, / Damning the tedious hours, laden with sluggish delay" (BB, I, 344:19–20). Did we not know Janus' filial devotion so well, we might suspect that he was being impudent.

The *vie littéraire* was not Nicolaus Everardi's only source of relaxation; he was happily married to the lady from Mechlin mentioned above, Elisabeth, née van Blioul (or van Bladel) and Latinized into Elissa Bladella, calling Vergil's Dido and *blanda* ("charming") immediately to mind. With her he fathered eighteen children, if we are to believe a poem in which Nicolaus Grudius laments the passing of another son, Hadrianus (*DPB*, II, 647). At the time of the illustrious father's demise, only nine of his offspring were still alive (the others having died in infancy or childhood), six sons and three daughters. Of two of the three sisters, almost nothing is known. We catch a glimpse of them in the description of family life at Mechlin which Nicolaus Grudius left behind; an imaginary guest is told what sort of reception he has to expect from the vigorous girls: [5] "Casting their shuttles aside, dropping their labors, both seek to / Press your beloved cheeks, making a double assault." With their talent for kissing (which appears to have run in the family), the girls probably found husbands worthy of them. As for the third sister, Isabella, she took religious orders, eventually becoming the abbess of Saint Agatha at Delft. Here the father confessor was Cornelius Musius (1503–72), the author of a poem in praise of solitude and the cloistered life ("O beata solitudo, / O sola beatitudo"), and destined to be the victim of an incongruous fate: at the opening of the revolt against Spanish rule, he attempted to flee from Delft, fell into the hands of Count Lumey, the Geuze chieftain, and was tortured to death.[6] In his happy years, he had a fitting colleague in Isabella, to whom Janus—younger than she—addressed a poetic epistle (*Epistolae* I, 5): it is characteristic of Janus' attitude toward the Christian faith that he celebrates Isabella not for her holiness but for the splendid quality of her Latin.

Something of the same reserve can be sensed in what the young man had to say about one of the two brothers who had entered religious life, Petrus Hieronymus. The abbot in the

Premonstratensian monastery of his father's home, Middelburg, he died in 1530; Janus wrote an epitaph for him, the implications of which are not altogether clear:

> Peter, I lie here entombed; but now it's too late for your weeping:
>   I deserved your laments, when destiny's envious might
> Dealt me an unhappy lot—for what I now suffer is gentler—
>   Shutting the road that lay open to glorious honor.
>
> (BB, II, 125:4–8)

What had closed the way to honor? Death itself, or some physical frailty which had made Peter choose the monk's existence? We shall never know; we can only note the dexterity with which Janus once again avoids any hint of praise of the sacred solitude Peter had chosen, or into which circumstances had forced him.[7] What Janus thought of Franciscus, the other brother who left the world for the cloister, lies altogether beyond our ken, since Janus does not mention him.

Of the brothers who stayed in secular life—Everardus, Nicolaus Grudius, Hadrianus Marius, and Janus Secundus—the eldest, Everardus Nicolai (1498–1561) was the least interested in letters. As a young man, Everardus had begun as an advocate before the Council of Holland, and had been sent to Leeuwarden as a councillor of the newly established Frisian court of justice; returning to Mechlin in 1533 (or 1531: see note 43), he stayed there until 1541, when he was recalled to Leeuwarden. He capped his career by an appointment to his father's old post, as President of the Grand Council of Mechlin; a Knight of the Golden Fleece, again like his father, in his last years he was named a councillor to Philip II. Everardus, it is plain, took the father's place in the family; but Janus, it is equally plain, could be a good deal franker with him than he ever could have been with the awesome Nicolaus Everardi. There are four poetic epistles from Janus to Everardus, the first composed during a visit to the grandparents at Middelburg, the second (as well as, probably, the brief third and fourth) sent from Mechlin to Leeuwarden. The verse-letters are less lively than two later ones in prose: the youth is trying hard to impress Everardus with his skill at Latin description (of the Walcheren flood, in the first epistle) and exposition (concerning his notions of Frisian barbarism, in the second); in the third letter, with its accompanying

The Life, the Early and Occasional Verse, and the Itineraries 17

package, he demonstrates his mastery of another art to the dazzled Everardus: he has done a portrait-medallion of their father. (In the fourth epistle, Janus makes a poetic joke of the fact that he has nothing at all to say.) The verse-letters are the work of a likable showoff, bound to his brother by genuine affection. Janus had a pronounced taste for domestic situations, provided they belonged to others; he closes the second epistle with a pleasant passage depicting his brother's family—the letter, his messenger, has been charged to find out what Everardus, his wife, and their sons, that "miniature crowd," have been up to (BB, II, 32:49–50). (The "turba minuta" is a good touch, although it loses something of its freshness when we learn of its classical ancestry from the note in BB; Propertius [II, 29:3] uses it for the crowd of irate Cupids which, kidnapping him, lead him to the house of his mistress. Still, the loan could be looked at from another side: why not argue that Janus has given the words a new application and new life?[8]) A more pristine example of Janus' naturalness can be found at the end of the first prose-letter to Everardus from Spain: he can write no more, he says, because the air is filled with the ringing of bells, sounded for the funeral of matadors killed the day before: "they succumbed to their several wounds, and are thought to live in eternal glory (for here this is a splendid, festive, and, above all, solemn spectacle)" (BB, II, 277). Reading these lines, Everardus may well have felt a little dissatisfied with his brilliant career,[9] his Genoveva van der Goes, and his "turba minuta."

The brothers closer to Janus in age, Nicolaus Grudius and Hadrianus Marius, were likewise closer to him in gifts and disposition: both were poets of some stature, although their place in the history of Neo-Latin literature would be less prominent if they had not been the relatives of genius. Yet Janus also owed them a good deal; it was thanks to their efforts that the first edition of his collected works—*Joannis Secundi Hagiensis opera, nunc primum in lucem edita*—came out in Utrecht in 1541, five years after his death. It is thanks to them, too, that we know what we do about his last years: the *naeniae* of Nicolaus Grudius and Hadrianus Marius are good sources of information, as well as being expressions of heartfelt grief. After all, the three had had many experiences in common; although Janus was something of a junior partner (Nicolaus Grudius was six years older than he, and Hadrianus Marius four), all the boys had evidently begun their education with the same tutors, and may have been students together at Louvain. Janus made his poetic debut together with, and, as it were, under the protection of the others; it was a Latin verse translation of some of Lucian's dialogues with the title *Luciani libellus de non credendo calumniae . . . dialogorum* (Strassburg, 1529), to which the youngest brother contributed good-natured translations of "Doris et Galatea" and "Polyphemus et Neptunus." [10] He was so pleased with what he had done that he wrote an epigram (I, 38) on the little book, a tribute, by the way, to Lucian himself, "mocker of men and of the gods." And he shared each of his life's two foreign sojourns with one of the brothers, the year at the University of Bourges with Hadrianus Marius, the somewhat less than three years in Spain with Nicolaus Grudius, who had become one of the secretaries to Charles V.

Nicolaus Grudius himself was a curious amalgamation of the various talents which other members of the family represented separately. Like his father and his older brother, Everardus Nicolaius, he was gifted in affairs of law and state and learning. (He took the appellation "Grudius" because he was born during his father's Louvain years; the people of that scholarly town considered themselves to be descended from the Grudii, about whom Caesar reports in the fifth book of *The Gallic War*.) The Hapsburgs knew how to make use of his loyalty and his gifts during the Spanish years and later, in Italy, and paid him with a generosity which he deserved, according to almost all accounts. Made registrar of the Order of the Golden Fleece by Charles, and secretary of his privy council, serving Philip for a while in the same capacity, and then named tax-collector general of Brabant, he was sent by Philip on a diplomatic mission to Venice, where he is said to have died in 1571, to be buried amid pomp, circumstance, and reverence, "attended by the Senate and populace of the city." But there are dissenting voices which claim that Grudius did not share his father's famous probity: according to these, Mary of Hungary, regent of the Netherlands, discovered that Grudius was dipping his hand into the public till. He demanded and was refused a trial before the members of the Order whose registrar he was, fell into disgrace, and his trip to Venice was, in fact, a flight from debts.[11] As a humanist, Grudius had widespread connections: he was an epistolary friend of the Bishop of Alba, Marcus Hieronymus Vida (1490–1566), the author of the *Christias*, the Vergilian epic of Christ's deeds; he corresponded with the German Johannes Stigel (1515–62), the young poet-friend of Luther and Melanchthon who put "A mighty fortress" into Latin; and, owing to his long residence in Spain, he was quite at home in the world of Spanish humanism. As a poet, he tried the customary erotic line and wrote both about Narcissus and about his own love affairs, where he is a paler version of Janus. Yet, unlike Janus, he had a strong religious urge; twice bereaved, and perhaps mindful of the charges of peculation, Grudius published his *Negotia, sive poemata sacra* and *Piorum poematum libri duo* in 1566. The *Negotia,* among much else, contain a hymn to the Virgin Mary, written at Montserrat while Grudius was awaiting the arrival of his wife, accompanied by Janus, from Flanders; as for the "pious poems," their whole first book, of about fifty pages, is a paraphrase of the Lord's Prayer, whereas the second, in Georg Ellinger's forbidding phrase, "steht unter dem Zeichen der Busse" (III:1:81).

Grudius was a child of Louvain, Janus of The Hague, and Hadrianus Marius, born between them, came into the world at Mechlin. He got his names not as the result of family tradition and birthplace, as Nicolaus Grudius had, but because of the date, September 8: at once, Saint Adrian's Day and the Nativity of the Blessed Virgin Mary. *Nomen est omen* sometimes, but not in the present case; Hadrianus Marius was not particularly devout. His best quality is a sort of proto-rococo elegance; we cannot imagine his being driven to a rash or desperate deed—a deed, for example, like the sensational suicide of Gaspardus Ursinus Velius, court historiographer to the Emperor's brother Ferdinand. Henpecked beyond endurance, Velius had cast himself into the Danube (*DPB*, III, 450). Hadrianus Marius mocked the late Velius in an epigram: "Bearing his wife no more, the fool threw himself in the Danube, / And with an eager mouth Velius drank his own death." Similarly, when Janus, longing for the chilly Netherlands, wishes that he could leave Spain's burning sun and parched plains (in a famous elegy, "Patriae desiderium," III, 11), and sends the poem to Marius, he gets a reply in the shape of a parody: "When, Father Bacchus, shall I be able to part from these reaches, / When shall I ever behold Spain's purple mountains once more?" (*DPB*, III, 426). Janus called his brother "ingenious," and that is what he was, a clever versifier who won a humanist-international and a Dutch-local reputation (Cats did him the honor of translation), with his *Cymba amoris* (*Boat of Love*), which Janus (*Elegies* II, 1:37–40) says will be immortal.

In his public career, Hadrianus Marius proved himself to be as true a servant of the Hapsburgs as ever his father and brothers were.[12] The legal training he got at Bourges was supplemented by further studies at Milan and Louvain; after a year of practice in the courts at Utrecht, Marius was called to Mechlin to take Everardus' place upon the latter's second call to Leeuwarden. At length, when he was chosen as chancellor of Gelderland and Zutphen, he may very well have concluded that he could spend the rest of his life in comfortable and honorable circumstances. This he did, resident in Arnhem, for twenty years, from 1547 to 1567. But then the Duke of Alba appointed him to sit as one of those twelve unhappy judges whose job it was to try the "instigators" of the iconoclastic riots in Brussels; he died on March 21, 1568, less than three months before the execution of Egmont, the most famous of the many victims of the special court. In his elegy on his brother's death, Grudius implied that Marius had been ill for some time, and that he was fortunate in his passing: "You will not see the fatherland's chains, nor behold the fatherland's ruin" (*DPB*, II, 647).

Despite the fact that Nicolaus Grudius and Hadrianus Marius were lifted up to their brother's level one last time in the collection which the Belgian professor and sometime poet Bonaventura Vulcanius (de Smet: 1538–1614) published in 1612, *Poemata et effigies trium fratrum Belgarum,* their popularity already depended on that of their brother. Janus Dousa put matters in their proper perspective when, in the obituary poem he wrote in 1592 [13] on the distinguished citizen of The Hague Arnoldus Nicolai, he talked of old Nicolaus Everardi, and his sons and grandsons. (Arnoldus, the son of Everardus Nicolai, had handsomely fulfilled the family tradition by serving as President of the High Court at The Hague.)

> And from this father sprang the poet called Secundus,
> Second to none, he stood, I think, in place of all,
> And from this father sprang the well-known Nicolaus Grudius,
> And Marius, gone away to the courts of Gelder,
> And then the great father's successor, Everardus.

Nicolaus and Marius are set on the prosaic level of Everardus—

The Life, the Early and Occasional Verse, and the Itineraries 21

who did not pretend to be a poet at all. What do we read by them today? Their poems on Janus. Otherwise, the document by which we know them best is not from their hands, but rather dedicated to them ("clarissimis viris"). It is the essay which Gulielmus Cripius, successor-to-be of the unfortunate Marius in Gelderland and Zutphen, wrote while resident in France—sometime, we guess, before Marius was compelled to become a hanging judge at Brussels. The essay [14] was printed only after the deaths of Marius and Grudius, in a collection that came out in Paris in 1582, *Poetae tres elegantissimi emendati et aucti: Michael Marullus, Hieronymus Angerianus, Joannes Secundus*, a pioneering attempt to see Janus in the context of contemporary Neo-Latin literature (although not the first: that laurel belongs to Lilius Gregorius Gyraldus, in his *De poetis nostrorum temporum* [1551], to which Cripius refers); [15] the words of Cripius are an appropriate foreword to the collection, in which Janus follows upon two distinguished predecessors in the humanistic love-lyric, the great Greco-Italian Michael Marullus (c. 1450–1500), and Hieronymus Angerianus (c. 1490–1535), whose technical claim to literary fame is that he devised the name of the genre, *erotopaignion* ("a playful love poem"), to which Janus' own *Basia* belong. In part, Cripius' intent had been to flatter the surviving brothers and to impress them with his devotion to the work of the dead Janus, as well as with his Belgian patriotism. Yet, one more time, the brothers are made aware of how important "vester frater" was, and what a borrowed claim to fame they had.

II *Childhood and Youth*

Janus Secundus was born at The Hague on November 14, 1511, two years after his father had been appointed President of the Council of Holland, Zeeland, and Frisia. The general location of the house where he came into the world is known; it was in the street called "North End" ("Noordeinde"), about opposite the present Royal Palace. Its precise site was forgotten by the seventeenth century, although enthusiasm for the works of the poet was at its height; we owe this announcement of missing information to Constantijn Huygens, who brings the matter up in an epigram addressed to Janus' descendant Adriaan Vergoes, "the worthy relation of my Secundus." [16] Some mystery surrounds the cognomen Secundus; while the notion has been advanced that it was bestowed in order to distinguish him from an uncle likewise named Janus [17] (as was the case with Germany's Petrus Lotichius Secundus), it seems more likely that he was called Janus Secundus in memory of an elder brother, one of those nine other children of Nicolaus Everardi who, not reaching maturity, fell into limbo. From his own pen there are few traces of his Hague childhood; the principal of these is a dreamlike passage in the thirteenth elegy of the third book, with an atmosphere that seems—if the mild anachronism will be permitted—out of Poussin or Lorrain. The reminiscence is part of the *propempticon* Janus wrote in 1534 for his new Spanish master, Cardinal Tavera, as that worthy set out for Compostela; summoning "goatfooted satyrs" to accompany the Cardinal to the holy town, the poet remembers the "satyrs" of his boyhood; he too has been in a Dutch Arcadia: [18]

> If, once upon a time, through the springtime twilight, I saw him,
>   I alone of my friends, I saw the mighty god Pan,
> (When at a tender age we dashed through my fatherland's gardens,
>   Where my Hague burgeons and greens, near to the Cyprian grove,
> Busily all through the evening blowing our pipes made of hemlock,
>   And with our little fists beating out time on our drums)—
> If then you first did inspire me, a child, with the breath of the poet
>   That I might sing of the woods, meadows, and rivers and birds,
> And if you placed on my head the first garlands, and if then the laurel
>   Pleased me less than the wreath made for me out of the pine:
> Tell me now how Pan appeared, and how his face was and his color?
> (BB, I, 209–11:17–27)

A smaller, if more realistic, view of The Hague may be detected —at least, this is what the local patriot, H. E. van Gelder, thinks [19]—at the close of the epigram which Janus wrote to his former tutor, Rumoldus Stenemola: he looks forward to a time—he is writing, we guess, from Mechlin—of reunion in the city they had known together:

> And that spot will be found by us together,
> Consecrated to Venus and the Muses,
> Where the linden, set on the lengthy concourse,
> Spreads, far-reaching, its set of broad-swept branches,
> Breaking the summer's heat, disarming sunlight.
> (BB, I, 334–35:13–17)

Van Gelder sees a special Hague detail in the linden tree, which calls the "Lange Voorhout," the long, linden-shaded esplanade, to mind. Otherwise the scene, like that of the satyrs dancing in the twilight, is part and parcel of the favored imagery of Neo-Latin verse, here, in fact, represented in one of its most common forms, a *locus amoenus*, inhabited by Venus and the Nine.

Attempting to reconstruct the world in which Janus Secundus spent his early years, however, we cannot limit ourselves to the two stylized vignettes. As the favored residence of the descendants of William, Count of Holland and Holy Roman Emperor (1227–1256), The Hague reached a bloom of late medieval courtly life during the reign of Albrecht of Wittelsbach (1330–1404), Duke of Bavaria and Count of Holland; after his niece, the unhappy Jacoba (1401–1436), had been forced to surrender the last of her lands to Philip the Good of Burgundy, the aspect of the little town changed. The Burgundians preferred a more central headquarters in the Netherlands and chose Brussels; in The Hague, the ruling house was represented by a "stadhouder," a post held, for example, for two years by Philip's son Charles, "the Bold" (1462–64), and, in the days of Nicolaus Evarardi, by Hendrik of Nassau, the mentor of the future Charles V, a widely traveled man, interested in the arts and letters. Around the "stadhouder," in his great "Binnenhof," there was an extensive bureaucracy which now set the tone; the Hague housed the instruments of provincial government—the Treasury, the Chamber of Accounts, and the Council of Holland, Zeeland, and Frisia, of which, as we already know, Nicolaus Everardi became president in 1509. (Another element in the town should not be forgotten, the weaving industry established by the Dukes of Burgundy.) The bureaucracy was a group, thanks not least to humanism, with strong international ties; as van Gelder puts it, a "somewhat foreign-hued culture. [with], even at the beginning of the 16th century, that special Hague cachet." Plainly, Nicolaus Everardi was a leader in this little intellectual world, eventually to be seconded by another trusted servant of the Hapsburgs, the Frisian Bernard Bucho ab Aytta, who was made Dean of The Hague and a member of the Council in 1519, for services rendered. (His nephew was Viglius ab Aytta Zuichemus, a sometime school-comrade of Janus and the recipient-to-be of one of the more informative of the poet's verse epistles.) Some other representatives of this Hague culture in process of becoming were the well-to-do advocate Cornelis Hoen and his good friend Willem Claeszoon de Volder, "Gulielmus Gnaphaeus," the principal of The Hague's grammar school, and the author of that most subtle of Latin school-comedies, *Acolastus* (1529). (In 1523, neither Hoen's wealth nor his station could save him and Gnaphaeus from imprisonment for heresy; they had been attracted by Luther's teachings, and Hoen had been in correspondence with Luther himself. Eventually, Hoen was freed, and died shortly thereafter; Gnaphaeus was also freed, only to be arrested again: by the end of the decade he had begun his German exile, which lasted until the close of his long life [1493–1568].) Returning to The Hague's establishment, we should mention the schoolman and bibliophile Joannes Harius (Jan Dirckszoon van der Haer), who became known under the attractive sobriquet "Joannes de libris." In 1531, "John of the books" presented his celebrated library to Charles V, to be placed at the disposal of the Council of Holland, an event commemorated by Hadrianus Marius and Janus in epigrams (BB, I, 324–25); it is fair to assume that both young men, thanks to their father's position, had ready access to this "Musarum domus."

In a letter which Viglius Zuichemus, now become a famous jurist, wrote to accompany the gift of Janus' *Basia* to his protector, Johann Jakob Fugger, of the Augsburg banking family, the Frisian spoke proudly of the fact that Janus and he "had been under the same masters and in the same house for many years." [20] The historian of the Collegium Trilingue Buslidianum of Louvain, Henry de Vocht, suggests that, perhaps, Nicolaus Grudius and, surely, Hadrianus Marius and Janus were the pupils, in their father's home at The Hague, of Rumoldus Stenemola, the young master of arts from Mechlin (only ten years older than Janus himself), whom Nicolaus Everardi had taken into his service. Then, de Vocht argues, after training with this "house-tutor," they were entrusted to the teacher of Viglius, Jacobus Volcardus, a Hague schoolman; in October, 1522, Viglius was sent to Louvain, in the care of Volcardus. "Certain it is that the three brothers also went to Louvain, where they enjoyed both [Volcardus'] tutoring and his board and lodging, as Viglius apodictically attests; the preceptor helped Nicolas and Adrian, along with Viglius, in their studies in Arts and, later on, in Laws, of which [sic] they took some degrees, and so did John

Secundus, who must have applied himself to Jurisprudence at Louvain, as otherwise he would not have been able to promote in that science at Bourges, where he hardly stayed one year."[21] De Vocht also calls attention to a turn of phrase in Janus' epigram to Rumoldus:

> Wont, as ever you were to test my spirit,
> Then, when I, but a child, beneath your guidance
> Sang my songs, though my tongue was all unwilling.
> (BB, I, 333–34:5–7)

It sounds as though Janus had been a very small fellow when he enjoyed the instruction—in writing Latin verse?—of Rumoldus.

In short, de Vocht's educational argument runs: Stenemola was Janus' first tutor, and then, together with his elder brothers, Janus was in attendance at Louvain from 1522 to 1528. However, de Vocht, who was a spokesman for the greater glory of the Collegium Trilingue, ignores the fact that Janus nowhere mentions a Louvain sojourn in his works,[22] and that, in his *Vita* (chapter 14), Viglius does not name Janus among the fellow students at Louvain. The time-honored belief that Volcardus was Janus' first teacher has support in the *naenia* on Volcardus' death,[23] where Janus addresses him as "the first shaper of my Muses" (BB, II, 116:33). Tradition,[24] then, would seem to have circumstantial evidence on its side: Janus was tutored first by Volcardus, next by Stenemola, at home in The Hague. Stenemola was certainly the closer to Janus' heart, as a comparison of the formal farewell to Volcardus with the lively epigram to Rumoldus will show: Janus has sent him his "hot new loves," that is, some erotic poetry, for his criticism (BB, I, 333–34). (In gratitude to Rumoldus for the excellence of his teaching, Nicolaus Everardi got him a secretaryship at the Court of Holland which enabled him to marry [in 1527] and to set up a home in The Hague.)[25]

Whether at Louvain or in the house at 'The Hague, Janus acquired a technical mastery of Latin; he did not wait long to try it out in poetic creation. Sometime in his middle teens—Ellinger (p. 28) conjectures it was when he was fourteen or fifteen—Janus began an ambitious project called "In laucem utriusque Cupidinis" ("In Praise of the Two Cupids," BB, II, 212–16). Like most such adolescent projects, it did not get very far—no farther, in fact, than a description of the two cupids (the one produced by his mother "under the branches of the Elysian woods in the dewy vales," the other "born amid the flaming furnaces of Etna"), and a longish description, telling what monstrous and impossible things would happen if the world were not held together by "single-spirited love," a display on Janus' part of the rhetorical device called *adynaton*. The fifty lines of verse are worth passing attention, though, because they show Janus perhaps inspired by Greek reading (Bosscha conjectures that the poem was indebted to the *Symposium*, where Phaedrus complains that none of the multitude of poets has celebrated so ancient and mighty a god as Love), and because they show the young poet learning his trade. The youthful *epyllion* would have described both heavenly and earthly love, the one born cool, the other hot; but, in his career, Janus gave all his attention to the second kind.

In 1528, Nicolaus Everardi and his family moved to Mechlin, where the father assumed the last of his posts. It was a good time to leave The Hague, which had entered a period of economic decline—the weaving industry in particular was in a bad way. The city had also been visited by more sensational calamity. Even in the early days of the family's residence, the city had known civil disturbance, mentioned by Janus in his obituary poem for his father; in the year of Nicolaus Everardi's departure, the condottiere Maarten van Rossem plundered The Hague (March 6–9).[26] We wonder if the removal of the family to the south took place before or after the unpleasant event. The raid of van Rossem, who was "field marshal" in the forces of Karel van Gelre, the emperor's persistent opponent in the north, was aimed in particular at the imperial officials in The Hague; after all, it was Nicolaus Everardi's Council of Holland which, in 1516, had condemned two Gelderland nobles to death for breaking a peace concluded between the Emperor Maximilian and Karel. Did Charles V mean to put Nicolaus Everardi out of harm's way by transferring him to a safer post?

The move to Mechlin was a homecoming to a prosperous spot, in the heart of the Hapsburg holdings, which had enjoyed a special importance ever since the establishment there, in 1473, of the Grand Council of the Netherlands. The children of the Emperor Maximilian and Mary of Burgundy—Philip the Fair and Margaret—spent part of their childhood in Mechlin; in 1507, as regent of the Netherlands, Margaret set up her court there.[27] Twice widowed, she devoted herself to the life of the intellect and the arts; it was the most brilliant period in the city's history, affording a Netherlandic approximation of the Estes' Ferrara, the Gonzagas' Mantua. Even before her regentship Margaret had had Jean Molinet, the author of a poetic of the French "rhétoriqueurs," as her librarian; her court poet in the first Mechlin years was Jean Lemaire des Belges, Molinet's nephew and a forerunner of the Pléiade; her resident humanists had been—until their deaths in 1517 and 1524—Hieronymus Buslidius and Remaclus Arduenna, the latter a friend of such disparate personalities as Nicolaus Everardi and Ulrich von Hutten. For brief periods, she sheltered the great Spanish humanist Juan Vives and the German Cornelius Agrippa von Nettesheim, that mixture of Latinist, mystic, physician, and satirist, who wrote a treatise in her honor, *De nobilitate et praecellentia foeminei sexus*, even as Lemaire had collected her speeches, poems, and word games in the *Couronne Margaretique*. She corresponded with, and was visited by, Erasmus and Sir Thomas More (and Anne Boleyn was a sometime lady-in-waiting at her court). Among her architects she had Louis van Beughem and Rombout Keldermans, a member of the Brabant building dynasty, and the Savoyard Guot de Beaugrant; her musicians were Pierre de la Rue and Alexander Agricola; among her artists were Barend van Orley, her "peintre en titre," Jan Gossaert van Mabuse, her court portraitist, and Jan Cornelis Vermeyen, called Barbalonga, who would become the painter of Charles V's expedition to Tunis, as Janus Secundus was supposed to be its bard. Her court sculptor was Konrad Meit of Worms, "der gut Schnitzer, den Frau Margareth hat," as Albrecht Dürer said of him in his account of his trip to the Netherlands. Meit and Louis van Beughem were the leaders of the "Flemish carvers, Lombard gilders, / German masons, smiths from Spain," who undertook the decoration of the church of Brou—Matthew Arnold's Brou— which Margaret, after the sudden death of her second husband, Philibert of Savoy, had chosen as her last resting place, at the side of Philibert and her mother-in-law. Janus Secundus passed very close to Brou, on his way south along the valley of the Rhone in 1533; strangely, he did not make the small detour in order to visit the glorious outpost of the Mechlin renaissance.

On August 5, 1529, Margaret had performed a useful deed for

the well-being of the Netherlands; together with Louise of Savoy, the mother of Francis I (and the sister of the lamented Philibert), she had brought about the "Ladies' Peace" of Cambrai between the two hotspurs, her nephew Charles and his French rival; freshly arrived in Mechlin, Janus celebrated the event in an elegy (III, 8) which gets directly down to cases: "See, the pact has been joined by France with magnanimous Caesar, / See, a pact woven well, fashioned by feminine hands" (BB, I, 190: 1–2), and which has a commercial Netherlandic tone in its vision of the deities following in the wake of Peace: "Then comes, blundering of step, and far to the rear of the others, / Plutus, a god although blind, guided by Mercury's hand" (11. 21–22). With his address to the youths of the two fortunate nations, finally, Janus gives another indication of what he is to become: "Wage the wars of the night in combat with hot-hearted maidens, / And, in that place you desire, deal them the wounds that are dear" (11. 43–44). His entry into Margaret's court was not an inauspicious nor an impersonal one. A little more than a year later, after having dictated a last letter to Charles, urging him to maintain peace with France and England, Margaret died, and Janus again did his duty. Of his two epitaphs (spoken by the deceased, in accordance with time-honored practice), the first is the better; Margaret tells about her lineage and her claim to glory:

> I am she who has ruled the Belgians with lenient wisdom,
> And by means of that treaty, forged by the true hands of women,
> Blessed with a tranquil peace the peoples whom discord had riven.
> (BB, II, 112:3–5)

Then the regent rather haughtily points the moral; if such as she can be laid low by death, then her subjects must accept their insignificant passing gracefully. The subjects might have retorted that she at least could take consolation in her deeds—she had left a lasting monument behind.

In his cultivation of powerful friends, Janus had not only Mechlin but Brussels, some eleven miles away, as his theater.[28] In 1529, when he was eighteen, he sent a poetic letter, in distichs, to Aegidius Buslidius (Gilles Busleyden),[29] of which the first purpose was to thank Buslidius for the gift of an edition of Xenophon. The book giver was not—as Crane supposed—the youthful friend of Janus, who bore the same name, but the youth's father, councillor of the Chamber of Accounts of Brabant at Brussels, and an extremely wealthy man. If we understand who the recipient of the poem was, and how much power he had at his disposal, we shall not be surprised at the poem's tone. It is typical humanistic encomiastic verse, indulging in the hyperbole endemic in the Latin literature of the age. The gentleman to be thanked is called the "most celebrated glory of the Buslidian clan" at the outset, the mildest example of laying it on too thick; then he is treated to lengthy chains of "tot/quot" comparisons ("as many fishes as lie concealed in the ocean's depths," and so on for a dozen lines, "so many thanks and more are to be given you for the gift"), and a natural *impossibile* ("sooner will a warm spring despoil the greening elms of their leaves," again spun out for twelve lines, than the "thrice venerable name of the Buslidian house will perish"). The boy was already quite aware of the way the humanistic world worked in practical matters. Aegidius the Elder was a good man to be on the right side of, and, if his own contributions to scholarship had been small, he was a brother of the late Hieronymus,[30] Margaret's humanist, ecclesiastical member of the Grand Council of Mechlin, and the donator of funds for the Collegium Trilingue; Hieronymus' donation gets a tribute at the heart of the poem (BB, II, 77:23–31). But Janus cannot be distracted for long from his main purpose; he will sing of Aegidius for ever: "So, oh most splendid man, I shall list you among the age's / Very Maecenases, likest, in fact, to the first" (BB, II, 78:57–58). Janus did not let it go at that; the virtues of the father were visited on the sons. In the ode, "Ad Aegidium Buslidium juniorem," the poet asks for the return of a portrait-medallion which he has made, in order to redo it—Aegidius will not miss it, he says, fashioned as it has been by a novice hand, and, besides, he wants it for a more personal reason: wherever the poet may be, the medallion will bring Aegidius junior to mind (BB, II, 8:37–40). Still another of the sons, Nicolaus, likewise had a medallion made with his prognathous face in 1530, and likewise received an ode from the maker. Later in life, Nicolaus Buslidius became a staid member of Hapsburg officialdom in Brabant; but, in his youth, he displayed musical and amorous talents, (as lutenist and serenader of his mistress), if we are to believe the praise he gets from Janus (BB, II, 14–16).

Another great Brussels house which stood open to Janus was that of Maximilianus Transsylvanus, secretary and councillor of the emperor. Transsylvanus had an unusual career behind him: probably a "Saxon" from the German-language enclave of Siebenbürgen (Transylvania), he was the protégé (and maybe the illegitimate son) of Matthias Lang, who had been a secretary to Maximilian I and was presently archbishop of Salzburg. His wealth aside, the merchant-prince Transsylvanus had won a niche in the annals of exploration by his account of Magellan's trip around the world, *De Moluccis insulis* (1523),[31] based on his interviews of Sebastian del Cano, the second-in-command of the expedition. Unfortunately, Janus passes by these interesting facets of Transsylvanus to talk about his Brussels mansion in a superbly empty poem (*Epigrams* I, 45): Transsylvanus had seen to it that "we Belgians shall be less envious of Rome." In 1530, Francisca de Haro, the wife of Transsylvanus, died; Janus gave her two tidy epitaphs. In the first of them, he remarks on her "mixed blood," her father a Spaniard and her mother a Belgian, a suggestion of the internationalism prevailing in the Southern Netherlands in those days; while, in the second, he describes her qualities—she was good and she was beautiful, and her husband, bereaved, thrashes about in his empty bed. The next year Transsylvanus married a noble lady of Brabant.

Surely, Janus wished with all his heart that the cultural riches of the Mechlin-Brussels axis might be increased by the long-awaited return of Erasmus to the Netherlands; his hopes soared upon hearing the news that Mary of Hungary, the emperor's sister who had been appointed as the late Margaret's successor, was engaged in an attempt to get the master to come to Brabant —a plan which she did not abandon, in fact, while Erasmus lived. Countless rumors were abroad about the aged celebrity, and Mary's project gave rise to still more of them; Janus contributed his mite with an elegy (III, 5) which strikes a modern eye as making a somewhat gloomy appeal to the old man. If Erasmus dies in his homeland, a stranger, come from afar, will say: " '. . . Happy you are, oh land, to have borne such an offspring! / In my regard you are not less than great Latium itself' " (BB, I, 173:23–24), a sentiment, come to think of it, which is not very different from what Janus said about the "magnificas aedes" of Transsylvanus.

To be sure, a humanist of international repute did loom on

the youth's Mechlin horizon: it was the German-Pole Johannes Dantiscus (1485–1548),[32] born a Flachsbinder at Danzig and quick to change his humble name for the more dignified city derivation. A student at Cracow, a priest, a soldier in the catastrophic war of King John Albert against the Turks in Moldavia, a traveler in Palestine and Egypt, he then entered the diplomatic service of Sigismund, John Albert's successor. In 1515, Sigismund met the Emperor Maximilian in Vienna, and loaned him his skilled negotiator to make peace with the Venetians: this was Dantiscus' first direct contact with the Hapsburgs. Subsequently (1522), Sigismund despatched Dantiscus to Spain, which he approached circuitously, going by way of Mechlin, where he first met Margaret; as time passed, his services to the House of Hapsburg and to Charles became ever more valuable, culminating with his presence in the emperor's retinue when Charles was reconciled with Pope Clement—later in the same year (1530), he accompanied Charles to the diet of Augsburg. In 1532, Dantiscus was recalled to Poland by King Sigismund; his sunset years—during which he cultivated an old friendship with Copernicus—were spent as Prince-Bishop of Ermland, at Frauenburg. Himself a poet and a protector of literary men, Dantiscus was not inclined to pay much attention to religious differences: at the Augsburg diet, he took up with Helius Eobanus Hessus, Luther's "rex poetarum," he corresponded with Joachim Camerarius the Elder, Melanchthon's friend, he played Maecenas to Gnapheus, the author of *Acolastus,* who had gone to Elbing in West Prussia as a Lutheran refugee (indeed, Dantiscus came over from Frauenburg to see a performance of the famous play), and he gladly received the visits of Georg Sabinus, the Latin poet in the service of Albrecht of Prussia and the first rector of the Protestant university of Königsberg.

Just how Janus Secundus came to the attention of Dantiscus is not altogether clear. The diplomat-priest had for a long time been in contact with the humanists of Margaret's court, in particular with Remaclus Arduenna, the secretary of Margaret's privy council; and he had had the chance to renew his Mechlin acquaintances, and make new ones, during the emperor's residence at Brussels, from January 24 to March 31, 1531, or later still—Dantiscus stayed on in the Netherlands, mostly at Antwerp, until the spring of 1532, when he departed for the East. It is almost beyond question that Janus made his personal acquaintance during this time, However, in 1530, Dantiscus had already included two poems on imperial subjects from Janus' hand—the elegy (III, 8) on the peace of Cambrai and an ode on the coronation of Charles at Bologna (Odes, I)—with the third edition of his own poem, *De nostrum temporum calamitatibus silva,* which Dantiscus had written for the formal reconciliation between the emperor and the pope: the two political pieces are thus the first original poems by Janus to appear in print.[33] A possible answer to the question which arises—how Dantiscus had heard of Janus before the beginning of his Netherlands sojourn of 1531–32— may lie in a letter which Cornelius de Schepper, Dantiscus' particular friend in the Netherlands, wrote to the Prince-Bishop in 1545: de Schepper mentions one Petrus Clericus as being among the Netherlanders who wish to get some word from Dantiscus, adding that Clericus was "your frequent guest at Bologna during the coronation of the emperor" (de Vocht, *Dantiscus,* p. 374). Clericus of Antwerp was the closest friend of Janus Secundus during the Mechlin years, and it is not unlikely that Petrus Clericus would have shown his host, Dantiscus, poems of the brilliant Janus with a close bearing on events to which Dantiscus and Clericus had just been witness.

The young poet had every reason to feel flattered by the attention which the "Regis Poloniae orator" had paid him, and by his inclusion in Dantiscus' timely volume; in fact, he may have hoped that Dantiscus, by his generosity, may have made the master of Christianity aware of his name. Janus repaid Dantiscus with an elegy (III, 4), in which he called him "the true adornment of a pious king" (a hasty bow to Sigismund) and a Phoenix who, after death, would have a new life by force of his generous spirit and sweet song. The poem is blessedly short; a longer address to Dantiscus is made in the poetic epistle (I, 7), which leads us into the world of plastic arts, and Janus' gifts on this line. Beforehand, however, some last remarks should be made about Dantiscus' literary contribution to the career of Janus.

In the epistle, as in the elegy, Janus celebrates the honor which Dantiscus has rendered the Netherlands by his very presence: "Guest, at your presence the Scheldt is captured by utter astonishment, / Thinking that it has become like to the Ister in might" (BB, II, 39:5–6). The mention of the Ister, the Danube, reminds us that, in his day and later, Dantiscus was reckoned as a member of Germany's band of Neo-Latin poets, not Poland's; and he may have served as the main channel by which Janus Secundus got to know the Latin verse of his next-door neighbors. Sadly, Conrad Celtis (1459–1508), who in the direct sensuality of his erotic verse resembles Janus, is not mentioned at all by Janus, and Petrus Lotichius Secundus was only eight years old when Janus died. One poem by Janus, the eighteenth elegy of the third book, tells almost all of what we know about Janus' readings, or acquaintanceships, in German-Latin verse: in it Helius Eobanus Hessus (1488–1540), in Janus' words, "the greatest bard Hessia has produced," is mentioned, as well as the Silesians Georg von Logau (1500–53) and his friend Ursinus Velius (1493–1539), whose unusual death has already been noted; farther on in the poem, Georg Sabinus (1508–60), is given what may be more than perfunctory praise, and it is amusing to remember that two of the best travel books of humanism, Sabinus' verse *Hodoeporicon itineris italici* and Janus' prose itineraries came into being at about the same time. The catalog of names in the elegy does not tell us much, to be sure, and we are almost wholly in the dark about the identity of the Joannes Ottingerus,[34] German and poet, to whom the elegy is addressed; but is it accident that Janus' list of German poets is a list, as well, of Dantiscus' German literary friends—Hessus and Logau from the Augsburg diet, and Velius through correspondence from the same year? Sabinus, to be sure, could have first entered Dantiscus' personal ken later, in the Ermland days; as Janus expressly states, Sabinus was brought to his attention by Ottingerus, during a trip he had recently made.

The seventh epistle of Book One (BB, II, 38–41), to Dantiscus, was intended to accompany some products not of Janus' pen but of his chisel, portrait-medallions of Charles V ("I send you the Caesar whom I cast into several forms") together with a medal bearing the features of Julia, the present object of Janus' affection. Janus was persistently modest about the products of his second muse, and he spends a good deal of space in the epistle to Dantiscus talking about his own ineptitude: "Alas, what can you expect from a poet who's turned to the chisel" (l. 9). Crane translates the closing words of the line, "a caelatore poeta," as "from a chiselling poet," and (although the painful ambiguity was not intentional), Janus is indeed disingenuous as he makes his pleas of faulty skill. For, as Dantiscus himself knew, Janus had been practicing these "new arts" for some time. If we assume that the epistle was written toward the end of 1531 (and a prose letter to Dantiscus, dated December 31, 1531 [de Vocht, *Dantiscus,* p. 123], refers to the sculpture of Julia, mentioned in the poem letter), then Dantiscus already possessed a portrait-medallion which Janus had made of him. Nor was this a beginner's work; Janus had done his first medallion in 1528—at any rate, the earliest medallion that has been preserved, in a copy. It is of Nicolaus Everardi, depicting him at the age of sixty-six, at the peak of his career, when, on September 20, 1528, he took office as the president of the Grand Council; a second medallion from 1531 also has "praeses Everardi" as its subject.

If Janus was able to do his father's portrait immediately upon the family's arrival in Mechlin, he must have received considerable training in the art form at The Hague. But there can be no question that the Mechlin atmosphere encouraged him; Janus' admiration for one member of "Madonna Margaretha's" stable of artists in particular, the Munich etcher and painter Nicolaus Hogenberg, is attested to in his verse, in the epigram he wrote for a series of engravings done by Hogenberg to commemorate the coronation of Charles at Bologna:

Gaze on the emperor's troops and the Holy Father's together,
    Ordered in ranks; then salute thrice that great cunning of hand,
Which was able to draw from the heart of obstreperous metal
    So many eminent names, giving them permanence here.
See, Hogenberg did this work, the artist, that all through the ages,
    Posterity, you could behold, living, this deed of the past.
(BB, I, 329:1–6)

How close an acquaintance Janus was of Hogenberg we do not know; we can be sure, however, that he became the intimate, in time, of another contemporary artist, and one of considerably greater stature—Jan van Scorel, who has been called "the greatest painter of the Netherlandic renaissance." He was born at Schoorl near Alkmaar in 1495, and was thus Janus' elder by some sixteen years; he had studied at Haarlem, then at Amsterdam, and finally at Utrecht (in 1517–18) with Jan Gossaert, the sometime ornament of the Mechlin court. In search of further training, he undertook a great journey which took him by way of Nürnberg (and Albrecht Dürer) to Carinthia, then to Venice and, finally, to Jerusalem; stopping off in Rome on the way back, he got the attention of the new pope from the Netherlands, Hadrian VI. By September, 1523, generous Hadrian was dead, and, a year later, Jan van Scorel (who had been given a prebend at Utrecht by his fellow countryman before the latter's passing) returned to the homeland. J. F. M. Sterck [35] assumes that Janus Secundus wrote the first of his two poems to Scorel, which bears the subtitle *propempticon*, summoning Scorel back to the Netherlands when Scorel was in Rome (1520–24); this would win for the *propempticon* the distinction of being probably the earliest verse (its rival would be the epic about the two cupids) we have from Janus' hand. The poem consists of only seven lines, of which the opening would not lie beyond a clever boy's power— "Go forth, happy of foot, to your native cities, / Oh renewer of art divine, go onward" (BB, I, 326:1–2)—while the middle portion is lifted from Horace's *propempticon* for Galatea (III, 27:5 and 15–16), and the remainder is again elementary. However, the poem's origin is more likely of a different nature. For one thing, *propempticon* is an inaccurate word, if we follow Sterck's argument, since it designates a poem meant to accompany a departing friend.[36] For another, Janus sent the same poem (with the second line changed, to "Oh, good aider of Phoebus' art") to Dantiscus in a letter of February 21, 1532.[37] If the poem was written (or recast) to accompany van Scorel away from Mechlin to Utrecht, in 1533,[38] after Janus' return from Bourges, the generic word would be used correctly (Scorel was on his way to his "native cities" of North Holland), and the splendid praise would be deserved. In a prose letter to Scorel, written on the eve of his departure for Spain (May 8, 1533), Janus speaks of the interest Scorel showed in him "when you were here." The author of the *propempticon* was not thirteen but twenty (thinking of the Dantiscus version) or twenty-one.

The acquaintanceship between Jan van Scorel and Janus was one in which the older man's approval was constantly sought; in his verse-epistle to the painter (BB, II, 81–82), Janus refers to their common "Batavian" heritage, calls him his teacher (Janus tried his hand at painting, according to his tombstone), mentions a "few poems . . . offspring of a devoted spirit," which he has recently "sung in harmony" for him, and says that he looks forward to visiting him in Utrecht, and to greeting him in Mechlin again. In the prose letter Janus tells Scorel that he wants an opinion of the portrait-medallion he has just made of

Jean de Carondelet, one of the emperor's most powerful ecclesiastical advisers: "I beg you, judge it sincerely, for I am hardly persuaded that the opinion you offered me concerning my portrait of Julia was accurate. Perhaps her image dazzled your eyes as it did mine" (BB, II, 273). (The reference to Julia's portrait is interesting; Scorel's much-discussed portrait[s] of Janus—see pp. 70–71—show Janus with the medallion of Julia in his hand.) Doubtless, Scorel had been flattering about the portrait-medallion of the lady fair; now, Janus is appropriately modest.

An appreciation of the medallion-art of Janus is made the more difficult by the fact that he used soft Kelheim stone for carving his dies, and the castings were often made in base metals: following the practice of the Augsburg medallion-makers, he turned out works that could not easily withstand the tooth of time. Of the eighteen medallions known to have existed (or nineteen, if we include the Erasmus portrait attributed to him), fourteen have come down to us: a small number of works, and in bad condition, by which to judge an artist. His contemporaries had a high opinion of this side of his production. Ronsard regarded the double artistry of Janus as a cause of his fame:

> Jean Second, de qui la gloire
> N'ira jamais défaillant,
> Eut contre elle la victoire
> Par ces armes l'assaillant:
> Dont la main industrieuse
> Animoit également
> La carte laborieuse
> Et la table dextrement. . . .[39]

(Does "la table" refer to Janus' efforts as a painter, of which no trace remains, or to the plastic arts in general?) Some moderns have been equally enthusiastic about his work as a *médailleur*, de Vocht claiming that "his talent as medallist . . . made him as great as that of poet [sic]" (History, II:348), and the numismatist Simonis, expressing an expert opinion, if somewhat colored by Belgian patriotism, says that he had "le rare privilège d'atteindre au sommet de la poésie et de l'art glyptique." [40] The literary scholar remains inclined to regard the medallions as ancillary works. They show the poet-artist in touch, here as in his poetry, with the small forms of classical antiquity; he was inspired by the Roman medallions contained in the collections of the regent, Margaret. They show how—as in the case of his Latin verse—he took what was in essence a fashion, even a fad, and, by energy and passion, made it into something peculiarly his own. Above all else, they reveal Janus as a renaissance man. Surely, Janus was a long way from being a Leonardo or a Benvenuto, but there are certain signs that, had he lived, he might have become more than a love poet and a brilliant amateur in the annals of a small art in a small country.

The medallions also offer a little aid to the investigator trying to fill in the empty spaces in Janus' biography. From the Mechlin days, he portrayed—in addition to the Busleydens, Carondelet, Dantiscus, his father, and, of course, Julia—some other acquaintances or friends. The medallion of Joachim Sterck von Ringelberg is from 1529, and is probably a souvenir of the polyhistor's visit to the Mechlin court the previous year. Some doubt exists that the Ringelberg medallion is in fact by Janus, although Simonis pleads the case strongly, and de Vocht (as usual) argues that Ringelberg had been a much senior fellow of Janus at Louvain; however, no mystery surrounds the portrait of Janus Lucius Brassicanus, a Swabian humanist from Tübingen and a friend of Dantiscus.[41] Janus wrote an accompanying epigram for the Brassicanus medallion, in which he engaged in some playful reflections on the "muteness" of the plastic arts—a statement which should be remembered: anxious for an exact expression of his experiences and emotions, Janus had good reason for choosing poetry and not Kelheim stone as his main instrument:

> I have sculpted whatever my hands and the heavens would let me,
>   Yet you behold a head lacking in spirit and voice;
> Though in this miniature image you long may endure through my efforts,
>   Gazing on ages to come, nevertheless you'll be mute
> Therefore, oh Janus, if you have a will to break the stone's silence,
>   Now, by means of your song, give it perpetual sound.
>   (BB, I, 348–49)

Still another recipient of both medallion and poetry was Franciscus Craneveldius (Craneveld).[42] Born at Nijmegen in

1485, a friend of Erasmus, More, and Vives, and, later, of Dantiscus, he had come to Mechlin in 1522 as a member of the Grand Council, a part of which body he remained until his death in 1564. The friendship between the humanist-jurist, a colleague of Janus' father, and the bright young man is a pleasant chapter; the latter was not put off by the former's age or station, and listed him (as he did another learned member of the Council, Gerardus Mulardus [Gerard Mulaert], of whom he may also have made a medallion) as being among his chief friends:

> Working for you with his prayers, and beseeching the powers of heaven,
> Good Craneveldius comes, first in the order of friends;
> Faithful for many a year, with a love that is like to a father's,
> Trusty Mulardus is next, guarding your family and you.
> (BB, I, 202-3:43-46)

This sounds sufficiently formal, whatever devotion shines through; the epigram to Craneveldius, though, shows that Janus felt close enough to him to make fun of him, and Craneveldius himself ("homme d'un abord agréable et d'un coeur excellent," Simonis calls him) was not the sort to be upset. Quite simply, Janus says, Craneveldius is a better man than he is a poet; the reader should note that the epigram (with some gentle irony?) is addressed to "Franciscus Craneveldium senatorem, poetam":

> As the swift wave of the river, suddenly come as a blessing,
> Cools the poor traveler's mouth, parched from the heat of the sun,
> In the same way, mighty man, your poem refrigerates swiftly
> Whatever flame's to be found, firing a passionate heart.
> (BB, I, 349)

Janus had friends of another sort as well—young men, of his own age, whom he did not need to learn from or to flatter, members of the circle of intimates slowly decimated by travel or by marriage (the second fate was worse, in Janus' opinion), but still maintained as a refuge for its surviving bachelors. After having seen Hadrianus Goesius—Adriaan van der Goes, a member of the distinguished family which produced painters, historians, and jurists—fall prey to "the soft chains of matrimony,"

Janus consoled himself and the other survivors with verses in the Second Asclepiadean:

> Meanwhile, since you have gone, and we are left to mourn,
> But a handful of comrades here,
> Friends unfettered by vows such as those you have sworn—
> While old age, silver-topped, is far,
> Let us garner the joys granted by love that's free.
>
> (BB, II. 11:28-32)

Among Janus' fellow gallants were Carolus Catzius, Petrus Clericus, and still another Catzius, Franciscus, who turns up only once in Janus' poems, in an ode where Janus assures a bereaved Isabella that an absent third party—Franciscus was in Louvain—will be faithful to her. Indeed, Janus is peculiarly solicitous of her well-being; his concluding compliment to her—"Oh, how lucky you are, beauty with torch-lit eyes"—should have been sufficient, provided she understood Latin, to make her forget the industrious Franciscus altogether. As for Franciscus' presumptive brother, Carolus, he received a New Year's greeting from his friend, on the theme of eat, drink, and be merry:

> Ancient god of a two-fold face, old Janus,
> He who makes new the sinking year in silence,
> Presently, dear Carolus, is upon us!
> Why delay? Let us live, and, nonbelievers
> In the future, capture the swift year's passage.
>
> (BB, I, 291-92:1-5)

These injunctions out of the way, Janus went on to say which goddess would be especially favorable to Carolus' prayers (the goddess born of the sea), and what rewards she would give him —lovely girls who seek out lucky Carolus, girls asking neither thanks nor money. Later on, the girls seem to have worn Carolus out; from the eleventh elegy of the second book we learn that he has joined the emperor's armies in order to escape them. But, Janus says, his dodge will avail him nothing, for battle does not free the soldier from the torments of love, and Venus, her passions afire, has never left the side of Mars. Janus spins out the joke: Catzius has made a particularly bad choice of army if he is resolved to be an ascetic, for Venus protects the troops of the emperor, the descendant of Aeneas. As a matter of fact, "In the

midst of the fray, when lightning shoots forth from Mars' aegis, /
Your sweet mistress's form sadly will rise up before you" (BB,
1, 155:19–20). But then Carolus Catzius returns to the darkness;
we learn no more about him from this elegy bearing his address,
since, pacifistic humanist that he is, Janus uses the rest of the
poem to make an attack on war in general and artillery in particular—the child of a simpler age, he found it to be an inadmissible weapon.

Setting out for Spain in 1533, Janus took solemn leave of his
friends, proceeding by age and rank; first come the venerable
Craneveldius and Mulardus, then the youths:

> Here is Petrus, who's shared my pleasures and moments of sadness,
>   Glad-hearted Petrus, who leads golden Apollo's great choir;
> Next comes Carolus—what polish, what morals are yours, white as
>   snowdrifts!
>   Even my judgment day will not give me cause to forget you!
> Live happily, friends, though I'm held by the ends of the earth in
>   confinement—
> Happily, though I may live, happily, though I may die.
>
>   (BB, I, 204:57–62)

No doubt Petrus Clericus—remembered by posterity because
Janus liked him so much—was the closest of all the friends from
the halcyon days at Mechlin. In Aragon, Janus wrote a poetic
epistle to Petrus, meaning it as an accompaniment to an allegorical poem of which he was very proud, the *Reginae pecuniae
regia;* the traveler gives expression to his feelings for the stay-at-home friend:

> Jesting, we're able to fill life's harshness with lingering laughter;
>   Marble-hewn castles of kings get but our smiles and our scorn;
> Yet, of a thousand ills, there is none which can hurt me more cruelly
>   Than the bereavement I feel when he is far from my eyes.
> I have known all of his games, and known all his moments of
>   graveness,
>   Just as he knows when I jest, and when my sombre side rules.
> I speak of him whose good name is preserved in that song of my
>   making,
>   When I have sung of the stars lighting my mistress's eyes.
>
>   (BB, II, 67:37–44)

This handsome tribute surely deserves a high rank, by reason

The Life, the Early and Occasional Verse, and the Itineraries 41

of its forceful succinctness, among humanism's countless expressions of friendship; in its last line, reference is made to a story which offers proof of mutual affection: the two friends were in love with the same girl, and their friendship lived to tell the tale. The girl was Julia of Mechlin, the inspiration of Janus' *Monobiblos* of love-elegies, one of the two pillars on which his literary fame directly rests; in its ninth elegy, "Ad Petrum Clericum," we are told more about Petrus' love for Julia:

Certainly, you have long known of the flame that is burning within me,
   For but one arrow of love pierces both your breast and mine,
And but a single girl's eyes gave the flame igniting the torches,
   Which the Idalian boy uses to sear both our hearts.
(BB, I, 65:19–22)

One or two details about the immortal story of Janus and Julia (and, to be sure, Petrus, who apparently loved more wisely than well) must be adduced here. The affair with Julia—if it can be called that, and not an unhappy, unfulfilled, and literarily productive infatuation—was placed in 1533 by Bosscha; the dating is made in Bosscha's commentary on a prose letter (BB, II, 270), written, Bosscha assumes, after Janus returned from Bourges in March of that year, and before he left for Spain in May. Adalbert Schroeter offered the same dating (p. 184), and Maurice Rat made the same mistake as late as 1939 (p. vi). For it was a mistake, as Ellinger suspected (p. 31), and as Crane then proved by close and excellent arguments (p. 12, note 6): the love affair should be placed in the spring of 1531, and the letter to Clericus probably comes from the same year. The matter is an important one, for the elegies of the *Monobiblos* had customarily been taken, Crane said, as "a contemporary record of an actual love affair, written when the poet was not yet twenty" (p. 13). Of a sudden, an inexplicable forward step, "ein unbegreiflicher Fortschritt," as Ellinger said, had taken place in Janus' verse: "das Erleben [löste] ihm die Zunge," Ellinger concluded (p. 31, p. 70).

However, the bloom was not altogether unprepared; it came after a work which, although of quite a different nature, demonstrated the same vividness and the same intensity—the "expostulation with Neptune" (*Silvae* II), written during a summer visit to his Middelburg grandparents which gave Janus both fresh air and a glimpse of the simpler life from which his father had sprung. The poem is a description of the terrible damage done by a storm which laid waste the Zeeland coast; Ellinger has dated the work at 1530,[43] by his discovery that a particularly severe storm raged that year. The sixty-odd lines of hexameter are an impressive display; Janus was overwhelmed by what he had seen, or heard about, and he was able to express his amazement with uncluttered directness:

Roofs and houses and cattle all mixed with the farmers that
    pastured them,
Sheep swept away with their shepherds, children and mothers together,
And those others whom fate has spared in their flight from the waters,
Find they've been saved for starvation, stranded high in some treetop,
Left on some lofty hill—and then they see, as they gaze downward,
Ghastly faces of wives or children or someone still dearer,
See them as they float past, and watching, the watchers must perish.
    (BB, II, 161–62:12–18)

Vergil and the raging sea of the *Aeneid*'s first book have helped out; but, in its terrifying detail, the poem forms a not unworthy beginning to the original contribution of Janus to Neo-Latin literature.

III *Travels*

After Walcheren and Julia, Janus got the chance to express his reactions to a third overwhelming experience, this time a mostly happy one. In March, 1532, his ailing father released him into the freedom of university life. In a poetic letter (*Epistolae* II, 5) addressed to Marcus Antonius Caimus, the model student among Alciatus' disciples at Bourges, Janus gives a summary of the mood which was upon him during the trip to Bourges, and the year spent there. Looking back, he tells poor Marcus, still sweating over his sweet studies, that he, the traveler, had found a far, far better way to spend time: observing the early day and listening to the matins of the birds ("e volucrum modulamine matutino"), meanwhile populating the fresh landscape with a band of naughty satyrs:

Seizing what girls they may spy as they wander over the meadows,

Dragging them off into wild groves, away to the uncharted forests,
Using their shaggy tool to pierce them, however they struggle.
(BB, II, 89:41–43)

So far, so good, albeit a little long-winded and overweighted with classical reference, but then, for forty lines more, the pleasures of hunting game are described. The epistle is useful comparative reading for the itineraries; the impulse (the pleasures of a life in freedom) is the same in both cases, but, in the one, the epistle, the poet cannot escape from humanistic verse practice—he has to show off his command of mythology, of nature description in the wake of Vergil and Ovid, and, especially, of the venatory vocabulary: is he trying to demonstrate that he has read Grattius Faliscus and Nemesianus? In the other case, however, he foregoes the writing of travel poetry (and of emulating Ausonius, Rutilius Namatianus, or the numerous authors of verse *hodoeporica* in his own day), and puts down his impressions in prose: the sense of freedom gets a corresponding freedom of expression. The *Itineraries* are reminiscent, in their liveliness, of Felix Fabri's account of his trips to the Holy Land in the 1480s, the *Evagatorium*, or the Swiss humanist's, Thomas Platter, story of his wanderings on the eve of the Reformation; yet they are less naive than the one, less sour than the other. It was not the venturesome sixteenth century itself but the seventeenth—a stiffer and more dignified time—which first had the chance to appreciate the little travel books of Janus. They were edited by the Dutch scholar, poet, and poetic theorist, Daniel Heinsius, and published at Leiden in the opening year of the Thirty Years' War.[44]

Hadrianus Marius and Janus started out for France in March; Janus prefixes a poem on the season to his prose: "Spring had come, and the earth, grown tired of the whiteness of winter, / Turned warm and fertile again, putting on vestments of green" (BB, II, 223). The brothers went first to Brussels; here they spent the night "amid wines and various entertainments," and "the cock announced the day when many of us had not yet caught up with the night." Their progress was held up by the bad road and by the fall of a traveling companion (Hadrianus?), whom "we brought to Mons, soaking wet and vomiting—together with mud—imprecations against the highway and himself and the gods." A jolly priest, who lived in Mons, showed the visitors the charms of the city; was it he—Janus does not say—who introduced the young gentlemen to the nuns of a new and rare order? Before dinner, they behave in a manner becoming their habits; but, postprandially, "they deck themselves out, they fix their hair, they dance, and I believe that they are accessible to us." On to Valenciennes the next day, accompanied as far as Quievrain by the obliging priest: Valenciennes was a magnificent town, too, and "by no means unpleasant because of the many beautiful girls there, with their black eyes and black hair." Janus was lucky enough to find a willing specimen in his inn that night, thanks to the protection of Venus; but he had time to observe other things as well: the great clock in the city square, the church—suddenly, Janus sounds like Barbey d'Aurevilly—"which had a perfume of great age, and seemed filled with the divine spirit, admitting light almost like that of a forest."

The travelers were disappointed by the "first city of France": the "city" was Ham; Janus, good Netherlander that he was, found it wretched—"dirty and run-down, with nothing of importance about it." After Ham came Noyon, on the etymology of whose name Janus reflected: making a strained connection with *noyer,* Janus said that it lay "submerged" in a valley. The following afternoon, on the way to Senlis, the travelers came across some enterprising children who earned tips by throwing themselves down a steep hillside in "a thousand different ways."

Arriving in Paris, after some bad weather ("for the month of March is variously turbulent"), Janus is not deserted by his affection for blood-and-thunder: he catches sight of the Tour de Nesle, and is inspired to write a poem (*Epigrams* I, 72), where he describes the awful events its walls have concealed. The tower of the "White Queen," the "wild queen of gloomy lust," is haunted; aware of the numerous murders committed within its walls, it atones for the impious deeds done by its lascivious mistress (BB, I, 354–55:12). (Isabeau of Bavaria, the helpmeet of Charles the Mad, had had her lovers flung into the Seine, once she had exhausted them.) The next day, finding his inn unbearable, Janus pretended to leave Paris altogether, but in fact went only as far as Saint Denis, from which he then returned to the capital and new lodgings. At Saint Denis, among other things, he beheld the tombs of Charles VIII and his successor, Louis XII; the descriptions (*Elegies* III, 17) of these

The Life, the Early and Occasional Verse, and the Itineraries 45

works, the one in bronze, the other in marble, show once again how much of the plastic artist there was in Janus. And, in the concluding prose comment to the elegy, we are again made aware of the sense of inferiority to the Italians, the descendants of Rome, which was so characteristic of artists, as of writers, in his age: "We deemed this very distinguished work [the tomb of Louis XII] attributable only to an Italian hand; and that was what we soon learned—that it was the work of a Florentine."

Back in Paris, at a new inn, Janus met old friends or made new ones—the physician and poet from Antwerp, Joachim Polites,[45] Balthasar a Kieveringen (von Künring), an Upper Austrian nobleman, the sculptor Jan Swerts, and Bartholomaeus Latomus, from the Ardennes, presently a lecturer at the Collège de Sainte Barbe; Janus evidently did not know, or care, that George Buchanan, Francis Xavier, and Ignatius Loyola were or had been members of Latomus' institution. After more sightseeing (which included "an ancient building of Julius Caesar"), the brothers went on to Etampes, a favorite hideaway of Francis I, where they had to listen to the "inexhaustible and dangerous garrulity" of some Frenchmen who had become their chance companions. (It was an interlude of peace [1529–1536] between the wars of Charles and Francis; but there were plenty of hard feelings on which to draw—Janus betrays them not only in the *Itineraries*, but in the snide epigrams on Francis [I, 25 and 26] and the mock lament for the Dauphin, to the effect that the boy was fortunate to have died when he did. Otherwise, he would have seen France laid waste by the emperor's hand [BB, II, 138:5–8].) At Orleans, luckily, they met a fellow countryman, Theodoric Bronchorst, who showed them the sights. Janus noticed on the one hand that "Orleans has more beautiful girls than any other city in France," and, on the other, that it was a popular religious center. "All the corners of the great church were occupied by more than two or three hundred priests, to be bought for two pennies, who had come together from the villages round about, to hear confessions."

The brothers wanted to get to their goal now—the "city destined for our repose and literary leisure." "Drawing near little by little . . . we entered, if I may say so, that best of havens. And I, in the very proximity of the city, poured out ['effudi': the verb is worth noting] these verses":

Bourges with your towers and walls, oh sacred home of the Muses,
We who have come from afar, from an alien world, now salute you:
Here Alciatus—at last, and after so long a time's passing—
Fits severe Themis' decrees to the very strings of the Muses,
Calling back life itself to the form of antiquity's Solon.

(BB, I, 342, and II, 235)

Born at Alzate near Lake Como in 1492, Andreas Alciatus had first practiced law in Milan and then taken a professorship at Avignon. An extremely popular teacher, he felt that the financial rewards of the calling were not commensurate with his gifts, and he returned to his Milan clients. However, he missed the academic life, and, in 1527, went back to Avignon, where he stayed for something less than two years, being lured away in March, 1529, to Bourges—a summons made by Francis I himself. The stay in Bourges was darkened by illness; in 1533, he withdrew to Pavia at the behest of Francesco, Duke of Milan and the last of the Sforzas. Alciatus never turned down an attractive offer; from Pavia he went to Bologna, from Bologna to Pavia, only to leave for Ferrara, responding this time to another Maecenas, Ercole II d'Este. In 1547, Pavia—which had passed into Hapsburg hands after the decease of Francesco Sforza—got Alciatus a third time, and kept him until his death in 1550.

Today, Alciatus is remembered not for his adroitness at changing academic positions, but for his propagative contributions to the literature of the sixteenth and seventeenth centuries. As a youth in Milan, he had studied with Janus Parrhasius, a friend of the Janus Lascaris of Florence who, in 1494, edited the first printing of the Greek Anthology which the Byzantine monk Maximos Planudes had assembled at the beginning of the fourteenth century. The Planudean Anthology, which Parrhasius no doubt used in his instructions, was thus familiar to Alciatus from his youth. In 1521, a distant relative asked him to put together a collection of epigrams suitable to be joined to illustrations, the words illuminating the picture, the picture illuminating the words. Alciatus chose a number of his translations (into Latin) from the anthology for this purpose, and, in 1522, the volume, *Emblematum libellus*, was ready for publication at Milan; however, it was first printed at Augsburg nine years later. It became one of the great publishing successes of the century, and, as well, a prime inspiration of both brief verse composition and of a special, "emblematic" kind of book-making, a collection of essentially didactic units—each made up of the opening motto, the woodcut or engraving, and the verse *explicatio* itself. The book was translated swiftly and widely, into French in 1536, into German in 1542, into Italian and Spanish in 1549, and into English in 1586.

The other work of Alciatus was related to the youthful emblematic project; the two were children of the same parent, the anthology. In 1529, there appeared at Basel a verse collection to which Alciatus had contributed about 150 poems, the lion's share. It was a book of Latin translations from the anthology: *Selecta Epigrammata Graeca Latine versa, ex septem Epigrammatum Graecorum libris (Select Greek Epigrams, Turned into Latin, From the Seven Books of Greek Epigrams)*. Janus must have studied the anthology carefully, if we are to believe the internal evidence of the *Basia* and his own epigrammatic verse. When, in the *Somnium* ("The Dream," *Elegies* III, 7), Janus made his review of Italy's Neo-Latin poets, his inclusion of his teacher at Bourges was altogether justifiable flattery (BB, I, 188–89:39–44).

The master of Bourges received his due of attention from the poetically inclined brothers during their years at the French university. Indeed, they went to the length of dressing up as the sun and the moon (it seems that Janus took the brighter role) in order to pay Alciatus a nocturnal call, and to present him with the following epigram:

> See how Phoebus, gold-clad, and silver Phoebe, his sister,
> Join their faces diverse, here in the silence of night.
> Oh Alciatus, the gods have given you this shining honor,
> You whose honor will shine ever in undying light.
> Are you astonished that Phoebus appears to you in the night's blackness?
> Why, he has heard your praise sung on the world's other side.
> (BB, I, 310)

Although Janus was able to obtain his doctorate of laws during the Bourges year (as his brother did), he had, apparently, plenty of time left over for the cultivation of Alciatus and for his own literary work: reading between the lines of the stilted tribute to "the school of Bourges, where Andreas Alciatus was teaching civil law" (*Epigrams* I, 1), we get the impression that Janus was anything but interested in his legal studies, an impression confirmed by the epistolary poem he wrote to one Andreas Baverius (*Epistolae* II, 2), concerning his training. Having wasted his youth on fragile verses and useless song (he says), he will now reform, taking leave of the dear muses (BB, II, 79:5–10). In place of Horace, Vergil, and Seneca he will peruse Baldus, Cynus, and other classics of jurisprudence whose barbarous name the Latin tongue blushes to repeat. (Baldus is Baldus de Ubaldis [1327–1400], Cynus is Cino da Pistoja [1270–1336], under whose *Lectura in codicem* Janus must have suffered; he had no idea that Cino was the vernacular love poet on whose death Petrarch wrote "Piangete donne, e con voi pianga Amore.")[46] The burden of such readings (too much for the back of an elephant, Janus claims) has made him lose his gift of song.[47]

Taking a quick look at the girls of Bourges, Janus decided they were worth very little trouble; the first book of the epigrams ends with an unenthusiastic description. Perhaps there are two or three maidens in the great city whom a "noble grace" keeps from being ugly, and:

Add to this number, say, ten, whom you would not meet with derision:
 But all the rest—what a crowd! Monsters are what you would
  call them.
Nonetheless, youths lie down with them, thinking them worthy
  opponents,
 For the waging of wars all through the length of the night.
(BB, I, 359:5–8)

The only woman whom Janus names in connection with Bourges is the poetess Jeanne de la Font,[48] who knew—Janus said in his epitaph for her (BB, II, 123)—everything France possessed of poetry. Caught between exemplary ugliness and exemplary knowledge, Janus turned to friendship. The friends Janus cultivated most sedulously at Bourges were principally sons of the land which he, like every northern humanist, wanted to visit, Italians who had followed Alciatus to his latest post. The brightest among them was the splendid Caimus who, Janus predicted in an epigram (I, 50), would be the academy's second glory, coming only after Alciatus himself; rather deceitfully, Janus also told Ansovinus Medices of Perugia that, "mighty at law and learned in language," *he* was the only one fit to occupy Alciatus' seat. (The epistle [BB, II, 41-44] to Ansovinus was written from Mennetou-sur-Cher, where the brothers had gone to escape the plague raging in Bourges; Ansovinus had fled even farther, all the way to Perugia.) Another Italian, with whom Janus had a greater community of interest, was the poet Hieronymus Monti of Milan, the recipient of the literary review mentioned above (*Elegies* III, 7); later, having received a copy of the *Basia* from Janus, Monti paid him the ultimate compliment: the poems will make "Italians admire the Scheldt and The Hague itself" (BB, II, 287:43). A learned compatriot at Bourges got almost as fulsome compliments as the Italians did, the Amsterdamer Sibrandus Pompeius Occo.[49] After leaving France, Janus wrote Occo an epistle (I, 11), which is the most exaggerated friendship-poem from his hand.

Some dark tones can be heard in the Bourges tale. One of Janus' colleagues was carried off by a singular fate, and Janus—whether moved by sadness or a native instinct for the bizarre—twice commemorated the event, in an epigram and an epitaph (BB, I, 353 and II, 123). A young gentleman of Milan, Hieronymus Moresinus, "strong, blooming, noble, of the Italian race," went out riding one day, and, together with his steed, fell into a bog, "Plunging the promise of youth to the muddy depths of the marshes, / Styxward he swam on his course, down through the waters that slay." Another death surrounded by strange circumstances was that of Carolus Sucquetus, a fellow Netherlander (from Bruges), son of the executor of the estate of Hieronymus Buslidius. Carolus had gone to Bourges in 1529, on the recommendation of Erasmus, one of the first students from the north to be attracted by Alciatus' presence; Viglius Zuichemus was another, and the two star pupils renewed a friendship from Louvain days.[50] Sucquetus was so gifted that he soon moved into a university post of his own, being called to a professorship at Turin in 1531. He visited his family (in Mechlin now) before departing for Italy, and Janus watched him set out for the promised land:

> I'd not shun hardships, Carolus, were you my guide and protector,

> Nor would I fear to walk down through the pathways of death.
> Willingly I would scorn the perils of deep Alpine valleys
> Which lie forever concealed, covered by white seas of snow.
> (BB, II, 37:1–4)

It could be guessed that Janus went to Bourges all the more willingly because it had opened the door to Italy for Sucquetus. The Italian journey was as dangerous as Janus had said; a message came that Carolus had perished in Italy, but it turned out to be erroneous, making Janus write him a second poetic epistle (BB, II, 83–87). Then the message came again, with proof: Sucquetus had died in Turin on November 3, 1532. Ever the cultural patriot, Janus issued some instructions to the motherland in a threnody: "Dry those unhappy tears, for he has given you glory, / Flanders, a gift that's the best earth is prepared to bestow" (BB, II, 133:59–60).

Janus and Hadrianus Marius had already got cause to think sobering thoughts. The plague had descended upon Bourges, and even the great Alciatus was laid low, although not with a severe case of the disease. Janus turned the unhappy episode into a handsome if somewhat discouraging compliment:

> Our Alciatus is failing; what profit is all of that knowledge,
> What good a glory that's spread over the lands and the seas,
> Now that pale fever is twisting him, trapped in his sickbed's
> tight limits.
> (BB, I, 197:7–9)

As we know, the brothers had sense enough not to stick by the bedside of the admired master. A little later, Janus sent Viglius Zuichemus a comment on the contaminated city:

> Bourges finds its walls are undone by the onslaught of ravenous illness,
> Bourges, where many a man lays his sweet spirit aside,
> And where many a maiden, yellowing, rosy no longer,
> Crossing the sallow-hued fens, enters the dark stream of death.
> (BB, II, 44–45:1–4)

He continued his epistle with an account of the brothers' premonitions concerning their father, who had been poorly when they left Mechlin in the springtime. Then (Janus' epistle says) a welcome communication from Zuichemus had come, raising their spirits: was this the letter of June 22 (see note 47)? At this point, trying our patience if not that of Zuichemus, Janus interjects a long panegyric on the distant friend; its only aesthetic reward is the climactic line, where Janus speaks of himself in the third person: "Non tecum ingenio, tecum contendet amore" ("Not striving with you in talent, he strives with you in his devotion" [BB, II, 50:75]). Yet before Janus had time to reply to Zuichemus, he tells him, the brothers' fears came true. They learned that Nicolaus Everardi had died at Mechlin on August 9, 1532: "Nor were we vouchsafed the chance to repay him the debts that we owed him, / On that last of his days, never to come back again" (BB, II, 50:95–96).

Their degrees won, Janus and Hadrianus Marius left Bourges on March 4, 1533; the journey northward was haster than the trip to Bourges had been. After protracted adieus to Alciatus (of whom Janus had made a portrait-medallion), the brothers headed for Paris, where they spent two days and a half in the company of their friends—Polites again, and others. These friends accompanied them out of the city, and to Saint Denis, where they paid a second visit to the tombs of the kings of France. Also, with their insatiable and not very selective curiosity, they beheld a unicorn's horn of tremendous size, and "we should have seen other things too, if darkness had not prevented it." At Clermont, they had to spend the night in the suburbs, since the city allowed no overnight guests; but it did not matter: the suburbs formed a second town. All of a sudden, they got a feeling that Flanders was nearby, since they found a "splendor beyond that customary in French cities." In Amiens, they paid the cathedral a visit—"the tallest and largest of all I have seen" —but, otherwise, were most impressed by "the head of John the Baptist," displayed daily a little after six. Riding toward Arras in a wind so strong that "it surpassed in unpleasantness all the other miseries of travel," they came upon a sad sight, the tomb of Reinaldus, the remains of one of whose murderers (the head and a leg) they had seen hanging from a tree earlier in the day. (The other evildoers had been burned.) Janus was moved—all the more because Reinaldus, a professional messenger from Ypres, had been bringing him a letter (with money) when he was slain. The result was a portrait of homely virtue, written on the spot—"this epitaph escaped me": [51]

> Here is the place he was slain—Reinaldus, coming from Flanders,
>   Bearing letters and gold, bound for the cities of France.
> Imagine: the cause of his death was not his but placed in his keeping,
>   Money he meant not to lose save at the cost of his life.
>
> (BB, II, 241)

At Lille, things brightened up: "we recognized at last the perfect cleanliness of Belgian cities"; the brothers' patriotic joy increased when they got to Menin (Meenen); there they heard people speaking "the tongue of Flanders" again—Janus' native language. The evening of the following day, "at six on March 13," they arrived at Mechlin; the trip to "die verriempt stat," "the famous town," as Felix Platter, Thomas' son, called Bourges, was over.

The stay in Flanders was not a long one; bereft of their father, the younger sons had to make use of their connections with the court of Charles V. The family decided to kill two birds with one stone. Nicolaus Grudius had gone to Spain, to serve as a secretary of the emperor; Janus would accompany Nicolaus' wife, Anna Cobella (Coebels), south, and try to make his own fortune there, in imperial circles. Laying his plans pretty carefully, Janus collected letters of recommendation; the informative letter to Scorel, of May 8, 1533, ends with a request that Scorel call him to the attention of the "Lord of Nassau": [52] "As I am going to Spain, where he too will be shortly, it would be of great advantage for me if in some way I might be insinuated into the good will of so great and good a prince." Janus does not forget the most important instruction of all; reference could be made to the late Nicolaus Everardi, "my father, whom he loved most warmly" (BB, II, 273–74).

Thus armed, Janus set out on May 28, 1533, for Spain; his mood was quite different from that in which he departed for Bourges a year before. To Joachim Polites, he wrote some very high-sounding words, saying that he would not fear death, once he had seen the world:

> Now the fates summon me hence, to Hercules' faraway pillars,
>   Where the sun's chariot sinks lazily into the sea,
> And I shall proceed from there, to explore other lands and still others:
>   This is the way of the world, this is the human condition.

> Surely, it's cause for rejoicing that, when the fates call for my spirit,
> I can surrender with grace, knowing what worlds I have seen.
> (BB, II, 55:57–62)

Elsewhere he sounded a great deal less brave, and, as he confessed, he was surprised at his faintheartedness. He takes farewell of Craneveld and Mulaert, Catzius and Clericus, with a brace of sad queries: ". . . Why does the burden of care press so heavy upon me? / Why does my spirit lie still, broken by grief of its own?" (BB, I, 198:1–2). The river Dyle, personified, comes bubbling up out of its waves, ministering to the youth with some wise words: the causes of his melancholy are many—he will miss Mechlin, sacred to Venus, Phoebus, and Father Lyaeus (Bacchus), he will miss his mother and sisters and brothers, and, most of all, he will miss Hadrianus Marius, "'without whom not a moment of your life has passed.'" But, the psychologically acute Dyle adds, the young man is much too skillful in seeking out reasons for worry. As Crane remarks (p. 17), low spirits and premonitions of death and disaster are an elegist's bread and butter; but, here, Janus appears quite genuinely to have fallen into a depression. At the opening of the Third Itinerary (written at the same time as the elegy just paraphrased), Janus, instead of plunging into the middle of things, puts down essayistic reflections on the resemblance between travel and death. "For if dying is that event by which you are separated from the company of men, so that in future you will not have anything in common with them or they with you, each one of us dies, as it were, with respect to the region from which he departs. Indeed . . . the salutations sent from afar are altogether too much like those offices—the prayers, the anniversaries, the memory failing and cold—which are rendered for the dead" (BB, II, 244).

As before, the first stop on the journey south was Brussels, and there, at an inn, Janus had his spirits lifted by a young lady who sang to her own accompaniment on the psaltery; it reminded Janus of a couple of lines from Ovid's *Amores*, which he misquoted mildly: "She with a nimble thumb tries out the strings' easy movement,/Tell me now, who can resist loving so skillful a hand." The numerous pleasures of the city did not make him forget serious matters, before all else the gathering of letters of recommendation—one from Charles Boisot, a member of the

Grand Council of Mechlin, to Nicholas Perrenot de Granvelle, the first councillor of the emperor, another from the Archdeacon of Arras, Claude de Boisset, to the same notable, and two from the exotic-sounding "Archiepiscopus Panormitanus," Jean de Carondelet, to the influential Granvelle and to Jean Perrenin, the emperor's secretary of state. (Carondelet, whose Sicilian archbishopric was simply a financial plumb, had succeeded Janus' father as president of the Grand Council of Mechlin; he had been given reason to want to help the young man out: Janus, it will be remembered, had made a portrait-medallion of him and, upon his arrival in Brussels, he had also presented Carondelet with a note or essay which he had written "super arte fusoria," on the art of casting.)

On May 30, the departure from Brussels finally took place; as usual, according to the pleasant custom, a group of friends—among them Carolus Catzius and the senior brother, Everardus Nicolaius—followed the travelers a short distance along their way. Passing through Valenciennes and along the edge of the Ardennes, the party arrived at the "last city of the Champagne," Troyes, the magnificent spaciousness of which astonished Janus; at Chatillon, he grew aware that he had come into the duchy of Burgundy, for "the houses . . . do not rise up as high as ours, they have a lower contour, like the houses of the ancients and those of Italy." Yet he found the inhabitants of Burgundy distinctly unclassical: "The people are almost all paupers and speak a coarse tongue." After considerable climbing the party got to Dijon, which had some earnest lessons to teach Janus. He beheld the tombs of Philip the Bold and John the Fearless of Burgundy, and found it sad indeed that "most courageous men, who had always repulsed the cruel attacks of all their neighbors and had lived in the most flourishing liberty, should now, dead, fall into the power of their foes and into servitude." (Following the death of Charles the Bold at Nancy, in 1477, Louis XI of France had taken Burgundy; Janus is aware that Burgundy's cause is Hapsburg's.) But not only the subject of Charles V speaks here; the strain of pessimism comes to the surface again: visiting the hospital which Nicholas Rolin, the chancellor of Philip the Good, had had erected at Beaune, for the care of the indigent ill, Janus reflects that "someday we shall no longer be the masters of ourselves and of our goods, for we shall be dead. Let our goods be used, then, to good ends, in keeping with Rolin's example."

The Life, the Early and Occasional Verse, and the Itineraries 55

The landscape grew more spectacular, and Janus' interest was aroused: "I have believed it worthy of note that I saw there the peaks of mountains surrounded by dense clouds." Still admiring the "most lovely mountains," Janus had trouble finding lodgings in Lyons because of the visit of Francis I, King of France. He was repaid for his discomfort; the next day, thanks to the intervention of a friend, he was admitted to the royal assembly: there were "various entertainments and dances of all sorts performed by the most noble ladies of France and Spain, while the king and queen presided over the whole, seated on a raised platform, like the stage in a theater." Janus was so impressed that not a single anti-French remark passed his lips. At Lyons, too, Janus chanced upon two Dutch friends, "Hilarius the poet and Cornelius of The Hague,[53] the painter"—the latter of whom may have been the means of Janus' admission to the king's festival.

The party descended the Rhone by boat; Janus enjoyed the trip—it was easier than riding, and, besides, what humanist was not infatuated with rivers, those links between civilization's centers, the cities? At Avignon, Janus took a good look at the palace of the popes and at the great bridge; "I have heard that it was constructed by a demon," Janus remarks, "but, on the spot, I was unable to find out anything certain about it." Also, forever curious, he visited the ghetto, placed in the dirtiest part of the city; "[the Jews'] work consists of making shifts cut of linen, artistically designed." Because of a fear that they bore the plague, the travelers were not allowed to enter the walls of Nimes; avid for traces of Rome, Janus had to content himself with transcribing inscriptions set above the city gates.

The group passed the Spanish border "in the worst sort of heat and on the worst sort of road." At "La Sausse" (Salses), they beheld a sign of imperial might at last, the border fortress expanded at the order of Charles V. Shortly, they began the ascent of the Pyrenees, spending the night in a hovel, quite unprotected against robbers. It was the beginning of July now, they had been underway for a month, and were glad to reach Barcelona after three more nights on the road. A physician named Florenas, who had expected to find his wife in their party, rode out to meet them. Madam Florenas had not come along, however; she would have been company for Janus' sister-in-law, Anna Cobella, who had been mute throughout the trip. At least, Janus does not mention her once in his account, and we might guess that the sister-in-law's presence had restrained the interest he had so richly demonstrated, on other journeys, in girls along the way. Florenas announced that Nicolaus Grudius, Anna's beloved spouse, whom the travelers had expected to find at Barcelona, had gone on to Monzón, some hundred kilometers to the west. Headed inland, the travelers made a point of climbing Montserrat, stopping at the Benedictine cloister, Janus was touched by what he saw there: "The monks have preserved a praiseworthy and attractive custom of the ancient fathers, offering all the travelers who come to them for the sake of greeting the Virgin Mother a gift of wine, of oil, and of bread." At Cervera, Janus left his temporary ball-and-chain, Anna Cobella, behind, so that he might hasten on to find his brother, her husband. Coming into the suburbs of the "celebrated city" of Balaguer at evening, Janus saw some riders approaching him in the dusk; one of them addressed him and a long conversation ensued before the brothers recognized one another. It was Grudius looking for his wife, "who he knew was not far away." The circumstances of the reunion made the brothers' happiness the more profound, Janus notes. "Toward ten o'clock the following day my sister-in-law arrived. Her husband received her with the greatest joy, and we lunched together happily." That is the end of Janus' *Itineraries;* concerning Janus' silence in prose hereafter, Prévot conjectures: "Le manque de temps, puis la maladie l'empêchèrent sans doute d'achever ses *Itinera* ou plus exactement de leur donner une suite."

Janus Secundus remained in Spain from July, 1533, until the winter or spring of 1535 or 1536. It is a time about which we are very ill informed. Janus appears to have been out of a job for the first ten months, accompanying his brother Grudius as he in turn followed the emperor—in fact, André Blanchard has built his account of the Spanish years on the comings and goings of Charles.[54] The trips are mentioned by Grudius in his *naenia* on Janus:

> How long was the span of the years when the fates let us two be together,
> Sometimes smiling on me, sometimes treating me ill;
> Carried wherever they pleased by their imperious power,
> I roamed through foreign lands, faithfully waiting on Caesar.

In October, Janus finished the *Reginae pecuniae regia,* and sent it to Petrus Clericus from Monzón, in Huesca Province; he was already tired of the Spanish weather and landscape, missing the "serpentine streams" and the "soft grass" of his homeland:

> [Muses], how often you've lain at my side in the sands of the desert,
>   Or in the mountains that stretch barren through Aragon's land . . .
> [Or] where the dry earth's exhausted, burnt out by heat's heavy burden,
>   Ceaselessly turning itself into a landscape of stone.
>   (BB, II, 65:7–8, 13–14)

According to his early editor, Scriverius, he also wrote the strange elegy to (and for) Gonzalo Pérez (see p. 60 and pp. 96–97) in 1533, at La Almunia, the little town just north of Monzón where the *Itineraries* ended. These two places of composition, Monzón and La Almunia, fit the activities of the emperor perfectly, for he held the *cortes* of Aragon at Monzón from July 12 to December 29. It would also be logical to place the emperor's stay in Saragossa, early in 1534, in connection with Janus' handsome short elegy to the city, which begins as follows:

> City that's held to the name, truly noble, of Caesar Augustus,
>   City of venerable age, built by the heroes of old,
> See, that captain of waves, the Ebro, sends you his waters,
>   Greatest of all the streams wetting Hesperia's lands.
>   (BB, I, 207:1–4)

As the elegy goes on, Janus takes the opportunity of bowing again to Charles, "Who returns to you now, having beat the barbarian foe"—in September, 1532, Charles had waited in Vienna for an assault which never came, the Turks having withdrawn after Nicholas Jurisics' heroic defense of Güns.

Charles had his headquarters in Toledo from February 13 to May 21, 1534, and we have, again, epistolary evidence that Janus was in Toledo in April of that year.[55] Scriverius ascribed this place and month to the elegy "Ad lectulum" ("To his little bed," II, 8), which names "Neaera"—elsewhere, "the hard-hearted girl"—in its eleventh line. Another "Toledan" poem with a nasty erotic intent is the epigram (I, 12) to the "Toledan Lycoris," a reminder that Janus knew his Martial. Lycoris is falling apart: "Should some filthy old man in her wide-open mouth seek his pleasure, / He'll be richer by far—he'll harvest a bumper of teeth" (BB, I, 299:11–12). The sentimental air of the earlier erotic poetry has vanished; and the process of sophistication is not limited to the realm of love. We can deduce from the letter (May 31, 1534) which Janus sent to Everardus, announcing his appointment as secretary to Cardinal Juan Pardo de Tavera, newly consecrated archbishop of Toledo, that he had become something of an intrigant, determined to succeed in the *vita aulica.* Janus had been reared in a world where connections and favors meant much; now his training could be brought to bear. "I shall be splendidly bold, and, if I do well, I shall be counted among the most prominent members of this little court. At a salary not to be scorned, with excellent perquisites and honors, a hope comes to me of the most ample benefits, a hope untinged by doubt: since he [Tavera] is a cardinal, all the dignities and benefices of the church which fall vacant throughout the whole year await his collection of them, so that he is able to provide generously from his holdings for anyone in any given week" (BB, II, 275–76).[56] Before closing the letter to Everardus, he tells his brother that he wishes to return home with enough money to support himself until his old age, "which I prefer, rather than having to depend someday on any of those people who are with the government there."

Janus had found an amiable sort of master, "a man most learned in all the arts, of a genial and pleasant disposition." (He felt obliged to justify his choice of an employer, since Everardus had warned him against taking service with a Spaniard.) Cardinal Tavera traveled extensively, and the letter to Everardus has the closing words, "We are going to Segovia"; by June 3, Janus wrote to Hadrianus Marius from that city, sending him a note smacking of haste and well-being and an elegy (I, 2), which, however, was of a surprisingly reflective nature, about the Julia-experience and Janus' own poetic calling (see p. 78). At Palencia toward the end of July, he wrote the elegy (III, 13) "On the Very Reverend Cardinal of Toledo, Making a Journey to Compostela." Oddly, the pilgrim, Tavera, gets rather perfunctory attention in the poem; Janus' real concern lies with his phantasies of his Hague childhood (conjured up in connection with the band of satyrs and nymphs which accompanies Tavera) and with an illness which has befallen him, making him leave the Cardinal's entourage:

The Life, the Early and Occasional Verse, and the Itineraries 59

Had not a troublesome fever, clinging tight to my bones' very marrow,
  Conquered the vows I had made, sadly shackling my feet,
I'd have gone on, mighty prince, and given no thought to my safety:
  He who's a demigod's friend fears not the wrath of the gods.
                                                    (BB, I, 212:49–52)

Still another elegy has been placed in the Palencia stay, in September, by Scriverius: the erotic elegy (II, 9) about the girl named Venerilla. The by no means farfetched proposal has been made, by the way, that Janus was a victim of venereal disease.[57]

In December, 1534, in Madrid, Janus wrote a propemptic ode to his friend Joannes Stratius (Jan Strass), a canon of Antwerp, who, having completed whatever business it was that had brought him to Spain, left the country very suddenly—at a time, Janus points out, when it is dangerous to cross the Pyrenees. Nymphs and dryads are summoned to hold back the fugitive, to make the Tagus and the Ebro flood, to lead Stratius astray in labyrinthine forests—but these strategies of Neo-Latin verse fail, and Janus admits that he can understand the reason for the flight. The Belgian earth calls Stratius, and a certain hot-blooded Antonia as well; describing her appetites, Janus drifts off into literary priapism:[58]

Chiefly, oh large-membered watchman, standing guard in the midst of
  green gardens,
  She's suspended huge wreaths there on your penis—in fear
Lest from the journey abroad his instrument, ruined by Spain's
  maidens,
  Might return drier to her, making its weaker way home.
                                                    (BB, I, 215:23–26)

But the poem's most important part is its opening, which implies that such northern humanists as Janus and his Antwerp colleague are, in fact, more Roman than the Spaniards: "But this barbarian earth, alien to those sprung from Latium, / Does it not know what he says? He speaks Ausonia's tongue" (BB, I, 212:3–4). The Netherlanders who served the imperial court in Spain were not especially popular among their Spanish rivals for episcopal or imperial favor, all the more because the former were inclined to boast about their industry and honesty; nor were the Netherlanders, with their excellent Latin, prepared to accept the condescension they—as Northern barbarians—got from their Spanish colleagues.⁵⁹ From the poetic works, it can be deduced that Janus maintained—perhaps—fairly friendly relations with Jerónimo de Zurita (1512–1580) and Gonzalo Pérez (?–1568). Zurita was the son of the emperor's physician, and, from Janus, the recipient both of a funny epigram against grammarians and an elegy (III, 16) of a personal-literary content (see p. 61); the elegy (II, 7), "written in [Gonzalo's] name," is based upon revelations the Spaniard made about himself (see p. 96). Otherwise, an epistle (I, 13) to Agustín de Zárate (?–after 1560), private secretary to the council of Charles V and a friend of Grudius, offers some indications that Janus has not met Zárate as yet, but wants to do so, because of what "a friend" has told him about Zárate's skill at love poetry, "ennobling a tender mistress in his verses." (Later on, Zárate was sent out to Peru as an imperial agent and witnessed Pizarro's rebellion against the distant emperor's authority.) ⁶⁰ Another of Janus' epistolary friends was equally distinguished, or rather would become so, as diplomat, historian, and poet. Diego Hurtado de Mendoza (1503–1575) told Janus to stop wasting his talent on light subjects; and Janus replied:

Why keep attempting, Diego, in vain to persuade this poor poet,
Long accustomed to lightness, to try out new measures of grandeur,
Solid songs, built for the lasting, songs that are laden with clauses,
Songs such as florid Lucretius, singing the great world's beginnings,
Liked to entone, fully using all of his mighty mouth's power.
(BB, II, 92–93:1–6)

He summed up his argument with a tag which proves that, capable of singing great themes or not, he had surely mastered Latin's pregnant brevity: "magnos magna decent" ("Great things become great men").

We have already noted most of the Spanish girls in Janus' life, or the names he gave their poetic transformations—Lycoris of Toledo, Venerilla of Palencia, and Neaera herself; a Lydia can be added from *Elegies* II, 4, whose frigidity produces flames on the poet's part. They are, of course, types from antiquity: the aging courtesan (Lycoris), the tease (Venerilla, with the diminutive name), the cruel beauty (Neaera), who, in Lydia, is reduced to a single conceit of Petrarchism, the icy source of fire. The chief of the experiences, as the tradition about Secundus has it, was with Neaera, to whose literary forebears and literary

The Life, the Early and Occasional Verse, and the Itineraries   61

existence we shall return in chapter 3. Here, concerned with piecing together a biography of Janus, we need only adduce the fragments of information we possess about the second woman whom Janus made immortal—if, indeed, she existed at all. He appears to have met her in the spring of 1534 (see p. 57); he mentions her again in the third of the solemn elegies which were his annual celebration of the events of May, 1531, when the affair with Julia had flowered. The Neaera to whom we are introduced here is a frightening sort, the latest agent of the importunate "Saint Cupid" to whom the elegy is addressed:

What's the more, I—thanks to you—have tasted the rigors of passion,
   Led to a realm filled with pride, ruled by a prideful new mistress,
Where fierce Neaera makes sport of me, using her cruel demeanor,
   Heaping up insult high on my poor suffering head.
                                                       (BB, I, 94:9–12)

Secundan scholarship of the past was much interested in Neaera's city of origin; Schroeter proposed Madrid, while Crane argued for Toledo. We have Janus' word for it that she was urbane, and made him feel something like a bumpkin. At the opening of the long Orpheus-eclogue, he describes himself as a "sad shepherd," up against sophistication; Lycidas (Janus' mouthpiece) forgets his flocks:

                                . . . but does not forget those passions,
Loves, which—and here was a man, at his ease in the quiet of
   meadows,
Wont to relax with the nymphs, taking their lukewarm embraces—
Came from the gray of her eyes, came from her hair, that was golden,
Came from the cunning and craft that polished Neaera commanded.
                                                      (BB, II, 173:8–12)

It is generally assumed that Neaera was a prostitute, although the poem which most clearly indicates her profession turns out, on closer examination, to be a literary construction. Casting about for some special praise to give his Saragossan friend, Zurita, Janus calls him a favored client: "And Neaera, in fact, preferred to have you before others. / Though her lips were still wet from all the kisses I gave" (BB, I, 224:5–6). However, the reference means simply that Zurita was the first to have a chance to read the *Basia*;[61] it is a parallel to the preceding distich, about the elegies to Julia (ll. 3–4), which Janus had given Zurita: "You in whose sensitive ears our Julia takes pleasure in singing / Songs with her tender voice, songs which have harvested praise." The rest of the poem is literary, too; Janus brags about his Latin reading (see pp. 72–73).

Whether Janus was troubled by a real "torva Neaera" or "urbana Neaera" or not, he had learned to make his way through the realities of Spain, finding the *entrée* to the entourage of Charles which he so long had wanted, having been only a hanger-on before. In a letter of February 28, 1535, to Everardus Nicolai, Janus reviews what has happened, and looks into the future. He has been struck by illness again; "Nevertheless I even now resist its threats bravely and spiritedly, so that I shall not keep to my bed or my dwelling, but think to travel outside Spain itself, lest my torpor nourish a torpid fever. The emperor is going to Barcelona the day after tomorrow, in order to send forth or himself to lead that enormous army he has assembled there, which he is to behold at last. And because it is believed that he will first go across to Italy, the Cardinal my master is sending me to accompany the emperor's court, first on its way to Rome, that I might congratulate the supreme pontiff on this supreme pinnacle of honors, and that I might also set forth other things in [the Cardinal's] name. Then [I shall go] wherever the emperor will go, that I may write down the history of memorable things, of which I have already made a beginning, roused by a certain martial fury. Here it is. [Janus now quotes eight lines of his military hexameters.] All men think to fight beside the emperor or for the emperor; nor, if things come to arms, shall we show ourselves to be unwarlike or cowardly, so that it will be somewhat the same case with my story as with the *Aeneid*: 'And I was a great part of these things'" (BB, II, 279–80).

The passage has its mysteries, which can partially be solved by taking recourse to the single detailed account we possess of Janus' last years, the funeral poem by Hadrianus Marius. It tells us that Janus had become a trusted secretary of Tavera, who placed his "secret notes, and things written in code" in the Netherlander's discreet hands, and who was delighted to use him as an agent of correspondence with the "great princes of Latium" and with the Pope, "the powerful master of the mistress city." Janus had been aware of Tavera's own papal ambitions before entering his service; the tribute to Tavera as a prime candidate, inserted by Janus nearing the opening of his *Reginae pecuniae regia* from the autumn of 1533, had been designed to call the prelate's attention to Janus' skills:

> Oh most generous protector,
> Tavera, pride of Hesperia, into whose hands high Toledo
> (Circled by winding streams, whose banks shine with gold in their glitter)
> Lately surrendered itself amid veneration and prayer,
> Giving its altar's rich rule into the blessed man's charge.
> Now, its waves turning pale, the Tiber envies the Tagus,
> And mighty Rome itself yearns to have him as its master.
>   (BB, II, 151:10–16)

Clement VII passed away obligingly and quickly, as Janus rather seemed to hope he would; "If anything should happen to the supreme pontiff, I do not know who would be able to fill his shoes better," Janus wrote to Everardus on May 31, 1534, and by September 25 Clement was dead. But his successor was not Tavera, "for whom Rome was sighing," but Alexander Farnese, who took the name Paul III. A politic man, Tavera decided to employ his gifted house Latinist for two purposes. He would lend Janus to Charles,[62] to be the monarch's Vergil in the expedition which Charles was planning against Khair-ed-din Barbarossa and his Tunisian pirates; however, since it seemed (according to Janus' letter) that the emperor would stop off in Rome on the way to undertaking the Christianization of "Carthage," it would be Janus' task, still working for Tavera although a member of Charles' retinue, to present the papal winner, Paul, with the good loser's wishes. In his funeral poem, though, Hadrianus Marius, with the advantage of hindsight, reversed the order of the events Janus had foreseen: the crusading Charles would seize Barbarossa's fleet and free the Christian slaves, and then, triumphant, he would set his course for Rome, where—the language of Hadrianus closely follows that of Janus' letter—Janus "might congratulate the supreme pontiff on these supreme honors, and the triple crown in the name of his master," that is, Tavera. But, note well, Hadrianus does not say that Janus had in fact done these things.

Charles had been given several opportunities to become familiar with the works of the gifted son of his trusted servant.

When Janus was only nineteen, he had written his ode, published by Dantiscus, in honor of the grudging coronation of Charles by Clement at Bologna, in which "all good men" are told to rejoice (BB, II, 2:11–12). Flattery of a wittier sort is to be found in the epigram on Charles' birth- and coronation day (February 24): Why is the day icy? So that Caesar's light may be reflected more brightly. Why is Phoebus so late in rising on the winter morn? Because Caesar sheds light enough (BB, I, 308). Janus also composed a poem of mourning on the death of the emperor's chancellor, Mercurino Gattinara, at Innsbruck; the architect of the Bologna coronation, Mercurino was given the same sort of high-flown lament which Janus would shortly apply to Margaret (BB, II, 111:14): "Cruel death with his scythe-bearing hand seeks out the stars of the sky." And when Charles, after the Diet of Augsburg, made his formal entry into Ghent, Janus provided another ode, full of the appropriate references:

> Oh, which god is it, greatest of emperors,
> Who's now returned you, many years afterward,
>   To these towns and skies—this sacred
>   Birthplace which fostered you in your childhood.
>   (BB, II, 12:5–8)

The poem, as commentators pointed out long ago, is a skillful imitation of Horace, *Odes,* IV, 5, to Augustus. After his arrival in Spain, Janus made an assault upon imperial favor with a double weapon; he did a portrait-medallion of the emperor, one side bearing Charles' head, the other his coat of arms, and then described his work in an elegy (III, 2). The remainder of the poem is comprised of an application of the formula of modesty to Janus' abilities as a sculptor, and, in addition, a heavy-handed defence of the portrait-medallion as an art form: the graven image of Nero tells posterity of his baseness; just so, Charles' noble profile will tell the centuries a different story, even though written records have passed away.

The Caroline poetry from Janus' pen is, for obvious reasons, of a formal nature; we wish that he had composed another of his itineraries for the days when he accompanied Grudius on his rounds. Yet we have only three obituary poems, snapshots, edged in black, of a boy and two men in the imperial court. The boy is Heduus, the emperor's cupbearer, who aroused too much

The Life, the Early and Occasional Verse, and the Itineraries 65

attention on the part of ladies and lords alike, so that envious Jupiter bore this Ganymede up to heaven (BB, II, 124). A passionate story of some sort must also lie behind the *naenia* for Jacobus Platpays Morinus, who was murdered at Monzón (BB, II, 118); the olive trees, "dripping with blood," weep for him, felled by a treacherous hand. And a more distinguished man passed away while Janus accompanied the court, Nicholas Hawkins, Henry VIII's ambassador to Charles, who died at Barbastro, north of Monzón, late in December, 1534, or early the next year (BB, II, 136–37). (By the way, should any propagandistic significance be attached to the fact that Janus mentions a plan of Henry to give Hawkins "the shepherd's gilded staff and the miter" upon his return to England? Henry's divorce of Catherine of Aragon, the aunt of Charles, had long since strained the relations between England and Hapsburg.)

Probably mindful of Janus' poetic gifts, Charles commissioned Janus to describe his African deeds in Latin verse. The poet made a stab at the task; there exists a fragment of verse in the letter to Everardus which may have been the epic's beginning:

Caesar prepares war anew, for anew the gentle youth's patience,
Put to the test too long, has by his suffering been vanquished;
Piety, savaged once more, has burst into flames of fierce anger;
Now I behold all the seas as they foam from the rhythm of oarstrokes,
See the earth shining with arms, and the heavens aglitter with flame.
(BB, II, 276 and 280)

The poem continues in this fashion for three more hexameters, instead of several thousand. Ever the eroticist, Janus also composed a little address to Elissa (Dido), telling her that a descendant of Aeneas was underway to save her realm: "You will say, surely: 'If I had perished for love of this hero, / Then my death's cause would have been worthier far than it was" (BB, I, 302:9–10). Finally, a piece of a letter to Hadrianus Marius has been preserved; it consists of a sentence of prose, describing Caesar's habit of schooling his mount (and those of his followers) in "equestrian games of all sorts," together with a few lines of verse, again showing Charles practicing horsemanship and war:

Now, with his crown slipped askew, he resembles the pug Mauritanian,

Now, mindful of Muslim hordes, he decks himself out in his armor,
Working his swift-footed horse, he could check the flight of the
   Parthians,
Eager, he deals from afar vain wounds to the reeds with his missiles,
Fleeing again, he breathes hard, bent close to the mane of his charger.
                                                   (BB, II, 282–83)

The vaguely comical charge along the beach reveals that the author of the *Itineraries* had not wholly lost his powers of impious observation. Janus had too independent a spirit for the task he was supposed to perform.

It has been assumed by various writers on Janus Secundus, Maurice Rat being the latest among them, that he made the voyage to Tunis with the emperor; the romantic Viennese, Budik, composed a colorful description of the great adventure: "Der Anblick des unermesslichen Meeres, das mit schäumendem Zorne die Sieger trug, das Gewitter der Seeschlacht erfüllte [Janus] Seele mit allen Schauern der Begeisterung" (I:246). Participation in Charles' summer war in North Africa would have been strenuous, to say the least, for a man in Janus' condition. The fleet left Barcelona on May 30, Goletta was besieged from June 15 until July 14, and Tunis fell on July 7; the emperor did not sail for Sicily, his mission completed, until August 22. The poetic evidence does not support the notion that Janus went along on the expedition. The scene of the emperor in training camp could most logically have been written while the troops were assembling for embarkation at Barcelona. As for the trip to Rome, Janus would surely have mentioned it in subsequent verses, had it taken place; like every humanist, Janus wanted to visit the Latin fountainhead. Some early scholars argued for an Italian sojourn: Foppens went so far as to say that Janus went directly from Bourges to Rome, where he became the secretary of Paul III; in this Foppens follows a statement made by Valerius Andreas in 1623 [63]—but Andreas, as Bosscha realized, had simply misread the *naenia* of Hadrianus Marius, failing to understand that Hadrianus spoke not of what had been, but of what might have been.

The turning point for the brothers in Spain was the death of Anna Cobella; the funeral took place at Madrid, late in 1534, and, according to Nicolaus Grudius' *naenia* for his late wife,

Janus spoke to the remains of "Sister Anna": "'Crossing the realms of the French, but lately I was your companion: / Why can I not aid you now, lighting the realms which you seek'" (*DPB*, II:623). If Janus himself undertook a *naenia* for Anna, it has not been preserved; his tribute is a portrait-medallion with Anna on the obverse and Nicolaus, looking considerably less dejected than she, on the reverse. The letter which Janus sent to Everardus from Madrid, on February 28, 1535, says that Grudius is still a member—perhaps not altogether willingly—of the emperor's entourage: "Having lost his wife, and less encumbered now, my brother does not see in what manner he ought or would not be able to obey the emperor, who is reluctant to send him away from his person; and so we both prepare ourselves for any and all eventualities, taking into consideration the great honor which will accrue to our family if from among its brothers, who have won fame for themselves lately by their good qualities, two will now also be known to have served strenuously in military actions" (BB, II, 282). Blanchard assumes that Nicolaus went with the army to Africa, and the epithalamium which Janus wrote for the widower's second marriage (to one Joanna Moysia of Antwerp, an event which Blanchard places in June of 1536) hints strongly that Grudius had taken part in the Tunisian adventure:

> Grudius, winning great fame afar in Hesperia's reaches.
>   For having sung of the tears wept by Narcissus himself,
> Faced down a thousand deaths as he followed the emperor's eagles,
>   Writing in secret script all of his sacred commands:
> Now he has gone home at last, seeking the land of the Belgians,
>   Tired of his empty bed, after the loss of his wife.
>   (BB, I, 151:19–24)

Crane was of the opinion that Janus stayed on in Spain alone until the spring of 1536 (because of the phrase "vere in medio," "in the midst of spring" in the description of the trip across the Pyrenees); but two pieces of evidence contradict this assumption: on September 16, 1535, Cornelius de Schepper, presently with the court in Spain, wrote to Dantiscus that the "Grudii fratres," unable to stand the climate, had returned to Belgium; again, on March 12, 1536, Viglius Zuichemus wrote to Hadrianus

Marius, expressing pleasure at the *Basia* and happiness that the brothers had returned safely from Spain.[64] Most likely, Janus left Spain in May of 1535, and Nicolaus Grudius followed later.

The faintest possibility exists that Janus touched a corner of Italy on his way north; Hadrianus Marius used the phrase "per Alpes" to describe his journey, but Janus himself speaks expressly of the Pyrenees:

Leaving the barren confines of Hesperia now in my illness,
 I seek the sweet homeland's soil, knowing it's mild to the touch,
Seek my friends too, at whose side I know it is better to perish;
 Why does the land I detest try to delay my escape?
Why do these mountains stand here, blocking the way of departure,
 Why does cruel winter strike now, here in the midst of the spring?
Snowy, the Pyrenees turn into water, and send down a floodtide,
 While a damp Jupiter adds rain to the wet of it all.

(BB, I, 306–7:1–8)

He reached France,[65] and then had to rest for two months in Poitiers; we know some details about the stay thanks to the researches of Henry de Vocht. He was a guest of the poet-priest Cornelius Musius, the Hollander who later would become the father-confessor of Janus' sister Isabella; presently studying in Poitiers, Musius wrote an epigram on a portrait-medallion which depicted his ill young friend: "He did not give him his due who gave him the name of Secundus, / For by all rights he should be titled the first of us all." Joachim Polites, the Zeeland poet and physician, whom Janus had seen in Paris in happier days, turned up too, among Musius' friends, as did the Belgian classical scholar and jurist, Julianus Aurelius (Julien d'Avré).[66]

IV *The End*

Sometime during the last year of his life, Janus wrote a work of a different character from most of his other poetry. On July 6, 1535, Thomas More was executed at the Tower. Janus had already essayed propaganda poetry with his feigned reply, made as it were by Henry VIII, to Catherine's feigned letter (written by Francesco Maria Molza [1489–1544], the Italian humanist best known for his poetry of love, not conjugal hatred); now he undertook his long *carmen heroicum* on the death of More. The poem was distributed in handwritten copies to friends; in the month of Janus' death, it was published as part of a book commemorating More, but attributed by the editor, Hieronymus Gebweiler of Schlettstadt, to Erasmus, himself lately deceased. (The volume also included Janus Secundus' epitaph for More, correctly ascribed.) The poem was accepted as Erasmus' own work by Germany's humanistic world—it would stand to reason that Erasmus had been moved by his old friend's passing, and Gebweiler, furthermore, had been a personal acquaintance of Erasmus. Hadrianus Marius caught sight of the poem, flying its false colors, and was enraged; he got the bookdealer Servatius Zassenus of Louvain to bring out a rival edition in December, 1535. It was called, appropriately enough, *Naenia in mortem clariss. viri Thomae Mori, Autore Ioanne Secundo, Nicolai F. Hagieñ, falso antehac D. Erasmo Rot. adscripta ac depravatissime edita*.[67] Apart from the *naenia*, "falsely attributed to Erasmus and most iniquitously edited," it also contained the More epitaph, an epigram on More's death, and an epitaph on the death of Catherine of Aragon (January 7, 1536). The Erasmian authorship of the More *naenia* continued to lead a ghostly existence, however, although the poem was repeatedly included in editions of Janus' works; such serious verse did not jibe with the libertine reputation Janus had acquired. In 1928, André Jolles proved beyond any doubt that the poem came from the young love-poet rather than from the old master-humanist.[68]

At Mechlin, Janus was greeted by the tears of his family, which was torn between grief at seeing him in such bad shape and joy at seeing him at all. Evidently, his health improved: he was able to write the epitaph for Catherine and the verses on the deaths of Erasmus (July 12, 1536) and of Francis of Valois (August 10); he wrote, as well, the two epigrams (BB, I, 311–13) against Francis I for breaking the peace by his invasion of Savoy in February, 1536.[69] According to Hadrianus Marius' poem, he acceded to the wishes of his brothers and his mother, none of whom wanted to see him go back to the "deadly heat" of Spain and to the court of Tavera, however much he wanted to; instead, he took a "similar position" as secretary to Georges (Joris) van Egmond (1504–1559),[70] recently (February 26, 1535) named Bishop of Utrecht and the pro-abbot of the Benedictine abbey of St. Amand, then in Hainaut and just south of the present Belgian-French border. In September 1536, he left

Mechlin for Brussels, and wrote to Hadrianus from there on September 13, promising a quick return.[71] Shortly thereafter he arrived in St. Amand, came down with a fever on September 20, and died on September 24. He was buried at the abbey church with an epitaph, on the tombstone, "put there by his mother, his brothers, and his sisters," which called the reader's mind not only to his poetic genius, but to his skill as a painter and a sculptor, his legal training, his service with Tavera and Egmond, and to an invitation he had recently received. "A little before his last days" a letter had come to him from Nicholas Perrenot de Granvelle, summoning him to the emperor's side once again, to serve as his Latin secretary. Hadrianus' *naenia* says that the letter came while the emperor was visiting the cities of Italy (thus in May, 1536), and Janus prepared to accept the call. It will remain a mystery, then, why Janus went to St. Amand to join van Egmond, if he was about to set out for the south again. Did he plan to tender his resignation?

A good many scholars (van Hasselt, Sterck, van Gelder, de Vocht, and Crane) have assumed that Janus went to Utrecht sometime in 1536, and, while there in the bishop's service, sat for a portrait (or portraits [72]) by his old friend, Scorel. Recently, Alfred M. M. Dekker has advanced the proposition that Janus did not go to Utrecht at all: Georges van Egmond was consecrated bishop of Utrecht at St. Amand, and remained outside his bishopric. Scorel did in fact make a portrait of Janus, but at Mechlin in 1533,[73] while Janus visited his home between the trips to Bourges and Mechlin. In Dekker's argument, this portrait, kept by the family and eventually lost, was employed by Scorel in doing a second portrait of Janus, painted in 1541 at the commission of Bishop Georges, to be hung in the church at St. Amand: this portrait, likewise lost, was the source of three extant copies, and of numerous engravings.[74]

On August 25, 1566, at the beginning of the uprising against Spanish rule in the Netherlands, a party of Huguenots rode down from Tournai and laid waste the abbey, destroying the tomb. A new tomb was erected by the abbot Charles de Par, at the urging of the canons Denys de Villers and Jerome de Winghe (all three of them have their only claim to immortality because of this good deed); in its inscription, apart from mentioning the worthy gentlemen just listed, attention was called to the "most celebrated poet, second to none"—time had put the rest of Janus

Secundus' glories in proper perspective. But this tomb also disappeared; in 1797 the abbey church was sold, and, a year later, torn down.

However, Janus' immortality had been established long since. The *Basia* were printed in 1536, without the last poem in the series, based upon a copy of the poems made by Michael Nerius, a friend of Janus; this edition was shortly followed (1538, 1539) by two more, again the work of Nerius. By 1541, the Borculo edition of the works, taken care of by the faithful brothers, appeared; this was followed by still others—that of 1561, from Paris, of 1581 (together with the poems of Michael Marullus and Hieronymus Angerianus), again from Paris, that from the Elzevier press of 1612, together with his brothers' verse, and finally the great Scriverius editions of 1619 and 1631.

CHAPTER 2

The Elegies

I *Background*

JANUS Secundus was not a venturesome reader: Xenophon is the only prose writer of antiquity he ever mentions. The style of the *Itineraries* offers few hints about his favorites in Latin prose; it has been observed that, in his clarity and liveliness, he resembles the better pages of Cicero and Pliny the Younger, and that, in the *Itineraries'* single reflective passage—the meditation on travel and death—he appears to echo the style of Seneca the essayist.[1] On the side of Latin verse, we have a relatively full picture of Janus' rather simple set of models. A misleading review of some of Janus' Latin readings will be found in the epistolary elegy addressed to Jerome Zurita (III, 16), where he lists the authors he would like to pore over with his Saragossan friend. First, he mentions the *Aeneid,* paying special attention to its later and duller parts; he turns to the poet "who makes the terrible rages of Caesar resound" (Lucan), he throws out a reference to Claudianus' *Rape of Proserpine,* and he would like to pass through the diverse forests ("varias per silvas") of the "singer of Parthenope" (the Statius of the *Silvae*) until he arrives at the "high walls of Amphion's lyre," in other words, at the *Thebais.* The list should be taken with a grain of salt: the Netherlander had the intention both of impressing the Spanish humanist with a display of learning, and of flattering him with the references to the Spaniard Lucan, and Claudianus, in whom Zurita was particularly interested. A similar case of showing off can be found in the "springtime" elegy (6) of the Third Book; the lucky poet, seated in his *locus amoenus,* lists the poets to be recited (Vergil and Pindar) or to be read there (Lucan). That Janus could in fact "recite" Pindar is doubtful, since the first printings, with Trissino's Latin translations, had only lately appeared;

The Elegies

Lucan gets the same pat phrase as in the elegy to Zurita: ". . . infestas qui Caesaris intonat iras" (III, 16:19; III, 6:15)—hardly a sign of burning enthusiasm on Janus' part. Lucan's topic of civil war was more likely to appeal, as it did, to the patriotically minded German, Petrus Lotichius Secundus, than to Janus, whose topic was love, not war.

In both these cases, the poem to Zurita and the springtime elegy, Janus gets around to the poets for whom he has a genuine affection once he has fired off his heavy guns for impression's sake. He goes on to tell Zurita that, together, they will read of Lesbia, Corinna, Delia, Nemesis, and Cynthia ("the first love of the Latin Callimachus"); respectively, these are the literary loves of Catullus, Ovid, Tibullus (responsible for the third and fourth names), and Propertius. The springtime elegy also ticks them off, this time in a somewhat different order, Ovid, "lascivious Catullus," "elegant Tibullus," and "the one from whose words Cynthia has her fame." Still unnamed, Propertius is the last and best again.[2]

Janus paid the three of them—excluding Ovid—extended homage in the third elegy of the third book, "In libellos Catulli, Tibulli, et Propertii": "Here you behold, undefiled, the splendors of Latin before you, / Togaed solemnity joined to a proud sweetheart's delights" (BB, I, 161:1–2). Then he has the immortal beloveds themselves parade before the reader, Lesbia saddened by the death of her sparrow, Delia with her sensual step, Nemesis at her side, and—the Propertian finale once more—proud Cynthia, shooting fire from her eyes. Why Ovid and his Corinna were omitted from the poem, it is hard to say. Surely, it cannot be the result of Ovid's having contributed less to the poetic language of Janus[3] than did the other elegists and Catullus; there is no Roman poet whose turns of phrase (and mythological references) Janus echoes more frequently; and, if Ovid was a great phrasemaker, Janus tried hard to rival him.[4] Probably it is because of the very diffuseness of Ovid's influence that Janus leaves him out of the accolade. But, more important than what "In libellos" tells us about Catullus and Tibullus, and what it fails to say about Ovid, is the rank it once more accords Propertius. Without question, Propertius is the main literary force behind the Julia-elegies. Yet Janus did not try to imitate some aspects of Propertius' poetic personality at all (for example, his bitterness), and there is a temptation to propose that it was the creation and not the creator that fascinated Janus; in an epigram (I, 20), Cynthia shoves her unhappy lover offstage altogether:

Cynthia, after black death had taken you from us and sprinkled
   Darkling shadows where once starlight had shone from your eyes,
Truly Laconia feared that she would fall prey to like darkness,
   Feared that a like cloud would bring weakness and failing and fall:
Each time the turn of the earth banked the fires of the goddess's brother,
   Terror took hold of her heart, as she remembered your fate.

(BB, I, 308)

But this suggestion slights Propertius, whose monomaniacal devotion Janus imitated so successfully in the elegies. In fact, it is Janus' Propertian singleness-of-mind from which he draws his peculiar strength; the humanistic poets were often all too easily distracted—discursiveness is a besetting vice of theirs.

A pattern of shifting literary affections can be discerned in Janus. The schoolboy follows Lucretius (*In laudem utriusque Cupidinis*), Vergil (the early letters to Everardus and the *Expostulatio cum Neptuno*), and Horace (the celebratory odes). Propertius becomes the model for the Julia-elegies and Catullus for the *Basia*, although Ovid and Tibullus constantly offer aid to the formulation of what Janus feels and thinks. There is a hint, in the poem to Diego Hurtado de Mendoza, that Tibullus gained a special importance as the poet perceived what he thought he could and could not do. The famous tag from Tibullus' first elegy, "parva seges satis est" ("a small field's harvest suffices") says what Janus tells Diego: that he is a poet of small themes, and knows it. This progression does not mean that Janus was an eclectic poet, judged by the standards of his day. Ellinger pointed out long ago that borrowing from the classics is a wholly legitimate technique of the Neo-Latin poet.[5] The miracle is that—out of the classical Latin parts and models—Janus shaped a style readily identifiable, in the best poems, as his own. He had few contemporaries for whom the same claim could be made.

Paul van Tieghem divided the Latin literature of the Renaissance into three periods,[6] the first of them comprised of "the fifteenth and the first quarter of the sixteenth century," the sec-

The Elegies

ond—much shorter—has its beginning in the Reformation and extends, roughly, to the sixteenth century's final quarter, and the third of them stands under the aegis of the Counter-Reformation and Protestantism's reaction to that religious and cultural movement. The first period, in which the hegemony is held by Italy and then by the Netherlands, with Germany as an ally, is by far the richest in works of genuine poetic value; the second sees the division of this "international" literature into two camps, where it is made, particularly on the Protestant side, to serve polemic purposes, while the Catholics become more cautious in their use of "pagan" references and thus more "Christian"; the third possesses a large body of what might be called informative and speculative prose, while poetry becomes paler, more artificial. Many corrections could be made in Van Tieghem's scheme; he is particularly unfair toward the virtuoso lyric and drama (by Jesuits and others) of the *Spätzeit*. But, taken large, the outline is still useful. The first period, of course, absorbs our attention, for at its very end, there stands Janus Secundus. He sums up the best of its potential in the lyric; he is, as it were, the child of Italy's Neo-Latin poets of the *quattrocento*.

A catalog of Janus' knowledge in this field is given in the elegy (III, 7) addressed to Hieronymus Monti; the mistress of ceremonies in the poem is the Elegy herself, personified, with her "uneven steps"—the dactylic hexameter and pentameter of the distich. (The poem does not reveal, by the way, which sort of elegy—mournful or more directly amorous—it is that speaks. Janus indulges in mystification by allowing two elegy-goddesses, the one sad and bearing a cypress branch, the other redolent of the myrtle, to appear; but only one of them—we are not told which—opens her mouth. However, he reveals his bias in the matter by noting a resemblance between the spokeswoman-elegy's odd gait and Venus' famous limp.) Elegy makes her way through the annals of Italy's Neo-Latin verse in accordance with chronology: she opens with the great Joannes Pontanus (1422?–1503); then proceeds to the "Strozigenae," Titus Vespasianus Strozzi (c. 1425–1505), who spent his life polishing and repolishing his *Erotica* (they finally appeared in 1514), and his son Hercules (1471–1508), who practiced his father's craft with somewhat less success; there follow Michael Marullus (c.1450–1500), the native of Constantinople who became a chief ornament of Italian-Latin verse, Pietro Bembo (1470–1547), man of the cloth and the flesh, poet in Latin and Italian, Grudius' admired Vida (1490–1566), the epicist of the *Christias*, Jacopo Sannazaro (1458–1530), again an author both in his mother tongue and in "the old Ausonian" one, famous for his *Arcadia* in the first department and his *Piscatoriae* (together with his osculatory verse) in the second, and finally, as we know, Alciatus, who had been the teacher both of Monti and Secundus. Leaving Alciatus aside, who had made his impact through personal acquaintance, it was no doubt Pontanus (see chapter 4, *ad fin.*) and Marullus who gave the most to Janus. We are poorly informed about the meeting of spirits between Marullus and his Dutch reader: from Janus' own hand we have only the reference in this elegy, and the epigram written to accompany the return of a volume of Marullus' verse to Franciscus Hoverius [7]—a new edition of the *Epigrammata et Hymni* (first published at Florence in 1497) had appeared at Paris in 1529, with an introduction by the Alsatian humanist Beatus Rhenanus, and it may be guessed that the good Hoverius had passed this printing along to Janus. Did the loan by Hoverius provide Janus with his first contact with Marullus, or had he read him before? The answer cannot be found in the epigram to Hoverius; from it, we learn only how highly Janus thought of Marullus and his "everlasting treasure," his "masterwork" (BB, I, 317, Epigrams I, 32). The epigram closes with a reference to Marullus' "pious praises of the ancient gods," praises which had aroused, incidentally, the ire of Erasmus, who found the Greek-Italian much too pagan; but they did not disturb Janus, himself inclined to a large tolerance in such matters, and, besides, Janus was probably less interested by Marullus' hymns, where these pagan tendencies are displayed at length, than by the "epigrams"; here, Marullus' ability to talk about his love for Neaera without ever repeating himself must have aroused the admiration of Janus:

Lately fair Venus beheld Neaera and saw she was woundless,
    And to her offspring she said: "Why do your darts slack their task?"
To her the boy-god replied, his eyes all dejected and weeping:
    "Mother, she catches my darts, hurling them back at my heart." [8]

The review of Italy's Neo-Latinists in the poem to Monti must have been composed during the stay at Bourges; Elegy, personified, remarks that—thanks to Alciatus—the "urbs Biturix" is not

The Elegies

foreign to her. It was written, as its title says, to thank Monti for the "gift of some epitaphs and elegies." We wonder if Monti's gift was itself a *quid pro quo*, and if, from Bourges, Janus had sent Monti a copy of his *Julia Monobiblos*. In his elegy on the death of Janus, Monti made a point of mentioning the late poet's experience with Julia, underlining the tenderness of Janus' age when that little tragedy of love took place:

Julia captured you when, long ago, you were green and unwary,
    Julia sowed the first spark, setting your spirit afire;
It was from her that you learned to write your sad poems of loving,
    And it's from you she will get fame that will live evermore.
                                (BB, II, 287-88:45-48)

Monti placed his passage about the youth of Julia's lover last in his poem, an envoy not to be overlooked; and we should do well to bear in mind what Monti said as we examine the *Monobiblos*, the first of Janus' two masterpieces of love poetry. Like *Werther*, it is a book about a world which will go to pieces—the disappointed lover thinks—unless he gets the girl he wants. In this respect, of course, its fiction is not the same as that of the elegies of Propertius which inspired it. Cynthia was a courtesan, from whom Propertius obtained what he wanted, whenever Cynthia was in the mood to give it; the fascination of the poems lies in their depiction of a sophisticated relationship—the two, Cynthia and Propertius, tormented each other with their various acts of faithlessness. Julia, though, is assumed to have been the respectable daughter of a respectable citizen of Mechlin; she was not generous with her favors, and the story ended with her wedding to someone else.

II Julia Monobiblos *and the Solemn Elegies*

The *Julia Monobiblos* takes its name from the first book of Propertius' Elegies, which was likewise called *monobiblos* (a book filling a single roll of script) by its first editor, Philippus Beroaldus the Elder. Like Propertius' *monobiblos* (with the exception of its concluding poems, XX–XXII), the *monobiblos* of Janus tells the story of the poet's passion; unlike Propertius' book, however, it is clearly a poem cycle, designed to recount the affair's events in chronological order and with some completeness. As Ellinger remarks (II:1:32), Janus paid careful attention—like Goethe—to the sequence in which the reader would confront his poems; the fruits of that labor can readily be seen in the *Julia* cycle and the *Basia*. The cycle begins with a conversation between the poet and Cupid, in which the former says that others may sing of war and heroic deeds; he will sing of the "winged boy with his blessed mother." (The motif is scarcely original with Janus; Ovid had made it the program of the *Amores*.) Unfortunately, Cupid is not mollified by the flattering news; instead he continues to sharpen his arrows, which gives Janus the chance to turn a handsome phrase —a modified *epanalepsis*—about himself: "Tuus est; laedere parce tuum" (1. 16: "He [the poet] is yours; cease wounding one of your own"). Unmoved, Cupid lets his arrow fly, telling the poet and the reader that he provides the lucky-unlucky victim with a rich store of literary material, "Accipe quae, dixit, multa diuque canas" (1. 18: "Take it, you'll make many songs from it a long time to come"); he points to his pedagogical intention—"Formaque quid valeat disce decentis herae" (1. 20: "Learn what the beauty is worth that a fair mistress can give"), thus introducing the second of the main characters (if we leave out Cupid himself) in this tale of love. The poem ends abruptly, with a promise or a threat: ". . . et una / Cum jaculo in venas sensimus isse Deum" (11. 21–22: the poet "sense[s] / That with his arrow the God found his way into my veins"). Divine gift and poison all at once, combined in a superb verse; if it is a recasting of Propertius (I, 9: 21: "quam pueri totiens arcum sentire medullis," "[You will much rather approach Armenian tigers] . . . than to feel so often the boy's bow in your innermost self"), as Burmann-Bosscha claim, who cares? The new version is the property of the young poet.

A story lies behind the second elegy of the *Monobiblos*. It was not composed in 1531, as a part of the "contemporary record of an actual love affair, written when the poet was not yet twenty" (Crane, p. 13), but was finished at Segovia on June 3, 1534, and was sent to Hadrianus Marius with a covering letter, in which Janus tells of his decision to add it to the "book written about Julia." "Forgive me if you find something turbulent in this elegy: the largest part of it has been poured out [*effusa est*] while I was riding, these last days. You—who are yourself composed—must strive to make it smooth, and return it to me

The Elegies 79

in a more sedate shape. For I loathe nothing so much as the reexamination of my own poems" (BB, II, 278). There is something of the fairy tale here: appearing to the fates when Janus was born, Cupid had claimed the baby for his service; then the god uttered a prophetic charm over the cradle, which the nurse ("filled with icy terror") heard and recounted later on. The child, grown up, would find a girl "worthy of the couch of the gods," a girl who would prefer him both to the gods' embraces and the wealth of the Indies; in return, she would be raised to the stars by his poetic genius. The baby is pretty well frightened by these views of the future beloved (her bright eyes will send "secret flames to your heart"), and begins to howl. First, Cupid tries to quiet his little listener by telling him to save his tears, since he will need them later on; then, changing course, the god informs young Janus of the pleasures which await amid the sufferings of love: as Cupid says, he himself has learned his lesson well from the tutor, Ovid, whom his mother hired for him—and so has Janus: the echoes of the *Amores* and the *Ars amatoria* come thick and fast. The allusion to Ovid not only gives the work added validity, by the lights of the age; it also allows Janus to indulge in the equally typical humanistic practice of self-praise; as Ovid, "by his loving," has added to the fame of the Pelignians, so Janus will not lack honor among the Belgians. Next, echoing Tibullus (I, 1:75–78), Janus adduces a catalog of expensive things which are altogether worthless without love, an inversion of the theme introduced by Cupid's prophecy, early in the poem: the riches which love will bestow upon the lover. Then (and our interest picks up) there is a policy statement by the poet—he is more suited to write of love than of weightier themes; even the possibility of Caesarian epic is touched upon and rejected:

Let it not be your concern to sing of earth or the heavens,
   Nor of the swollen waves Tethys sends forth with a roar,
Nor of the signals which show us the stars in their rise and their
    falling,
   What place they hold in the sky, whether it be high or low;
Nor let it be your task to sing of the triumphs of Caesar,
   Though he's a scion, they say, sprung from my fair mother's womb.
But, in slow-tempoed verse, develop the elegies' sweetness,
   That they'll be able to make my loving softness submit.
                        (BB, I, 16–18:87–94)

The theme of riches has returned, and the theme of the poet's assigned fate is expanded. We may complain at the poem's *longueurs,* but we cannot deny the soundness of its construction; we have been led from the poetic gift to love's riches to the poem's center piece, the prediction of the sufferings and pleasures of the lover, and have then been taken back, past riches again, to the gift and its dimensions. An alphabetical scheme could readily be made: a/b/c/b/a.

The second elegy is a justification, then, made three years after the fact, of the beginnings of Janus' career as a love poet. In the third elegy we return to 1531; it is a shortish poem, of forty lines, about young men in love. If they are ashamed of submitting to the "servile chains" of a mistress, there is something distinctly wrong with them; as for Janus, he is ready to endure all sorts of things, since the mistress is beautiful ("cum sit formosa"): wind and rain, silence of night, deserted streets. (However, he does not walk alone; he is accompanied by the pseudo-Tibullus of *Elegies* IV, 13:10.) Indeed, he will even go to places where neither the wheel nor the ship can pass, if the beloved wishes his company. Finally, if this were not enough, Janus hopes (like Tibullus in I, 1:59–62) that his mistress will be with him on his dying day, so that his departing spirit, caught by her lips, will return to the beloved herself, the source of its existence, "spurning the Elysian fields and the blessed vale for the kisses of so sweet a mistress." It all hovers on the border of the *adynaton,* to which Roman love-lyricists, and Neo-Latinists, had constant recourse in order to express the strength of their feelings, and to show off their inventiveness. But here the piling up of exaggerated statements is justified by the poem's place in the cycle; there is a psychological aptness about the expression of such feelings at the opening of the love affair.

The fourth elegy, briefer still, shows the lover from a different, happier, and quainter side. There is a practice, Janus says, according to which people who walk abroad in the month of May must bear a greening branch; caught without it, they must pay a forfeit. Now ready to offer something more real than *adynata* to Julia, Janus proposes a bet to her: if she catches him out, then he will give her a necklace (whose resting place he will envy, he says); should she lose, she must give him kisses, kisses which—a link to the end of the preceding poem—would "be able to stop a fleeing life, where no hopes remain for recovery." With a low

The Elegies

voice, but with eyes that say a great deal, she promises him kisses indeed, and something that he will "think much better than her kisses."

After the imaginary sufferings of Elegy III, and the pledged pleasures of Elegy IV, the fifth elegy gets down, at some length, to persuasion. Janus says, in sum, that he cannot continue to live in his present state, and besides—a handsome compliment both to Julia and himself—"In mortal company's ranks there is no place for a god." He tells Julia that he does not possess the stuff of which heroes are made, and begs her to let him live: "I am not one of those from whose death triumph goes forth." Having thus both kept and eaten the cake of his argument, he asks, like Catullus, for a hundred or a thousand kisses, or: "Give me, my light, something more, and I shall be a god." Unhappily, Julia is not prepared to follow the first suggestion, let alone the second; and so Janus tries the threat of age against the beloved, as so many other poets had and would—Propertius, Ovid, Ronsard. "Tempus erit," a time will come when she will be a crone, on whose mute threshold no lover will sing. Then the element of Janus' mounting passion is reintroduced, and there is a counterpoint of commonplace (beauty cold and ruined) against commonplace (lover hot and alive) which succeeds by its obviousness. At length, having had a vision of Julia's arrival in Hades (where—Janus is not a logical arguer—the shades will rush forward to greet her loveliness, which he has just taken such pains to destroy in verse), the poet turns the screw one final time, giving Julia a picture of love's ultimate delights, all entwined, like the syntax itself—only to cut off the scene with another warning about mortality: "Death approaches, its head encircled by clouds everlasting." But the poem is still not finished; a coda seems to mock its storm and stress—youths notice that Janus is in a bad way, and laugh at his drunken words. ("Ebria verba" have been used with great cunning in the poem.) Still, once they know his suffering's source, these youths will say: "Non infeliciter arsit," an intentional ambiguity, suggesting both "He burned, but not in a worthless cause" and "He did not burn in vain." It is a final reference to the poem's opening themes: death from love unrequited and life from love fulfilled.

The sixth elegy moves away from emotional choices to those of an artist's means of expression; Janus employs his customary modesty concerning his attainments in the plastic arts to his own amorous and poetic advantage. He wishes he had the fingers of Praxiteles and Mentor, the hands of Lysippus and Phidias—all four of whom are lined up in the first distich—in order to do justice to Julia's beauty: "Julia would like me to draw her face, gold itself, with my burin, / And not to have her fair name stand in my poems alone" (BB, I, 40:3–4). His skill, as we might guess, is not up to the task, nor are his tools and materials; his eyes, his hand, his spirits fail, and he becomes (artistically) as impotent as the man in Stendhal's *De L'Amour* who becomes so overwhelmed with a lady's beauty that he cannot take it when it is offered to him. A last compliment ends the poem: "Oh, no mortal's allowed to capture the face of a goddess: / Failing in mind and in hand, I am no more what I was" (BB, I, 42:19–20). This is a fib, at least as matters turned out; he finished his medallion of Julia and asked Scorel for his opinion of it (see p. 36). He liked to mention the "sculpture" of Julia made by the "poet's hand" (for example, in the poetic epistle to Dantiscus [BB, II, 41:46]), and his friends regarded the portraits of Julia as a part of his love cult, and his fame. In two copies of Scorel's portraits of Janus,[9] he has a medallion of Julia in his hand.

Cupid's promises of miseries, as well as grandeurs, come true in the seventh elegy. Hardly had Janus begun his work, he says (which work—the *Monobiblos* itself, the medallion, Julia's seduction?), when a rustic appeared, come from a distant city (Schroeter, allowing his imagination to run away with him, called the "rusticus" an "alter Satyr"), armed with honorable intentions. The audience is not told precisely what happened; instead, Janus pours out a string of curses, some his own, some, in transformation, borrowed from Tibullus and Horace, against the intruder. (For example, Horace's prayer to the gods to grant free passage to his Galatea, shielding her against woodpecker and crow [III, 27], is changed into a wish that these bad birds may bar the rustic's way.) The parting shot is a reminder that Julia's first lover belongs to a special class: may these punishments serve as a warning not to tamper with the pleasures of poets, "vatum deliciis." The rebuke delivered to Julia is similarly literary—so literary, of course, that it will make the reader smile, as he is intended to, at the mock rage of the whole scene. Julia has not only condemned herself by a swift word to eternal misery (she evidently said yes to the rustic's proposal); she has also deprived herself of membership in the immortal band of Corinna, Delia, Nemesis, and Cynthia—to which, for good measure, Janus adds another name, Lycoris, the beloved of the first Latin elegist, Gallus. Indeed, had she been true, young men and women would have made a cult of visiting her grave.

Since the Julia of the elegy remains unmoved by this prospect of a life after death, Janus is given the opportunity to provide still another catalog, this time about the immortality of classical poets: Vergil, Horace, Propertius, Ovid, and Tibullus pass in review again, and the recitation would be boring, were it not for the lines which open and close the list. Janus lets the cat out of the bag: he would have had a brilliant poetic career, were it not for this accursed marriage ("male faustus Hymen"). A lost Julia is bad enough, but a career ruined because of a lost source of inspiration—that is worse still. After all, had not the goddess with the myrtle branch and the unequal step (the mixture of Venus and Elegia) promised him immortality? We see the germ cell of the "elegy on elegy" to Monti (III, 7), but, more important, we see what a Julia and, later on, a Neaera, meant to Janus.

What follows may sound like frustration's wish-dream, but it is as much a part of the Renaissance literary tradition as what has gone before—Janus calls up *la bell' età dell' oro*, which allows him to say, rather boldly, that things were better by far before Hymen was added to the company of the gods, when—before the servile name of marriage was known—our ancestors practiced the free art of Venus. Since this "first age" cannot return for the general public, Janus suggests that Julia may want to recreate it for herself and him; no one will blame her if she makes the life of her spouse miserable. An unworthy husband is rightly cuckolded by young lovers (a theme which had recently received a classic expression in Piccolomini's *Euryalus et Lucretia*); then Janus turns to Propertius again—soon the rustic will tire of his prize, and Julia will lie alone, waiting in vain to be embraced by Janus ("Julia, I shall not come"). Finally, when the husband returns, worn out by wandering loves ("peregrino lassus amore"), he will be able to do nothing for the lonely girl. Any number of charges could be brought against the seventh elegy: it is rambling, it is self-contradictory in its attitudes, it depends too much on tradition for its effects. But, leaving the last of these charges aside (it can be brought against every Neo-

Latinist), it may be retorted that the poem is long-winded, disjointed, and sometimes absurd precisely because it is a statement of emotional upset—an upset which seems to mock itself at first, but which then becomes more and more in earnest.

The awful day of the wedding came, Janus galloped off to Brussels. Riding in the rain, he poured out the eighth elegy, twenty lines long; we are informed about the conditions of its composition in the letter which he sent to Petrus Clericus from Brussels, where the elegy is quoted entire (BB, II, 270–72). The gods were displeased at what was happening, and thus were altogether willing to comply with Janus' request for a storm. The downpour gives the poem the air of an antiepithalamium, because a standard feature of the marriage poem was to wish the bride and bridegroom good weather. Yet the poem has one other charm, apart from the story of its writing and its parody upon a typical feature of nuptial verse: once again it is the mixture of blind heat and calculating cold in Janus' attitude. He will be forced, he says, to take his passion elsewhere, an accurate sizing-up of the situation; yet, at the same time, the romantic aspect of his passion gets its due: "No one was ever loved thus, nor will ever be so much beloved, / Whether my days will be few, or will be many to come" (BB, I, 63:5–6). Even though we are aware that a part of the distich belongs to Catullus ("Amata nobis quantum amabitur nulla," 8:5, "No one will be loved as much as [you have] been loved by me") we are interested, borrowing or not, by Janus' conflicting emotions. It is no wonder that a commentator of an earlier generation, Ellinger, saw a resemblance between the young Janus and the young Goethe. Today, we might be more inclined to say that Janus had aped—or learned well from—Propertius, with what Einar Löfstedt called the Roman's mixture of "passion" and "drastic realism." [10]

Rainer Maria Rilke used parts of his correspondence for portions of his novel, *Die Aufzeichnungen des Malte Laurids Brigge;* either he had an exceedingly good memory, or he copied out striking passages before he sent the letters off. The ninth elegy may have a similar root; the letter to Petrus Clericus (BB, II, 270–72), in which Janus presents his friend with the eighth elegy, in fact bears close resemblance to the ninth poem in the cycle, and it is to Clericus, for the rest, that the elegy is addressed. The Clericus-letter opens with an extended encomium

The Elegies

to Brussels: "Here we are in the most celebrated city, here we are in the company of most learned men, and our eyes and ears lack nothing which will please them." But then the bottom falls out: "And we are here, nonetheless, against our will." The elegy begins in just the same way; the city-encomium is expanded to sixteen lines, including comparisons of Brussels to Athens and Rome, but the message of praise is similar, and the edifice of compliments is similarly destroyed: "Here are myriad things which can capture my hearing, my vision, / None of them captures my eyes, none of them captures my ears" (BE, I, 65:15–16). The letter to Clericus continues: "None of the others believe this, perhaps you will not believe it either, you who are aware of my passion." And the poem says: "No one, save you alone, can offer belief to my story, / And, if your belief fails, you must believe nonetheless" (ll. 17–18). At this point a no doubt unanswerable question arises. In the letter, after one more sentence, in which Janus reflects on the slim chance of his expelling Julia from his heart, he quotes the final six lines of the ninth elegy. Had he already composed the whole poem, and made a prose reduction of its ingressus for the letter to Clericus? Or had these last six lines (in which he tells of a possible replacement for Julia—"Candida quantumvis, et non deformior illa" ["Very beautiful, and not less lovely than she"]) come into being first, and then were inserted into the letter to Clericus? In this case, the remainder of the poem—its first fifty-eight lines—would have been written later on, perhaps with the aid of the letter itself. It is always instructive to look into the poet's creative process, however brief the view. The letter to Clericus may also be useful in another respect: it offers a first version of the elegy's conclusion, in which Janus described the "vicina" ("neighbor") who had now captured his attention—"Saepe meos oculos in se moretur" ("Often the neighbor girl draws my eyes to her"): which then becomes, in the printed text, "Saepe meos oculos in se Domitilla moretur." However seriously we may take Janus' emotional upset (and scholarship was once inclined to take it very seriously indeed), he was quite prepared to improve, and to stylize, his outbursts. The letter of the brokenhearted youth ends with suggestions for emendations in the seventh and eighth elegies, which had already been sent along to Clericus.

Ellinger regarded the ninth elegy as one of the best in the set (III:1:34). The opening tribute to Brussels could stand alone as a representative of a genre the humanist-poets loved, the praise of the city, their natural habitat; but the encomium serves another purpose as well—as a bright preparation for the poem's dark center. For, after the transitory passage in which Janus talks to Clericus directly (and from which we learn about the often-noted story of Clericus' own uncomplicated attachment to Julia), we are brought to the poem's heart, in which we are compelled to make a double comparison: between Clericus' light affection, readily healed, and what we are told is Janus' unflagging passion, and between Brussels, "casting forth eternal waters from its fountains," and Mechlin, emptied of the object of love but quite full of memories of her. (Julia has gone away with her husband "where the Scheldt rolls its green waves into the sea"; was the "rusticus" in fact a merchant from Antwerp?) Again a phrase in the prose letter appears to be the source of a passage in verse; in the former Janus writes: "Sed abcessit illa: quid tum? tum? restant vestigia; et propinquior aliquando istic illi futurus sim" ("She has gone—what then? What then? The traces remain, and the thought that sometime I may be closer to her there"), and in the poem:

> She has gone, and I must suffer. What is left? Only her footprints,
>   And the places which put lingering joys in our care.
> And if I go there again, I shall be closer to her presence.
>   (BB, I, 66:31–33)

The prose goes on to say that Clericus may think these things foolish, and the verse repeats: "Esse putas haec tu ludicra? magna loquor" ("You think I am speaking in jest? I speak here of serious things"). His point is proved, then, by a passage which captures the essence of the elegy in the sense most familiar to us, the poem of longing for something irretrievably lost:

> When, at evening, a score of new carriages stopped on the marketplace,
>   When the vessels returned, brought on the slow tide of night,
> In my foolhardiness I would inspect all the vessels at dockside,
>   Go through the carriages' ranks, gazing at them one by one,
> Thinking this hour perhaps would bring back to me my beloved,
>   Whether in Venus' car, drawn on its sweet-sounding wheels,
> Or borne along in her shell, that shines through the crystalline waters,

The Elegies

Or from the roses sprung forth that cover the Cyprian's lap.
(BB, I, 66:35-42)

The real Brussels seen by daylight is to be compared, by the reader, with the dream Mechlin seen by twilight; and then the reader is brought back to reality again, this time a nasty one. For, while Janus roams Mechlin in his genuinely elegiac mood, Julia is pressed down by the weight of her husband. To be sure, that is not exactly what the poem says next; Janus makes the reader imagine her actual situation by constructing, paradoxically, a quasi-consolatory dream. Venus had substituted a wretched whore ("scortillum turpe") in the bridal bed, and "the barbarian holds her in his odious embraces," preserving the true Julia intact for Janus "in the Idalian groves." Thus the sudden turn of Janus to the figure of the "vicina/Domitilla", mentioned above, will be seen to be a part of the poem's structure, or a last variation upon its theme of reality-and-dream. If Julia's fleshly parts are transformed into the little whore, "scortillum," then Janus has simply turned his own flesh toward another diminutive, toward Domitilla, "Oscula quae facilis ad me sponte venit" ("Who so readily comes, glad to receive my embrace"). Reality, which has started off so grandly in the poem, in the view of Brussels, is now clearly smaller and less valuable than the dream—but still very much worth having. Indeed, we have to possess its little pleasures in order to bear its distresses (of an empty Mechlin, and of Julia in another's bed). Yet, set against Brussels, bereft Mechlin, and the "barbarian's" Antwerp, the dream is what triumphs: a twilit Mechlin filled with visions, Julia whisked away by Venus to a never-never land of classical allusion.

The tenth elegy grows out of the exalted strain in the ninth; now the dreams of the ninth have no tangible connection with reality. However, the dream—the poem's title is "Somnium"—is prepared for very carefully; Julia is restored to that primacy she once held: "Prima mihi quae fax, quae mihi serus amor" ("She who was my first flame, and will be my last love")—a line plainly fathered by the most famous of Propertius' remarks about Cynthia, "Cynthia prima fuit, Cynthia finis erit." And now she is completely in his power, to which she accedes altogether willingly. The reader will recall the return of the golden age, proposed in the seventh elegy; here, in the "Somnium," the details of the world of perfect erotic freedom are a good deal homelier—another of Janus' effective uses of contrast, between unbridled emotion and the practical details of the imagined assignation. Julia's mother, the guardian of her daughter's morals, is absent; "Sola jacet mecum semoto Julia lecto"—"Julia lies alone with me in a remote bed." Alone, that is, save for Venus and her son and perhaps even the other gods, who are asked not to be envious of the lovers' pleasures, just as Janus, presently, is not envious of theirs. The preparatory play in the imaginary bed so excites Janus that he indulges in chiasmus: "Te teneo, mea Lux, Lux mea, te teneo." ("I hold you, my light, my light, I hold you"), a statement which is turned directly into a series of questions: "What can I say? Is it true? Is Julia here in my arms? / Am I asleep? Do I wake? Is it true, or a phantom of slumber?" Are these things true or dreams? The word "somnium" predominates in the reply: "If they are dreams, let them last for a long time." Unfortunately, they do not; the poem ends abruptly with a blessing for those who have not disturbed him. In other words, the climax of the love novella has been reached, intercourse with the imagination.

Like the first of the elegies, the last (eleven) is addressed to Cupid. The son is given a votive offering of these "primos ignes" ("first flames") while his mother, "sancta Venus," gets "primitias" ("first fruits"). That the word "primus" is made the kernel of a wordplay at the opening of the cycle's last poem is clever, of course; it also reveals what the poem's burden will be. In the cycle, which Janus pretends is his first poetic outing, the lover has had a bad time; but he knows what he has gained from it— his poetry—and his heart stands open, ready to receive new wounds. He has some hard words for Hymen, as before; the marriage god, not Cupid, caused the catastrophe. Thoughts of Hymen lead him into the contrasting center of the poem; making a variation upon the theme of votive offerings, "primos ignes" and "primitias," he likens himself to a farmer who, looking at the green husks, believes that golden ears will shortly come, only to have these "vota" (simultaneously "wishes" and "vows") destroyed by hail and rain. Plainly, the one set of fruits of love, to be had in bed with Julia, has not been harvested; but the other and more valuable harvest, the poems, stands ready. Janus returns to his presentation speech—the dedication of the *Monobiblos* to the deities who inspired it—and holds out the

The Elegies

elegies once more. He asks for certain guarantees, to be sure: that he will not be the talk of the wineshops (a fate that Propertius also wanted to avoid), and that next time his "pain of love" will be more protracted. Finally, his eye fixed on his and Julia's shared immortality, he has his deathbed lines ready: "'Such was the maiden who got splendid fame from my small verses: / Julia was first to possess booty that came from my heart'" (BB, I, 83:55–56). "Prima . . . Julia": the play on "primus" is made a last time in the address to the deities of love which closes the poem; they are asked to accept "these elegies, monuments of a first passion," "primi monumenta caloris."

For the next three years, Janus kept the memory of Julia alive by means of the "Elegiae solennes" which form the appendix to the *Monobiblos*. A review of the chronology of the affection for Julia is in order here: the happy days fall in the winter and spring of 1531, the marriage of Julia took place the same year, and the three solemn elegies were written in 1532, 1533, and 1534, the last of them containing unmistakable references to Spain. They do not have the immediacy of the cycle to which they are affixed; Janus does appear to have been unusually dependent upon fresh experience. Despite the obviously artful or constructed aspects of his poetry, of which we are particularly conscious today, he can still fairly be called an "Erlebnisdichter"; it is this quality which endeared him to the nineteenth century, with its exaggerated zeal in seeking out the "event" behind the poem. Janus "makes" his poems, of course; it was, after all, the practice of his time. But a major attraction of his work is the interplay between his restatements of classical love elegy, his employment of common rhetorical devices, and his not inconsiderable desire to present a statement about himself, and his frame of mind.

In the "Solemn Elegies," with the Julia-experience receding, the poems draw more and more heavily upon familiar material from well-known Latin verse. The first of them begins with a description of Maytime which reminds the reader a little too forcibly of the corresponding passage in an Horatian ode (I, 4), and closes with the same moral as Horace's poem: Horace tells his friend Sestius—and Janus tells a whole "flowering band of youths in the flowering month of May"—that life's springtime had best be made use of directly, for death comes all too soon. (In fairness, it might be pointed out that the poem's last line is memorably gloomy: "Morsque tenebrosa nube revincta caput" ["Death, too, its head bound about by a dark circlet of cloud"]; but the line is a reworking of a verse he had tried not long before, in the fifth elegy, "Mors venit aeterna cincta caput nebula" ["Death approaches, its head encircled by clouds everlasting"], which may in turn have been fathered by Tibullus, I, 1:70: "Iam veniet tenebris Mors adoperta caput.") What there is of genuine interest in the poem lies in its middle portion, which tells how the May rites were inspired:

This month, you see, was the first to behold how my face lost its color,
    And how my heart, overwhelmed, suffered the torments of love,
When both my eye and my step betrayed how the winged god had burned me,
    Wandering the lonely ways, careless of where I might go;
Guarding my mistress's gate, I feared not the troublesome rainstorms,
    Nor did I fear the fierce threats Boreas hurled at my head.
(BB, I, 85:15–20)

Does this mean that Janus first fell in love with Julia in Maytime, or that he first realized how cruel she was in the month of May? After a placatory remark that May also gave him "a thousand pleasures from the gentle eyes of his mistress," and after a promise to Cupid that he will receive more such songs, "wrapped in the myrtle leaf," the poem comes to its sententious end.

The second solemn elegy has an ingressus quite like that of the first; the signs of spring remind the poet that it is time to take up his annual task. For the sake of variety, the festival is somewhat changed; the servant boy is told to bring flowers, wine, and, most important, a new playmate, a "fusca puella," a brunette; she is part of the *tableau* which also contains the Muses, Hermes (the son of the May goddess Maia and Zeus, and the inventor of the lyre), and, of course, Cupid, who is invited to send a new flight of arrows at the poet. The poet, in turn, having performed his rites, will hang his songs from the myrtle tree, with a dedication to Cupid. It is plain that Janus had difficulty in maintaining the gravity of the project; what the poem turns into is an anacreontic game.

At the opening of the third memorial poem, it briefly appears that a conflict may develop between Janus, presently tasting the fleshpots of Spain, and Janus who tries to keep Julia's

The Elegies 91

memory alive: "far from his sweet homeland," he has become the prey of "torva Neaera," "cruel Neaera." The poet must placate Venus and Cupid for having broken his vows; he would first ask Venus for pardon, and then give her son a gift: putting up a statue of the naked boy, done by his hand, and placing beside it a medallion of Julia. After this reminder of his other *métier*, the poet forgets the prospective struggle, giving the elegy over to praises of the month of May, its goddess Maia, and her companion Flora, the "florum dea versicolorum," the "goddess of many-colored flowers" (the adjective contains a pun on "versiculus," "little verse")—just as the Romans held games in Flora's honor ("ludi florales"), so Janus, in Hesperia, will sing songs for her. Thus we are brought back to the Spanish setting, and, somewhat forcibly, to the celebration of Julia's memory. There is another parade of deities; Venus, Cupid, Bacchus, and Phoebus are asked to allow "these monuments of a flaming passion" to live forever, a passion inspired by the trembling glance of the girl who "has been granted a great name by my little book." The poem could be called an extended advertisement: of the *Julia Monobiblos*, of Janus' attainments as a plastic artist, and of the *Basia*—Neaera's book—to come.

In 1911, scholarship was able to add a scandalous footnote to the story of Janus and Julia. P. C. Molhuysen published a letter which he had discovered in the Leiden University Library,[11] written to Hadrianus Marius and Janus Secundus, lately arrived in Bourges; the letter was by their brother Grudius, who had not yet departed for Spain, and was dated May 29, 1532. After talking about a belated *carmen sepulchrale* he has written for the death of Margaret of Austria, describing the preparations for his trip to Spain, and thanking Janus for his "hodoeporicon," he closes with an account of Julia's latest adventures. She has suffered an illness of the eyes and other parts of the body. There are those who suspect it to have been the "noble disease"—that is, syphilis. But now she is in much better shape, with a good color, agile, most elegantly dressed. "And if you wish to know what's going on, she's busy, together with her mother and her sister, and, something that's a sign of good health, a good female organ: she continues to do the work of Venus in various forms, and to wriggle her flexible tail with gentle art, until artful Venus flows dropwise through her very marrow, and she collapses, tired from the sweet labor." The passage, in Molhuysen's opinion, proves that Julia was not a respectable young woman, but a prostitute, "of the same sort as the Corinnas, Lesbias, and Cynthias who inspired the Roman poets." The letter allows this interpretation, an interpretation which, in turn, has considerable implications; for it could indicate that the story supporting the *Monobiblos* and the solemn elegies was to a great extent a fiction. Of course, the passage in the letter could be cast aside as a kind of supportive sour grapes on the part of Nicolaus Grudius; knowing that his brother had already said that Venus had substituted a "scortillum turpe" for Julia in the marriage bed, Grudius decided to help Janus get over his loss by embroidering the poetic statement. However, such an explanation does not account for the presence of an unencumbered Julia in Mechlin in the spring of 1532. What had become of the "rusticus"? A possible answer is this: that the "virtuous" Julia was a character in Janus' literary play, that Julia was in fact a prostitute—which would not have kept her from marrying someone in a class lower than Janus' own. (Janus himself had no plans of marrying her, as he makes clear.) As for the devotion which Janus showered upon her in his verse, that is indeed a main part of the fiction—a literary devotion to a love only in part real. That Julia was a whore does not destroy the *Monobiblos* as an interesting and even moving work of art; in fact, the possibility enhances its fascination. And, for those sentimentalists who would still prefer to think well of Julia, there is always the chance that Grudius was indeed indulging in malicious slander. In his *naenia* for Janus, Grudius devotes several lines to Julia, without hinting in the least that she had been what he said she was in his letter. Yet, in the *naenia*, she is, again, a figure of literature, a part of Janus' fame, not the girl from Mechlin:

There, stepping forth from the others, Julia would mourn her poet,
    Julia herself, who had been, brother, the first of your loves;
Beautiful maidens around her, she'd conquer them, turned to a
        goddess,
    Thanks to the gift which the bard gave to her once in his love.
Casting her branches of myrtle and rose on the pitiless tombstone,
    She would soften that grave by means of her tears as they fell,
And she would press her mouth, still swollen from terrible weeping,
    Onto the dead poet's cheek, giving last gifts to his love.

III Elegies, Books Two and Three

The second book of elegies bears the title *Amores* in Scriverius' edition; there is no single leading lady: the girls who appear in elegies two through nine have various names, or no names at all. Yet they are of a single type, affording Janus the chance of living up to Boswell's dictum: "Be Spaniard: girl every day." The collection, then, is a kind of Spanish journal, in which Janus gives glimpses of Hesperia; the first and the tenth elegies (a tribute to his brothers, and a poem for the new marriage of Grudius) provide a background of orderly familial circumstance against which Janus' adventures are played. The final poem, to Carolus Catzius (eleven) is by way of being a postlude.

The opening elegy sets the tone: it is another of Janus' programmatic statements about his intention to follow the light muse, as long as his health and vigor may last. When his fires burn out, he will try to ascertain the laws of nature (an allusion to Lucretius, for whom Janus had a weakness); Vergil, Homer, and Hesiod may rest easy, as far as he is concerned—it is only the "Umbrian poet" whose shade he asks for protection, and so the stage is set for an eight-line tribute to Propertius. Having got these apologies and tributes out of the way, Janus arrives at what may have been the most important question for him: the immortality of this new little book, written, like its predecessor, under the aegis of Venus and Cupid. He does not have such high hopes for it as for the *Monobiblos,* and, should it fail to live, then he will console himself with the immortality of Hadrianus Marius and Nicolaus Grudius. The tribute to their works, the former's *Cymba,* the latter's poems on Montserrat and Narcissus, goes on a good while, finally letting Janus return, in more specific terms, to the Spanish setting of which he had given a hint at the poem's opening. Janus has thus afforded his brothers a nice write-up, in accordance with the humanist practice of praising one's colleagues in hope of praise in return; also, in doing so, he calls new attention to the statement of the poem's opening Unlike his brothers, Janus will attempt only small things.

The following elegies (2-6) illustrate his point. Elegy II is about the girl whom Wright called "the pocket Venus," Venerilla: the first section of the poem is a *pysma*, a question-series arising from her failure to come to an assignation. Is she making fun of him? Has she assigned the time to someone else? Is she trying to increase his appetites by the delay? Then there is a first climax, an erotic fantasy which is cut short by what Janus thinks are Venerilla's footsteps. He is wrong; out of his disappointment there arises an antierotic vision (of Venerilla and the other lover, laughing at him), which is then turned, once again, into more pleasant thoughts by a second advance of footsteps: "Now at long last she will pass all adorned through the door of my chamber: / Do I mistake what I hear? Does Hylax bark at my door?" (BB, I, 109:29–30). Hylax is the dog whose barking may, or may not, herald the coming of the beloved Daphnis in Vergil's Eighth Eclogue. The Vergilian allusion is a happy one; just as the reader of the Eclogue is left in doubt (*aporia*) about the lover's coming (a situation which Janus' audience of Latinists would recall), so Janus is left in doubt about Venerilla's approach. The uneasiness which is the prevailing mood of the poem is never resolved—to the poem's great artistic advantage.

In the third and fourth elegies, the poet's stratagems are more obvious and work less well, although they again proceed from the tormenting question. The lover of Elegy III tries to decide why his mistress, having excited him with her glance of flame, is so cold herself. Because Cupid hesitates to wound such a lovely creature? If so, he should light his extinguished torches at the flames of her eyes, and then, while she is asleep, set her afire with them. It is amusing to watch Janus string conceit upon conceit. Yet he is aware of the virtue of moderation (here, as in the use of classical allusion), and stops his variations upon the theme of hot-and-cold after twenty-two lines. The fourth elegy is simply a pendant, an epigram where Pseudo-Petronius' Julia and Paul the Silentiary's Hermonassa are turned into Lydia, who has struck her lover's breast with icy snow, a snow from which flame is born—a flame which cold cannot take away.[12] Lydia is requested to fight fire with fire instead: "Burn with a fire like to mine, and you'll lighten my miserable passion; / Lydia, it's by your cold that you cause me such pain without cease" (BB, I, 113:9–10).

Ellinger had the notion that the hot-eyed, icy-hearted girl of Elegy III was Neaera, who clearly has the center of the stage, or bed, in the fifth elegy. Jealousy has upset Janus, who, abandoning his oxymora, becomes the self-analyst familiar to us from the Julia-poems. He begins by admitting that he has only himself to blame: if nature had not given him such a soft heart, and lazy complaisance, he would not have put up with present humiliations. Even as he praises Neaera, someone else, a barbarian, embraces her, "stimulating [her] by my verses." With his poet's imagination, Janus has a painfully clear vision of Neaera *post coitum*: "I see your eyes half asleep, and your throat disfigured with teeth marks, / And—surely not a good sign—bedclothes all rumpled and crushed" (BB, I, 114:13–14). The vision hurts him the more because he has believed what Neaera told him about her virtue, and has written about it; this failure of his perspicacity makes him call himself a "vates vanus," an untrustworthy or inexact poet, and now—a failure both as a man and artist—he has got what he deserved: "Oh, how cruel Cupid can be—and you are crueler than he is! / Yet whether you're hateful or not, you are Neaera the fair" (BB, I, 115:23–24). The pentameter is the poem's watershed; before it self-accusation, after it a search for a way out. He will harden his heart, he will shake Neaera off, he will no longer follow her; finally, a distich from the first part, where he attempted to find out the reasons for his subjugation, is repeated:

> Dura puella, puella meis indigna Camenis,
> Alpinis animum frigidior nivibus.
>
> Hard-hearted girl, girl unfit to be part of the song of my Muses,
> Having a soul to outfreeze even the snows of the Alps.
> (ll. 37–38)

Now, however, it is uttered with a variant—"Neaera" is substituted for "puella." The effect of the distich's repetition, with the slight change and in the new ambience, is to intensify the poem's mood, and to mark the beginning of the poem's final section: a list of settings in which he might reject her. The catalog has an ironic twist, though, in that—even as it seems to posit a prouder Janus—it in fact conjures up further situations in which he could be humiliated.

The sixth elegy, like the third and the fourth, is an artful inlay between longer personal poems; it is evidently written in imitation of an epigram by Alciatus: the arrows of love and death fall into the wrong hands when they are withdrawn from the body of a dying lover. Shortly, the world is topsy-turvy: young people are struck down by what Cupid thinks are his arrows, and old folk, pierced by Death, become the happy victims of senile sexuality. At length the two archers realize what has happened, take new arrows—and now comes the *pointe* for the sake of which the somewhat macabre story has been told: "Good! But the bow of the boy-god was filled through and through with a toxin: / That is the reason he's dealt death to so many with it" (BB, I, 120:23–24).

By its telling in the third person, the little tale seems less autobiographical than the elegies which have gone before; the process of distancing is continued in another way in the seventh elegy, "written in another name and as a favor to Gonzalo Pérez, the Spaniard." Gonzalo Pérez was a notorious Don Juan, in which capacity he fathered, out of wedlock, the gifted Antonio Pérez, in maturity to become an intimate of Philip II. Furthermore, Gonzalo had the odd habit of collecting not only girls but love poems, written in his name and based on his experiences. Here, though, instead of learning how to be a successful lover, Janus became privy to the story of one of Gonzalo's less brilliant campaigns. As the poem's preamble says: the youth who goes to sea for the first time expects to drown, but how terrible shipwreck is for the old salt whose ship founders in sight of the homeland. In a poem from his middle years, "Man muss sterben weil man sie kennt," Rilke remarked that the experienced sailor on the sea of love keeps quiet, and "die bestandenen / Schrecken spielen in ihm wie in zitternden Käfigen." Gonzalo, however, reacts in just the opposite way; confronted with defeat by the lovely Justine, he cannot stop talking—in Janus' poem—about what has befallen him; in a style quite unlike that of Janus, who employs the extended simile only rarely, he compares himself to a soldier who keeps on fighting, unaware that he has been dealt a mortal wound, and falls dead only at battle's end—just so, love goes slowly through our veins, and, in our passion, we do not notice that we have been slain by it. In fact, Gonzalo-Janus is not yet dead; he suffers palpably, though, from the Petrarchan *nosos*, the disease of love, and only a willing Justine can restore him to somewhat doubtful health: "It is that thing beyond words, which men are wont to call loving: / Uneasy pleasures, which tears moisten again and again" (BB, I, 128–29:57–58). The distich would have provided a suitably ambiguous end; Janus elects to go on, flattering Gonzalo with a rehearsal of the latter's life and travels (it is this account which has led to erroneous conclusions

The Elegies

about Janus' own journeys), and repeating a point that Janus—and the whole Renaissance love-lyric—frequently make: no matter how far the lover travels, he cannot escape from love. Gonzalo (the local patriot notes) even gets as far as Belgium, "those unique fields which are farmed by Venus and by her son," where he finds himself surrounded by a hundred lovely forms; but the thought of Justine renders Gonzalo immune. Janus brings the poem to an end with an *aprosdoketon*, a surprising scene in which Gonzalo is on the very brink of being rewarded by Justine when a hag interrupts the busy pair. It has been assumed that Janus recounts an episode told him by Gonzalo; still, it should be remembered that the situation is one of Janus' favorites from the *Monobiblos*—the dream of erotic pleasure, broken off at the point of fulfillment.

Cynthia granted Propertius a few happy moments; he opens a description of one of them (*Elegies* II, 15) with a triple set of blessings: "Oh, how happy I am! And how sweetly this night shines upon me! / Oh, little bed, you are blest, made as you are for delight." In Janus' next elegy, though, the little bed is a place of torment, not delight: "Little bed, you must remain ignorant of every pleasure; / Lacking your master's sweet friend, you bear his dull weight alone" (BB, I, 133–34:1–2). Like the second and fifth elegies, this is a jealousy poem; but Janus' criticism is now aimed outward, away from its owner. Neaera is tricky (selling the night to three lovers, spending it with none), venal (casting her admirers aside like old gods in ruined temples), a corruptor of youth (a rosy-cheeked boy "Whose smoothish loins are unsullied by the least little trace of a hair"), snobbish (she would have nothing to do with ordinary men, "Once she had got to know what tribunate tools could be worth"), changeable (feigning headaches, religion, and fury), and so lustful that she wears her bedmates out:

Straightway the lover departs, with his coffers exhausted and empty,
　Straightway there follows a boy, very unusual to see:
Dragging his bent legs along in a gait mixed of trembles and totters,
　Nestor of Pylos could claim him as his grandfather now.
(BB, I, 138:59–62)

(Considering the tone of the passage, it seems likely that Janus allowed himself a *double-entendre* with the "coffers" of the first line.) After this outburst of polished obscenity, the imagined revenge on Neaera seems almost insipid; it is a familiar threat—that Neaera will end as a lustful old woman, the stock figure of fun. The description of the dilapidated Neaera is brief, as well; Janus closes with a hope of reconciliation, not with Neaera, but with love itself. Upon the execration which makes up the body of the poem there follows, in effective contrast, a hope for his own happiness:

Meanwhile, I hope that my heart may burn with a passion that's better,
  As long as life's springtime endures, as long as my fate will allow.
Oh, may the tranquil breath of a love that is placid breathe on me,
  May the disquiet of care be ever far from my heart.
Let joy and laughter be mine, and the shifting fortunes of travel,
  Give me the lyre and the cup, roses made damp by the wine,
Give me a day without clouds, and give me not night but its shadows.
  Give me a night without dark, brides brought to bed without vows.
Give me a strife without hate, and that battle in which there's no wounding,
  Give me a Venus who drifts, conquered, to slumber at dawn.
                                            (BB, I, 141–42:83–92)

The poem is particularly memorable for its surprise, its shift from the scurrilous to a nobler tone, and for a conclusion which mixes bravado, serenity and wistfulness, at the same time intimating that it is a *percursio*, a rapid review of the charges made above against Neaera. At his best, Janus was a poet of considerable emotional complexity.

The ninth elegy, "For Driving Away the Sleep of the Girl Lying With Me," has the same locale as its predecessor, a bed; but, according to Scriverius, it was written on horseback. Like the other Venerilla elegy (II, 2), the ninth depends heavily on repetition; just as there the lover thinks repeatedly that he hears his mistress approaching, so here he thinks repeatedly that she is about to wake up. The poem has a double opening, a few words of blame against sleep, "the lazy brother of shadowy death," and a suggestion that it try to find some more appropriate victim than Venerilla—a love-starved girl, perhaps, or an unsatisfied wife; after all, slumber does not hesitate to violate a little girl who vainly summons her mother to her defense. This last image, at once shocking and homely, is a happy invention, and, with its air of the nursery, contrasts nicely with the boudoir scene that follows: again, Janus has a skillful hand with abrupt changes of key. As for the remaining three-quarters of the poem (the description of the girl pulling herself out of sleep, at her lover's urgings, only to succumb to it once more), there is no need to recount its skirmishes and feints: the lover tries all sorts of remedies. They do not work, and "I can do nothing, for she will give herself over to slumber; / Safe in her torpor she'll lie, knowing the rosy dawn's far" (BB, I, 146:51–52). Growing disgusted, the lover repeats and extends some themes from the opening: wives should lie thus asleep, and ugly girls, and "women who offer foul acts, causing disgust, to tired men." For once, though, the struggles of love turn out well for Janus; Venerilla wakes up, "noch sanft vom Schlaf," as Rilke says, and the poem ends in a fireworks of mythological references.

The last poems in book two are the epithalamium on the second marriage of Grudius and the reminder to Catzius that soldiering does not provide a sanctuary from love; their function in the *Amores* would be to show conjugal love and love's inevitability. The epithalamium is a restrained and formal exercise; Janus was writing for a respected brother, lately bereaved. The address to Catzius is by far more lively, a variation upon Ovid's "Militat omnis amans," and makes an apt coda for a book about love's wars; otherwise, the *Amores* are arranged like Chinese boxes: fraternal references (1 and 10), the Venerilla poems (2 and 9), and the Neaera poems (3–8).

The third book does not have a title and the poems' subjects are as mixed as the times of composition. The elegies on Charles V (2), Dantiscus (4), Erasmus (5), Hieronymus Monti (7), the Peace of Cambrai (8), and Alciatus (9) are from the spring of 1533; those on the departure for Spain (10), homesickness (11), Saragossa (12), Tavera (13), Stratius (14), and Zurita (16) come from the next period. The brothers, no doubt responsible for the arrangement of the poems, worked according to rough chronology, beginning their series with efforts of the apprentice. The first elegy, overloaded with classical material is a traditional address to Orpheus and the power of poetry, the third is the tribute to Janus' Roman models, the sixth in praise of spring, again with the authors, gods, and places of antiquity prominently displayed. The sole problem in chronology arises from the latter part of the book, where there are the poems on the *Theseus* of

Jeanne de la Font (15), the Abbey of Saint Denis (17), and the mysterious Johannes O[e]ttinger (18); two are from the Bourges trip, and the third cannot be dated: were these items found among Janus' papers after the order of the other elegies had been established, and so were simply tacked on?

The poetic value of the third book is relatively low; as Wright says, "[it] is far less interesting than the other two" (p. 29). However, exception should be made of the "Patriae desiderium" (11) [13] and of the vision of a satyr-inhabited Hague (in 13). Furthermore, even when Janus is not at his most interesting, he is still clear, direct, and, for the most part, brief. The tributes to the Latin love poets and the poem on the imagined return of Erasmus are cases in point.

CHAPTER 3

The Basia

THE jurist Hugo Grotius [1] called Janus Secundus a discoverer, an inventor: with the *Basia*, he devised a new kind of verse, an accomplishment of importance in an age which set great store on questions of genre: "Nothing is more pleasant than the *Basia*, which sort of writing [genus scribendi] he discovered and established." Bosscha followed Grotius' opinion—he speaks of the "new kind of song, which [Janus] himself also invented, and in whose merit he is said to reign so supremely that all who, in his wake, have attempted the same or a similar idea, Dousa, Bonefon[i]us, Lernutius, would remain inferior to him by far" (p. xxxvi).[2] Oddly, it was the first commentator on the *Basia* who discerned wherein the poetic virtue of the *Basia* lay. While Janus was still alive, the *Basia* were circulated in manuscript among his admirers (and, the story goes, many took the trouble to learn them by heart); in the spring of 1536, his school friend Viglius Zuichemus wrote to Hadrianus Marius: "I have read the *Kisses* of your brother with great pleasure . . . and am filled with extreme admiration both at their multitude and their inventiveness, then at their charm and at the fact that Venus herself, who must indeed have been propitious to him, has made so many and such sweet suggestions about kissing to him."[3] Certainly, one of the virtues of the *Basia* is their inventiveness, the way in which they treat a single and not particularly rich theme in a variety of ways without boring the reader. Furthermore, where Tissot believed,[4] almost three centuries later on, that inventiveness somehow canceled out "chaleur," Zuichemus was evidently of the opinion that Janus combined the two qualities in a happy and satisfying unity.

The weightiest charge to be raised against the *Basia* is that of their lack of originality. Basing his study on the annotations in Burmann-Bosscha and on Ellinger's introduction to his edition of

101

the *Basia*,[5] German Joos has called attention to the many borrowings by Janus from the poets of antiquity: "Our poet is most indebted to Paul the Silentiary, Catullus, Tibullus, Propertius. Ovid and Horace emerge in the second place, and then Vergil a few times *en passant*."[6] Joos also adduces the poets of the Renaissance: "Sannazaro, Marullus, and Pontanus, partially Beroaldus and Crinitus, too." And he states: "Thus this *eroticus* appears to us to be someone who has let himself be led by the commonplaces and the generally prevalent motifs of the love poetry of the ancients and of the sixteenth century, in order to develop and to adorn his thoughts, which have reality as their basis." There is no denying that Janus stands in the debt of others; we have only to glance at the first lines of the seventh Basium—"Centum basia centies/ Centum basia millies"—to know who the generator of the cycle is, the Catullus of "Da mi basia mille, deinde centum" (*Carmina* 5:7), and "Quaeris, quot mihi basiationes/ tuae, Lesbia, sint satis superque" ("You ask me how many kissings of you are enough and more than enough for me, 7:1–2), is another plain example.[7] As for the lady who gets the kisses, her ancestry is equally plain; her grandmother is the Neaera of whom Horace has such bitter things to say in the fifteenth epode, and her mother the Neaera to whom Marullus pays assiduous attention in his epigrams. Also, the reader of the *Basia*, remembering the introduction which Alciatus had given Janus to the Greek Anthology, will see how its authors have been plundered: Meleager, Paul the Silentiary, the anonymous poet of V:305, Pseudo-Plato, Callimachus of Cyrene. The first of the *Basia* is built on a situation out of the first book of the *Aeneid* (another source everyone can detect), and there are, as usual in Janus, the echoes of Propertius, Tibullus, Ovid; maybe Martial (VI, 34:1–8) has been used too, contributing to the thousand kisses. As for the poetry of the Renaissance, Ellinger—long before Joos—told that story in greatest detail, giving particular attention to Philippus Beroaldus the Elder's "Osculum Panthiae," to Petrus Crinitus' "Ad Neaeram," and to Sannazaro's "Ad Ninam."[8] To these readily provable charges the same retort must be made as before: the derivative nature of Neo-Latin poetry, whether the sources are classical or contemporary, must be accepted as typical. The point, again, is that Janus Secundus makes poetry which can readily be recognized as his own, however much it owes to others. It is only when his strength departs or his interest flags, as in the last of the *Basia*, that he descends into nondescript verse. Ellinger—who, for all his work on "influence," was keenly aware of the special originality of the *Basia* —notes that Beroaldus made a formulation similar to "O vis superba formae" (8:49, the cycle's most famous line, thanks to Goethe's praise of it). The author of the "Osculum Panthiae" has (1. 33) "Tantum forma valet." The notion may belong to Beroaldus, but the inimitable style—the outcry, the ambiguities of "vis" and "superba," the climax of "formae"—is the work of Janus.

That the *Basia* comprise a cycle, carefully arranged, is plain from the outset. The first poem tells how kisses came into being; the poet, by the reference to a passage [9] that every schoolboy once knew, the tucking-into-bed by Venus of Ascanius (*Aeneid*, I:691-94), takes the reader back not only to the birth of the human activity he plans to describe but to the reader's own childhood. At once love-goddess and mother, Venus looks at little Ascanius asleep and decides that he resembles a former flame, Adonis. Fearing that she will disturb the boy's slumber with an embrace, she plants her mouth instead on the white roses which are his mattress. The novel gesture is returned with a bonus: "Every rose that she touched gave birth to a kiss, born as quickly, / Giving the goddess delights, doubled and doubled again" (BB, I, 247:13-14). Thus having learned a new thrill, the goddess, pulled by her swans, sets out on a flight around the world, to share the blessings she has just acquired with "suffering mankind." The little narrative is over; the poem's final section begins with an address to the kisses, these means of tempering ("moderamina") the poet's unhappy flame. (Each poem in the cycle has an envoy or apostrophe, the most of them directed to Neaera.) Then the poet makes a formal introduction of himself, of his task, and of the sweet Latin tongue which Cupid (or Janus) will employ: "Mindful of that cherished race which sprang from the loins of Aeneas, / Eloquent love will speak Rome's gentle tongue in these lines" (BB, I, 248:25-26).

Neaera appears in the second Basium, introduced by a simile which calls attention to her classical ancestry. In the fifteenth epode (11. 5-6), Horace tells how Neaera once pledged her faith to him: "Clinging [to me] with arms that held closer still than the ivy, / Embracing tight the lofty holm oak." The simile, expanded with some help from Paul the Silentiary (GA, V,

255:13–16) and the *Heroides* (5:47–48),[10] is used by Janus to present *his* Neaera:

> Just as the neighboring vine plays wantonly over the elm tree,
>   And round the lofty holm oak's trunk,
> Berried the ivy wraps its measureless arms in embracement,

so Neaera might embrace him and he might embrace her. It is a vision of what might be, not of what is: if such an embrace should take place, then their two beings, joined, would be carried away to the "pale realm of Dis." The pale realm, though, would in fact be a landscape of eternal spring; the immortal heroes and heroines, "in ancient loves," would surround Janus and Neaera, granting them the first place among their numbers. The clumsy imitators of this popular Basium, Weckherlin and Bürger,[11] appear not to have understood that the poem is all a dream; even Ronsard, closer to Janus in time and in talent, made it a vision of the attainable: "Tantost nous dancerons par les fleurs des rivages/ Sous maints accords divers." [12] The poignancy of Janus' poem lies in its view of the future as a dim possibility, not a probability; the dark undertone in the Horatian epode (of faith pledged but not kept) is maintained: faithful lovers are immortal—but what lovers are faithful?

In the third episode, Janus transforms his theme, the plea for love, by means of contrast; the heroic praise which flourished in the dream is replaced, at the outset, by a direct demand: "Da mihi suaviolum, dicebam, blanda puella" (literally, "Give me a little kiss, I said, alluring girl"). The narrative signals of the *Basia* are more carefully concealed than those of the *Monobiblos;* the past tense of "dicebam" is a subtle reminder that a story is being told. The reaction to the proposal is scarcely what an immortal lover should expect; Neaera brushes his mouth with hers; then, as if she had stepped on a serpent, she jumps back and runs away. The last of the three distichs of the epigrammatic poem rearranges the elements of the first: no kiss has been given but rather the "sad desire" for one.

In the interval between poems three and four, Neaera—or so the reader must infer—has changed, still another of the cycle's series of abrupt transformations:

> Nectar comes from Neaera, not mere kisses,

The Basia

> Perfume borne on her breath, all filled with fragrance,
> Thyme and spikenard and cinnamon and honey,
> (BB, I, 252–53:1–3)

and so on. The passage, with its atmosphere of the spice-cabinet, was vastly attractive to Janus' admirers and imitators, giving a tip to Ronsard and de Baïf, and more than that to the Neo-Latinists Buchanan, Dousa, Relandus.[13] The nectarine kisses were not Janus' invention, however, having flourished in classical antiquity and in Renaissance poetry before Janus.[14] The description of them turns out to be another of Janus' familiar wish-dreams; after the flatly indicative statements about the quality of Neaera's kisses, the subjunctive returns in line eight. If he were granted the privilege of discovering such good things, he would be immortal, a thought which puts him—the foresighted player of the game—in a position to close his catalog of flattery with a brilliant move: an admonition (to take good care of the precious gift) which becomes, then, the poem's concluding address to Neaera. She must become a goddess too, for, without her, he would not want to sit at the table of the gods.

The plan works, and the fifth chapter is added to the implied story. Neaera provides not only the embrace dreamed of in the second Basium and asked for in the third, but a whole range of small-scale gymnastics:

> Then you take a small bite, and weep, rebitten,
> Then you send your tongue, trembling, hin and yonder,
> Then you suck my tongue, aching, hin and yonder . . . ,
> (BB, II, 255:6–8)

and the excitement grows; their breaths meet, their souls meet, but Janus has trouble maintaining the pace, so that Neaera must keep his failing breath going, both breathing her own sweet breath into him ("Aspirans . . .") and drawing his failing breath outward ("Hauriens . . ." can be ambiguous, "drawing out" and "consuming"). A panting effect is achieved by the present participles ("Aspirans," "Hauriens"), by adjectives in series with like-sounding endings ("mollem, dulcisonam, humidam," "soft, sweet-sounding, damp"), by *anadiplosis* (". . . nimio vapore coctam/ Coctam pectoris impotentis aestu," "by too much [damp] warmth seared/ Seared by my exhausted breast's [dry] burning"). The climax is an outcry, "O! jucunda mei caloris aura" ("Oh, my hot passion's happy breathing"), which, in its final word, repeats the central noun of the poem. After these verbal tricks, the poem is brought to a finish with a statement in the simplest language, the main force of which is put into the comparative ("maior") at the end of the last three lines:

> Then I'll say that 'The god of gods is Cupid.
> There's no god who— than Cupid—is the greater,
> Yet if any—than Cupid—should be greater,
> You alone—my Neaera—are the greater.
> (BB, I, 256:18–21)

The way has gone from implied wishes to their implied fulfillment, something indicated not only by the poems' contents but by their meters. The first and third Basia are in elegiac couplets, but four and five are in hendecasyllabics, the meter of Catullus and Lesbia. (The second poem, with its reminiscences of Horace's fifteenth epode, is couched in that poem's meter, the First Pythiambic, still another indication that Janus wants his audience to remember Horace's faithless Neaera as it reads his cycle.) In the sixth Basium a return is made to the distich, and to a world of the lover again more mournful than successful. A pact has been made for an exchange of two thousand kisses of the first quality, Janus has taken a thousand and given a thousand, but love by the numbers is never satisfying. A display of examples follows: Ceres does not count the ears of grain, Bacchus does not count the grapes, we do not count the raindrops Jupiter sends, nor does Jupiter count the crops he destroys in his anger; thus, since Neaera is a goddess, she should not count the kisses she gives. A foundation is laid for the poem's conclusion: if Neaera persists in counting kisses, she must count his tears as well, and if she does not count his tears, she must not count his kisses. The store of invention seems inexhaustible, but Janus knows when and how to stop by asking for infinity: "Give me then—though it be poor solace for all I must suffer— / Kisses that go beyond count, matching my countless laments" (BB, I, 259:25–26). The poem has begun with a clear sum, the two thousand kisses, and ends with the elegiac drift into a world where, "innumera innumeris," numbers exist no more.

Like Basium 6, the seventh poem deals with calculation, and

immediately calls to mind the Catullan "Da mi basia mille," the source of both of Janus' poems. It leads again into the realm of the impossible. But the meter—the Second Glyconic—provides a naively chanting quality that makes the lyric sound very much like a child reciting multiplication tables:

> Hundred kisses a hundred times,
> Hundred kisses a thousand times,
> Thousand kisses a thousand times,
> As many thousand thousands as
> There are drops in Sicilian seas,
> As there're stars in the heavens. . . .
>
> (BB, I, 259–60:1–6)

After a statement of the places at which the kisses will be aimed (rosy cheeks, swollen lips, talking eyes), line eleven—catalectic like line six, introducing a variation into the sing-song meter—brings the elaborations up short: "O formosa Neaera!" The chant continues but, at length, lush comparisons are supplanted by a practical problem. Kissing Neaera, Janus cannot see her mouth (nor cheeks nor eyes nor smiles), and the large numbers of the poem's outset are reduced to two entities, the eyes and mouth of the lover: "Oh, what battles are being waged, / Spawned between hostile eyes and lips . . ." (ll. 29–30). The occasional semi-rhymes (*homoioteleuta*), the refrainlike effect of the catalectic lines, and the ease with which the Glyconic may be read accentually, rather than as quantitative verse, may remind us of the poetry of the Goliards, just as the poem's climactic war might seem to be reminiscent of those medieval disputes between "heart" and "soul." It was probably Janus' simple intention, however, to provide a songlike interlude with the seventh Basium, bringing variety into the cycle by means of its form.

The eighth Basium has short lines as well, the meter which Henri Estienne made so popular a little later on with the publication of the Pseudo-Anacreontica (1554). Again, as so often in these poems, the material is love's warfare. Persisting in her violent habits, Neaera has bitten the poet's tongue; transposing the formula by which Cupid is asked why he is so cruel to the poet who sings of him so well, Janus wonders why Neaera gives such harsh treatment to the organ which sings about her:

> How often, at first sunlight,
> How often, at sun's setting,

> And through the tiresome daytime,
> And through the bitter nighttime,
> Did I recite your praises?
>
> (BB, I, 263:13–17)

The catalog of lauds is a lengthy one, made to seem short because of the fast-running Anacreontic lines; when it is over, the initial question returns: how could Neaera have done such a thing? The answer is Goethe's "schönes Wort von Johannes Secundus," "O vis superba formae!" [15] Beauty is cruel and tyrannical, but we cannot renounce it.

The girl who has bitten too hard in the eighth poem's apparently playful world and playful meter, is instructed, in the ninth, to be more restrained; as if to give a prosodic illustration of his intent, Janus chooses the most dignified of the strophic forms of the ode, the Alcaic, with which Tennyson addressed Milton: "O mighty-mouth'd inventor of harmonies,/ O skill'd to sing of time or Eternity." Yet the Alcaics of Janus should not be taken too seriously, any more than the Anacreontics of the preceding poem should be regarded as a sign of meaningless frivolity. There, beneath the joke, the frightening power of woman's beauty is hidden; here the solemn commands are to be taken lightly. Neaera is told to be chaste, and subjected to some moralizing in the Horatian style; in love as in life, there is a golden mean, or, more harshly put, a limit:

> A measure's set to all of life's sweet delights:
> The more a pleasure adds to our spirits' joy,
>   The closer it comes and the swifter
>   To dull satiety's final limit.
>
> (BB, I, 266:4–8)

The fifth strophe, the center of the nine in the poem, appropriately contains the turning point; running away at the poet's own orders, a Diana, Neaera will hide herself:

> And though you lie in lairs' deepest darknesses,
> And though you lurk in caves' farthest fastnesses,
>   I'll track you to the caverns' bottom,
>   Track you to lairs where they lie remotest.
>
> (ll. 17–20)

Perhaps we could suspect Janus of some indelicacy in his superlatives; but such physiological implications would not be a necessary ingredient of the joke. The poet, the "burning victor," will cast himself on his shrinking prey, and, with all his pent-up energy, punish her for having listened to his Horatian instructions. Neaera, of course, will swear that she would like to suffer more such punishments for more such crimes. Any of the poems in the *Basia* can stand alone, and they often have, in anthologies; but all of them lose by being removed from their setting. This is the case with the ninth Basium, where the wry notion of a shy Neaera can be fully enjoyed only if we recall the concluding line, on beauty's power, from number eight.

The tenth, a catalog of the kinds of kisses, uses the distich which is Janus' staple; it is a recitative inserted between the cycle's arias, but a recitative that momentarily grows impassioned. Wet kisses, dry kisses, mildly warm kisses, kisses placed on the eyes, the cheek, the neck, the shoulders, the breast, bruising kisses distributed to all these places, and especially—Janus repeats himself with different and diminutive [16] adjectives—the "little-white" shoulders, the "little-white" breast. (They have been merely snowy before.) As a climax, there are kisses on the mouth, by which deed two spirits are interchanged: "Making the soul of the one pass into the flesh of the other, / While love, sighing its last, languishes, ready to die" (BB, I, 270:13–14). But after this thought, which comes close to a spiritualization of the relationship, Janus immediately reminds us that we have to do with exhausted lovers who need stimulation. He returns to the notion of erotic inventiveness, and to a catalog, this time of forfeits for the failure to be inventive.

In the eleventh Basium, the poet peoples his stage—which, since the preamble, has been left to Neaera and himself—with critics, who say that he offers kisses of an elegance which "our rude forefathers" never knew. In other words, Janus, who must constantly inject variety into an essentially monotonous theme, brings feigned charges of indecent behavior against himself; his excuse is that, busy with Neaera, he did not know who he was or where. In this way, three distichs, half the poem, have passed; the remaining three are given over to Neaera, whose portion can be further subdivided: she puts her lover's worries to rest in three ways, one to a distich—a laugh and an embrace, a kiss (and Venus never gave a more lascivious one to Mars), and some words, to the effect that she, not a stern crowd, should be the judge. As in poems 6 and 7, Janus has drawn again upon Catullus' number five (here, the "complaints of severe old men"), and turned the Catullan lines into a full poem of his own, constructed with arithmetical symmetry; at the same time, he has added, by implication, an element to his fable about the affair. Janus and Neaera, as it were, have become compatible, a harmony to be deduced both from the answer Neaera gives the carpers, and from the balance of the poem's composition. We have come a good way from the turbulence of "Centum basia centies" (7) and "Quis te furor, Neaera" (8).

The theme of outsiders-versus-lovers is continued in the twelfth Basium, where Janus returns to hendecasyllabics, a meter last used for the perfervid statements of the fifth. Not only the meter is Catullan; the shocking word around which the poem is built—*mentula* ("penis")—is Catullan as well. The critics of the preceding poem have been replaced by a band of "matrons and chaste young girls." This watch-and-ward society has been upset by the subject of Janus' conversation; he assures them that he is really quite respectable. His songs are not phallic ("Nulla . . . carmina mentulata"), and a schoolmaster may read them to his pupils; a "chaste priest of the Aonian choir," he sings, in fact of "harmless kisses" or, literally, "weaponless kisses," "inermes basiationes." Again, the poem is divided into halves; nine lines are spent in protestations of innocence and nine in tormenting the ladies who have brought the charges. Because he has used the word "mentulatum," they have turned their faces, "vultus . . . protervos," toward him, just as, in the poem's first line, they turned their "vultus . . . pudicos" ("modest faces") away from him. The parallelism is not quite as simple as it seems; "protervus" can mean both "indignant" and "enraged" or "shameless" and "wanton." The "naughty band" is told to go away; Neaera is chaster than they are. A last ambiguous defense of his book's purity is offered: "Certainly, she prefers a book without a penis / To a poet who does not have a penis" (BB, I, 272:17–18).

The poem has two paralipomena, epigrams which continue to argue the theme of "mentula." The one, Epigram 24 in the first book, claims that Lycinna and Aelia make fun of his verse, calling him the poet of a "languid penis" because of the chastity of the *Basia*. His retort is that he does not sing for such people, and, in fact, has no penis: "mentula nulla mihi est." He sings instead to teach tender lovers. The epigram at first glance seems to be a puzzler: does Janus mean that his verses are intended as chaste, premarital instruction books? The key lies in "mentula nulla mihi est." With its lack of qualification, it is meant to make us sit up, take notice and laugh; the poem is a feigned protestation of innocence once again. In the second of the epigrams (58), his joking is more open still. The grammarians would use his poems for teaching if they dealt with great deeds; as it is, his "carmina lasciva" scare them away. The epigram throws still another light on a subject about which Janus evidently had a bad conscience, his inability to write lofty epic; but we are more interested by what it says about the *Basia*. "Wet kisses" dictate his song to him, he says, and his sexual organ frequently becomes excited by his verse; he offers a stimulus to young men and young women who want to please one another sexually. The main business of the *Basia,* then, is not kisses but what comes after them. The twelfth Basium and its two pendants are of some importance for the understanding of the cycle; until the twelfth Basium— indeed, until its concluding two lines—the gentle reader could sail along in the belief that all the talk was about kisses, nothing more. With the twelfth Basium, Janus calls attention to what he has done: the poems could pass for "casta basia," being "mentulata" all the while.

Now that even the most guileless member of the audience knows what Janus is up to, he can be franker. The thirteenth Basium tells a little story, using the past tense ("Tired from sweet combat, my life, I lay there languid, exhausted") for three distichs and the present perfect for two: Neaera has blown upon his lips and has led him back from "the Stygian vale." But a third present perfect verb ("I have erred") marks the poem's *volta*: he begins to mull over his condition, and to use the present tense. Charon's barge is not empty after all, and Janus' body, still lying on the bed, is enlivened only by a part of Neaera's spirit. Yet this "piece of [Neaera's] soul" ("pars animae .. tuae") also wishes to flee to its "pristina jura," its "ancient rights"—a dark phrase that has been taken to mean that Neaera wishes to die, too, to return to "Death's sad company" by Wright, or "zum Ganzen," rather cosmically, by Blei, or, romantically, "nach der Heimat" by Wiesner.[17] Her one breath will have to nourish the two of them until they pass away together: "Finally, after the last tired strivings of still unquenched passion, / Single, a life will escape out of our flesh's twin form" (BB, I. 276:21–22). These lines admit a romanticizing interpretation; Janus would seem to long for a *Liebestod* and there is surely a temptation to read the poem to Wagnerian orchestration; Schroeter says: "Das Thema hat hier seine schönste Verklärung gefunden." Yet the phrase about "the last tired strivings of still unquenched passion" brings us back to the poem's altogether physiological beginnings (as in the case of Basium 10); it offers, in fact, a familiar message about erotic technique: the poet would like to stay alive, sexually, until Neaera is also ready to experience love's little death with him. Nor is the basic conceit of the poem's climax unusual; it is a paraphrase of the thought that the one lover has no life save that the other lover gives him. But these platitudes are clothed in high-sounding, even noble phrases. Tissot has charged the *Basia* with occasional obscurity; here, Janus has made grandiloquence, if not obscurity, work for him.

The sequel, the fourteenth Basium, leaves no doubt about the plane of love on which it stands; the distich is again abandoned for the hendecasyllabic, and the Roman love-elegists for Catullus. Missing the point of the poem, Schroeter claims that the poet is "im vollen Liebesglück;" instead, he is ready for happiness, but cannot get it. Neaera—"harder than hard marble"—is only willing to provide some more harmless kisses ("osculationes imbelles," literally, "warless kisses"), which he refuses, since they do not lead to the battle of the bed. Indeed, they only make his situation the more uncomfortable; the male lover's present state stands in stark contrast to his total collapse of the previous poem. It is one of the notorious obscene passages in the *Basia*, making a play upon two kinds of hardness:

> For, each time that my supine member stiffens,
> Through my clothes and through yours I'm forced to prod you;
> Then, sick with a desire that gets no answer,
> Melting, I pass away, my hot vein with me.
>
> (BB, I, 277:6–9)

Commentators have called attention to the section's close resemblance to Catullus (32:10–11), Ovid (*Amores* III, 7), and Martial (XI, 16:5); but Janus scarcely needed their aid to describe the phenomenon. Neaera runs away, but he catches up with her;

the poem ends with a compliment corresponding to the accusatory *adynaton* of the opening: Neaera is now "softer than soft goose-marrow." Or, at least most translators have taken the words, "mollis / Mollior anseris medulla' as applying to her; others—Prévot, Wright [18]—have thought that the poet referred to the softness of his own mouth, and kisses, implying a contrast, as Wright said, to "the hardness down below," and not just to the hardness of Neaera's heart at the outset.[19]

In the cycle's narrative line, the male lover appears to be no better off than when the affair started; as a poet, he may be worse off, since the next Basium (15) shows signs of failing power. It is a mythologizing attempt to discover why, indeed, Neaera is harder than marble. Cupid was ready to shoot her with his arrow when he fell in love with her himself; after having given her "a thousand kisses," he implored the other gods never to do her harm again. Should we be astonished, then, that Neaera's kisses are so hot, and her heart so hard? It is a tired poem, following—to its disadvantage—upon a vital one. For once, the yoking of two treatments of the same theme—here, in 14 and 15, hardness—does not work its usual magic. And whoever looks up the lines of Marullus which seem to have been this poem's source, "Coming of late on my mistress, Cupid took aim with his arrow, / When of a sudden he fell victim to what he beheld . . . (*Epigrammaton liber,* I, 3), will find that Janus suffers by comparison; his version is longer than that of Marullus, fourteen lines against eight, and the extra length overburdens the already fragile conceit. Still, it is fair to call attention to the poem's function in the *Basia*'s total structure. Undeniably, it is a gallant compliment, and, following the *mentulae* (12), the worn-out lover (13), and the distended clothes (14), it may well have been intended as a device for raising the cycle's level of discourse.

Janus returns to Horatian strophes in the sixteenth Basium—to the double Asclepiadean with Pherecratic and Glyconic; the meter's appearance will make the reader wonder if the poem contains some surprise of content, some association with its most famous application in literature, the Bandusian ode of Horace. Yet the theme is all too familiar: how many kisses the poet will get. He starts out modestly enough; "Da mi basia centum" ("Give me a hundred kisses") will call earlier poems in the cycle all too easily to mind; then he provides a long list of other manners of measuring kisses which once more cheerfully reveals his debt to Catullus—as many kisses as Lesbia gave to her "much-demanding poet," and as she received, as many kisses as there are gentle Venuses and Cupids wandering through "your little lips and rosy cheeks." It is plainly tiresome; but suddenly Janus rises to one of those passages which bear his hallmark, clarity of style and ambiguity of emotion. He will have as many kisses

> As you keep, in your eyes, lives and violent deaths,
> Hopes and terrors and joys: pleasures all intertwined
>   Both with cares everlasting
>   And with sighs born of lovers' hearts.
>   (BB, I, 279:9–12)

A description of nuanced erotic practices follows the summary of possible emotional combinations; not kisses matter, but their prelude: caresses, words spoken aloud, whispers, smiles, embraces. The climax comes, or the several climaxes; the situation of Basium 13 is repeated, but this time the two lovers are given equal endurance. Ten strophes have gone by, from the stock request for kisses to satisfaction and exhaustion; Janus cuts the poem off in the eleventh, a Horatian sentiment to end the pseudo-Horatian ode (so very un-Horatian, in fact, in its unswerving progress and its growing emotional intensity, as opposed to the intentional meandering which is one of Horace's chief charms):

> So, my love and my light, let us pluck life in bloom,
> For old age comes too soon, bringing its miseries,
>   Pulling cares close behind it,
>   Joined to illness and awful death.

Schroeter thought that Janus expressed "eine Ahnung frühen Todes" here; instead, it is a standing formula—the admonition to make hay while the sun shines, to pluck the rose before it withers, or, with Horace, to seize the day.

The seventeenth Basium is the cycle's last piece of good workmanship, with tight construction and broad implication. Just as the rose, wet with dew, turns red at the morning sun, so the morning kisses ("Matutina oscula," that is, "little mouths") of his mistress grow red, having been dampened all through the night by his kisses ("basiolis"). Nature comes first, and then the comparison with Neaera, in two distichs; in the next two, the order is reversed—another of those feints, the most of them very simple, by which Janus continues to achieve variety. The mouth is surrounded by the cheeks' snowy whiteness, the violet contrasts with the virgin's white hand, and: "So the new cherry burns in its ruddiness under late blossoms, / And the tree all at once has both its summer and spring" (BB, I, 282:7–8). An element of the *aubade,* the dawn-song, is introduced; getting up, the lover asks Neaera to keep her lips red until evening. The final *pointe* ties the themes of paleness and ruddiness together: if Neaera's lips receive someone else's kisses in the meantime, he hopes they will turn as pale as his cheeks are now. Elegant indeed, but also filled with bawdy hints: if the lover is (sentimentally) pale with sadness upon leaving Neaera, he is also—as the *Basia* so often inform us—pale with exhaustion. Reobserved from a sexual standpoint, the poem's color scheme, of white and red, will be visible enough: exhaustion and readiness. The Basium, by the way, is fourteen lines long, and has the disposition of the sonnet: [20] eight lines of related images are offered, and then the turn, with the outcry at the start of line nine ("Me miserum"), to be followed by the commentary on the octet's images in the remaining six lines.

The poet has gone through the introductory torments of love to a first climax (1–5), has known the varieties of love (6–10), has met outside critics and lifted some veils (11–12), and had more erotic defeats and triumphs (13–16), leading to a well-made parting (17), which could have served as the tale's last chapter. In the eighteenth and nineteenth Basia, the poetic fatigue returns, of which the first signs were detected in the fifteenth poem. Basium 18 is a mythological potpourri. In a not altogether felicitous image, Neaera looks as though someone, with curious art, had adorned an ivory seal (her face) with coral pearls (her lips). Beholding this creation (which recalls Janus' practice of the *médailleur*'s art), Venus grows envious, wishing to know what good it was to have won the judgment on Mount Ida, if Neaera outdoes her, in the poet's judgment. The Cupids of her court are commended to take awful revenge: Janus is to be shot full of love's arrows, while Neaera will get a special anaphrodisiac dart. After the narration is over, Janus says that the plan worked to perfection: he burns, she is all icicles. Since it is Neaera's fault (Janus is punished for having sung about her), she would do well to join her "lips of honey" to his, drawing a little of the poison of passionate love from his wounds into her own spirit. She need not fear the gods nor Dione (Venus), since—Janus tries for a concluding line like the "O vis superba formae" of Basium 8—a beautiful girl commands the very gods, "Formosa divis imperat puella." But, lacking overtones, the line falls flat.

The last poem in the cycle, an address to the bees, was not included in the 1539 edition of the *Basia*, and even warm admirers of the *Basia* have trouble finding virtues in it, the customarily ecstatic Schroeter calling it shallow, and Tissot deciding that Janus' inventive powers had simply vanished. As usual, the makeup of the poem is uncomplicated; it can readily be divided into two parts, of six and five distichs. In the first, the bees are asked why they persist in drinking from flowers when Neaera's lips are available, lips combining the perfumes of a number of plants. In the second, Janus regrets his suggestion, and asks them not to drink too much from the source he has proposed, lest the well run dry. Also, the bees are told to beware of stinging Neaera; otherwise, she will send similar darts from her eyes: "Hear what I tell you: she'll not endure any wound without vengeance. / Gently, you harmless bees, gather your honey and go" (BB, I, 288:21–22). Ellinger called the poem a "wirksamen Abschluss" to the cycle, and some arguments could be presented for its use as a muted finale. The personified kisses which filled the stage at the opening are replaced here by another nonhuman chorus, again addressed by the poet; thus the cycle is enclosed within "unreal" episodes, and the interior poems (2–18) present the story of the lovers. Furthermore, two major themes of the cycle are intertwined in the poem—the celebration of the kiss itself, and of Neaera, with her "vis superba." Yet the nineteenth lacks the material which is the main strength of the *Basia*. The intense perception and representation of physical love by Janus have kept the *Basia* alive, and not, when all is said and done, his ingenuity, his elegance, or even his coinage of phrases, however important these qualities have been in his literary survival. The nineteenth Basium could have been written by many of Janus' contemporaries, or by his many imitators—Buchanan and Beza [21] before they devoted themselves to Calvinism, the Netherlanders Lernutius, Dousa, and Eufrenius,[22] the Frenchmen Muretus [23] and Bonefonius, or the late German humanist, Caspar

Barth (1587–1658). Barth's *Erotopaignion* shows what became of the kind of erotic poetry which Janus popularized with the *Basia*: Barth plays the game of verbal eroticism in a detached and exaggerated fashion which can either be called manneristic or grotesque; Janus has played the game, too, and played it brilliantly, but not to excess, and, more important, his display of wit has been supported by a constant and entertaining self-irony —Montaigne (*Essais*, II, 10) called the *Basia*, together with the *Decameron* and Rabelais, "dignes qu'on s'y amuse." The *Basia*, for all their virtuosity, still speak of recognizable human experience, a claim which it would be more difficult to make for Janus' many imitators.[24]

CHAPTER 4

The Other Poetry

MAURICE Rat was of the opinion that Janus runs the danger of being thought a "petit maître," because of the preeminence of the *Basia*; whoever takes the trouble to go through all the works will find "en Second un grand poète, infiniment varié, d'une profondeur et d'une ardeur de sentiment incomparables." [1] Looking at the "other works" of Janus today, we are inclined to agree with a part of Rat's argument: they are extremely important in judging the range of Janus, and in providing a basis for guesses as to what he might have done, had he lived. The *silvae* in particular offer glimpses of the future that did not come. Still, there is no escaping the fact that he did his best work in his cyclical erotic poetry. The odes and epigrams, then the *funera*, and above all the epistles have been used extensively in the biographical part of the present study. In the paragraphs that follow we shall try to find out what ones among the "other works" have some poetic value.

There are twelve odes extant from the hand of Janus Secundus.[2] Like the elegies of the third book, the odes were evidently arranged by the brothers in chronological order; they open with the poem on Charles' coronation, which is followed by a picture of springtime, and odes to Aegidius Buslidius junior, an unnamed friend, and Hadrianus Goesius, about to take a wife. The sixth ode is that on Charles' return; then there come poems to Nicolaus Buslidius, to Franciscus Catzius and his loves, and to Petrus Bausanus.[3] Looking through these nine odes composed between 1530 and 1532–33, we are more impressed by workmanship than by inspiration. The Catzius poem is an exception; we have already seen (p. 39) how an extraneous interest carries Janus away—he likes Isabella so much that he forgets Catzius. The result has more the air of being "poured out" [4] than "made," quite different from the next ode, the sedate, orderly, and dull poem on the joys of friendship addressed to Bausanus. Here lies the cause of Janus' failure as an odist: while he is a master of the virtuoso love poem, where he confronts and masters problems of variety, piquancy and suggestiveness, he has difficulty in laying out the thought pattern of an ode, where the poet must move, often with an apparent obliqueness, from one topic (or aspect of the main topic) to another.

Two of the collection's last three odes are successful, eminently so, while the third is a "curiosity," in F. A. Wright's word. In "Ad amorem" (10), Janus first asks if he shall spend the rest of his life "free of sighing love." Then he says that he regrets the time he has lost; he waits for love to come. At the conclusion, he states with utmost simplicity (in a Latin so lucid that even a beginner could read it) what his future will be: he will live between quarrels and kisses, between laughter and tears, between hope and fear, between life and death. The *anaphorae* and doublings at the opening of the second strophe ("Jam, jam remissi paenitet otii; / Jam, jam . . .", "Now, now I regret time lost, / Now, now . . ."), the parallelisms in the third ("rixas inter et oscula, / Interque risus, et lacrymas graves, / Spemque et metum, vitam necemque . . . ," literally, "between squabbles and kisses, / Between laughter and heavy tears, / And hope and fear, and life and death . . .") are not rhetorical devices introduced for their own sake (as is so often the case in humanism's poetry), but seem perfectly natural, and perfectly convincing.

The eleventh ode, "In choreas ab se spectatas" ("Concerning a Ball He Beheld"), stands alone in the works of Janus, and, to the author's knowledge, in Neo-Latin poetry. It is a picture of a girl dancing; the keenly observant eye of Janus (used so well in the *Itineraries* and too infrequently in the lyrics) is at work. Once again, the ode begins with the hint that all is a dream: "jam nescio quo loco" ("I know not in what place"). Out of the crowd of dancers, one catches his attention, a girl whose white cheeks are flushed, and whose forehead is covered with golden curls— and we grow fearful that Janus will list the stereotype details of Renaissance beauty. But he does not; instead, led at the outset on the arm of a young man, the girl then takes command of the dance floor and the poem:

> Alone and freed from his well-meant companionship
> She wandered, looking this way and that, and in

> Her bold game's moves she swiftly captured
> This youth and that, then approached a third one.
> (BB, II, 20:17–20)

Janus brings the poem to an end by expressing envy toward the very boards she dances on, saying that she is altogether welcome to make her turns on his breast and face and eyes. There is a suggestion, in "Ad amorem" and the ball scene, that Janus might have had it in him to transform the humanistic ode, to make it something different from the instrument for praise, celebration, and reflection it usually was. He takes his start, no doubt, from Horace, in the latter's most erotic moments, say, in I,9, with those famous whisperings, or II,4 about the slave girl. The result, however, differs from the mass of would-be Horatian verse; it describes without digressions, and it never—that economy, again, which sets Janus off from the vast majority of his Latin-writing contemporaries—shows off learning.

The last of the odes, "Ad deum optimum maximum, cum tumultuarentur anabaptistae," bearing the date 1534, tells little about what the Anabaptists have done, although Janus, with his interest in the bloodily melodramatic, might have done some good odic *reportage* here. Instead, it dwells, at length, on the good deeds of God, a catalog of benefits that quickly grows tedious. Yet, the poem's air of technical experiment is interesting —its recasting of the message of Psalm 18 ("Caeli enarrant gloriam Dei") in Horatian meters. Historians of the literature of the sixteenth century have paid considerable attention to the *Paraphrasis in Librum Psalmorum* of George Buchanan (1566),[5] the rendering of the whole of the Psalms in Horatian meters; Janus Secundus, proving himself to be *rerum novarum cupidus*, had taken a step in the same direction a generation earlier; indeed, it was in 1566 that the zealous reformers destroyed his tomb. Would Janus have become a religious poet, had he lived?

I *The Epigrams*

The first book of epigrams is made up of seventy-six items, the second of seventeen; the first contains "original" creations, the second is made up of renderings from the Greek Anthology, and probably came into being under the tutelage of Alciatus.[6] The "second" book, then, is interesting principally as a preparatory exercise for the best of the epigrams in the "first" book. The majority of these were written in Spain, in the tough school of Charles' court and of Toledo; the Spanish pieces have, in turn, been framed inside Bourges poems: the opening epigram is a tribute to Alciatus, the closing is the abusive observation on the girls of the university town. The seventy-four poems coming in between are a mixed lot. A third of them are tributes, to Charles and Alciatus, the monarchs, respectively, of the political and literary worlds in which Janus lived, to Janus' father, to teachers, friends, and acquaintances. A dozen or so have topics which may be called literary: the early poems on Lucian, the portrait of Propertius' Cynthia, attacks on grammarians, attacks (not very scathing) on one Bubalus, a bad poet. A few deal with contemporary political events (for example, the hard words to Francis I, for his renewed hostility to Charles). Some are a kind of emblem poetry, written as texts to pictures ("On a picture of Icarus," "On a picture of Phaeton's fable," "On a likeness of Hercules"); some are directly moralizing—the limit to be placed on pleasure is announced, while an equally unconvincing homily lists the three greatest evils which can beset man: "femina, flamma, fretum" ("woman, fire, flood"). Elsewhere, Janus— forgetting flame and stormy water—concentrates on woman: love is an incurable disease, impervious to every herb, resisting every physician. In his epigrams, as elsewhere, Janus shone best when he talked about love, or lust. The epigrams contain a handful of pleasant little amorous poems: the two derivative but graceful *epicedia* for Glycera's pet sparrow, the hate-and-love tribute to fierce Neaera ("Your shining beauty has caught both my eyes' light and my soul") and—a *hapax legomenon* in Janus—a piece of sound advice to a bad-tempered matron, on how to keep her husband's love:

Streams which you let wander freely, making their way down broad courses,
Follow their tranquil path, brushing their banks in sweet silence,
But if you would restrain these same streams in narrow confinement,
Swiftly they'd burst into floodtide, making a terrible sound.
(BB, I, 337:3–6)

A different kind of abandonment of restraint is recommended to the lovers who keep a tryst in church. In its small space, the epigram combines two of Janus' sterling qualities, his simplicity and his gift for the apt phrase:

> Take your stations, youths, with these lovely maidens,
> Joining your right hands, let neither church nor altar
> (However reverend) keep you here asunder:
> Why not blaspheme against the gilded altars,
> If in exchange you'll get girls' golden kisses.
> It is a sin and a shame to let shame stop you.
>
> (BB, I, 337)

This mild and relatively subtle humor fits well with Janus' poetic personality; nonetheless, a much more bitter kind of erotic satire forms the second largest grouping, after the tributes, in the *Epigrammata:* in these poems, Janus is always vivid, and sometimes amusing, sometimes not. The little vignette on a *ménage à quatre* is unpleasant, brief, and quotable; with the obliging husband out of the way, Marullus and Varius can do what they like with Septimilla, when they like:

> Safe, they frequently do it at sun's rising,
> Safe, they frequently do it at sun's setting,
> Safe, midway in the day they take their pleasure,
> Marullus and Varius on Septimilla.
>
> (BB, I, 298:8–11)

At times Janus likes to linger over his black eroticism, imitating Juvenal more than Martial. The prostitute Gellia, growing old, must work harder, since someday, not too far off, she will have to pay young men for their services. Gellia gets a long poem, of seventy-two lines; Janus can cast off neither the tradition of antiquity, by which the lustful old woman was a figure of fun, nor the attitude of his age, which, in Latin and vernacular literature alike, delighted in mocking the woman whose beauty had vanished. It is to Janus' credit, however, that we perceive the glimmering of a human sympathy beyond the strictures of the tradition and the age; seeing herself in the mirror, Gellia is forced to behold her beauty's ruin, and: [7]

> Then at last you must weep, pitying so your plight,
> And you'll curse all these days that fail,
> Poorly burgeoning now, Gellia, lacking fruit.
>
> (BB, I, 322:52–54)

But it is only a glimmering, no more.

What is there in the epigrams which Janus alone could have written? The reply may be couched this way: Janus is himself, at his best, when he forgets that he is writing epigrams, when he does not try too hard to be witty. The Gellia poem is dragged back to a cruel convention again and again by its central, bad joke; the poem instructing lovers not to be ashamed in church succeeds because Janus can limit himself to gentle incongruities of phrase and to a simple statement of the situation. Here, putting the natural above the accepted norm, he offers a modest counterpart (in the erotic sphere) to a famous poem of German humanism, Conrad Celtis' "Ad Sepulum disidaemonem" ("To Sepulus the Superstitious," *Carmina* I,16).

II *The* Epistolae

The nineteen *epistolae* of Janus are divided into two books, of thirteen and six, respectively. The reason for the division is a metrical one, between "elegiac" and "heroic" song, as Scriverius says on the title page of the section in his edition; the first part is in distichs, the second in dactylic hexameters, modeled upon the epistles of Horace. It is regrettable that Janus, who was a lively letter writer in prose and whose *Itineraries* can be taken as long letters home, does not prove to be a better correspondent in verse. Wright says, correctly, that the epistles are "primarily . . . poetical exercises, . . . frequently diffuse or trivial"; Ellinger's enthusiasm for the "charm" of the poems is all the stranger because he prefers the first book to the second. The second book contains the epistles enlivened by Janus' irony—the joking to Baverius about the exchange of a poetic gift for a mess of legal pottage, the attempt to tease the model boy Caimus with the account of a hunt for game and girls, and the deft putting-down of Mendoza, with its splendid-sounding Lucretian tones. The other poems in the second book, to be sure, are like those in the first—pompous, stiff, and self-conscious, run-of-the-mill flattery verse, however informative they may be about Janus' life (and they take a great many lines to offer relatively little information). When Janus means to impress a correspondent, he directly loses his appealing lightness. With Baverius, Caimus, Mendoza, he feels confident enough to relax; but he evidently thinks he is at a disadvantage with the distinguished Buslidius, the painter Scorel, the golden boy Sucquetus.[8] How much bad Neo-Latin poetry has been written because of the author's apprehensions about the recipient's judgment of it?

III *The* Funera

Humanist poets were expected to write *epistolae* as means of formal, and publishable, communication with their relatives and colleagues; another formal use to which they put their skills was the commemoration of their distinguished or beloved contemporaries' passing, or, simply, the writing of verse epitaphs in the style of the Greek Anthology. There are twenty-nine poems in the *Funerum liber* of Janus; of these, one, by far the longest poem in the collection, is called a *querela,* or lament, on the death of Nicolaus Everardi, while four, of middling length, are termed *naeniae,* burial or grave songs: these are for Janus' teacher Volcardus, the poetess Jeanne de la Font of Bourges, Charles Sucquetus, and—the climax of the collection, as the *querela* is its overture—on the death of Thomas More. The other poems (with one exception, the short and early poem on the death of Mercurino Gattinara, which has been given no genre title at all) are all *epitaphia,* fifteen of them couched in the third person, describing the departed who lies, as it were, in the tomb below, and nine in the first person: the departed speaks for himself. (One is in the second person: the unhappy Francis of Valois is harangued by the Francophobe, Janus.) With the exception of the poem on More, there is nothing startling in the poetic treatment the notable dead received: Janus is cognizant of their virtues, he knows that death is the great leveler, he is aware of the special poignancy of dying in a foreign land, and he has a gift for dwelling on small domestic details, as in the *naenia* on Jeanne de la Font, a simple and moving poem, in which the poetess, speaking herself, laments the anguish her death has caused her husband. (The pendant epitaph on Jeanne, in the third person, is considerably less affecting; it pays attention principally to her literary accomplishments.)

These funerary poems have provided material for the biography of Janus, and that is why we know them so well already. Another group of epitaphs, however, those dealing with simple people, may tell something about Janus which has not been noticed before—although an inkling of this sympathy downward was given in the itinerary of the trip from Bourges to Mechlin. There, it will be remembered, Janus recounted how he and his brother had written epitaphs for the messenger Reinaldus, killed while defending the money entrusted to him. The epitaph, rewritten, appears as number 22 in the *Funerum liber;* it is one of the important handful of poems celebrating those favored neither by birth nor by talent, but only by character. The book, to be sure, contains a couple of epitaphs on unimportant dead of a different sort: Faustinus, "having been burned through and through by the flames of a passionate Venus," lies extinguished beneath a water spout (like Hardy's Fanny Robin), and a certain Menelaus has been torn away from his labors by lascivious death. Such heartless witticisms are common in the quasi-tombstone verse of the Renaissance; an epitaph such as that for Reinaldus is rarer, and may again be an indication of a deepening sensibility. The epitaph of Old Michael is likewise something of a novelty—a man of simple heart who has spent his life in quiet service:

> In a forgotten village I led little boys through their primers,
> Meanwhile serving the church of Mary, the Mother of Jesus,
> Many a year and more, as vigilant guardian and sexton,
> And in obscurity led an obscure life, without blemish.
> (BB, II, 126:2–5)

Steadfastness, of the high and the low, was a quality which Janus evidently admired—the steadfastness of Reinaldus and Michael, or of Nicolaus Everardi, who remained the poor but honest judge, and of Thomas More. Of course, it is not only admiration of this moral quality which led Janus to write his *naenia* on More's death. Catherine of Aragon, the sanctity of whose marriage the English humanist died defending, was an aunt of Charles V; and it has been pointed out by Jolles and by Blanchard that More's martyrdom was an event that Charles could use to his own political ends. Still, it is striking that Janus, who otherwise chose his themes from what lay close at hand, should have turned to England, and that he, a sick man, should have given himself to the writing of the great poem about More. It would not be altogether outlandish to suggest that, at this juncture, illness and disappointment had darkened Janus' view of life, and that here, if anywhere in his brief career, there is a sign of a change of orientation.

The *naenia* for More, 163 lines long, opens with an invocation to the Muses, a request that they join the poet in weeping for the "murdered bard"—a term applied to More several times in the poem's course: "mecum vatem lugete peremtum." Janus writes of More first of all as the fellow humanist and poet, a member of the international elite who has been done to death— "vatem canimus vates" ("A poet, I sing of the poet"). Having presented the honored dead, Janus, the sometime eroticist, and avid collector of the sensational, does not shy away from a lurid account of Henry Tudor's misdeeds. He digresses twice, once to tell about the family tree of abandoned Catherine, in the course of which account he bows toward her nephew, Charles, and again to mention Henry's establishment of a new, heretical faith:

Now for himself he usurped the pope's rights and his sacred title,
Wielding them however far the confines of his kingdom extended,
And, in his sacrilege, slew the whole of the ancient religion.
(BB, II, 142:67–69)

Janus concludes this passage with a *polyptoton:* "Et gravius peccat, ut non peccasse putetur" ("And he sins all the worse, lest he be thought to have sinned"). Then, having given Anne Boleyn ("the wanton whore") a horrified glance, he thinks of More again, and simultaneously, it may be guessed, of his own father. More has been an ornament of the realm, and his monarch's closest adviser; "no judge administered justice more fairly." Janus is quite aware of the tragic element in the case; More could have saved himself, if he had been willing to quell his conscience: "You were able to lead a life unharmed, but to be less honest." Nor does Janus let the matter go at that; More's conscience is worth a much longer description, in Janus' opinion, than was Henry's uprooting of the old faith. If More had wished to protect his life with a false oath, "applauding defilement and base ambition," then he would have sullied "his customs and his prior life"—and have destroyed all that he had been. And so he decided, by his own free will ("sponte sua")—is Janus engaging in a little Catholic propaganda here?—to place his head on the block. In other words, Janus appears to have had a clearer notion of what it was that More died for than did Erasmus, with his remark: "If only More had not involved himself with these religious matters, and had left theology to the theologians."

Furthermore, Janus entertains a more complex view of More's death than did the great German-Latin odist, Jacob Balde, who wrote a poem on the same topic a hundred years later. For Balde,[9] More was a monolithic baroque hero, an almost superhuman figure, who immediately perceived the right way to go:

> All England, weeping, followed the final march;
> Yet one did not weep: harder than marble, he
>   Beheld his fate with haughty visage,
>   Cheerfully greeting the gloomy headsman.

Balde's More is indeed like a statue, harder than marble; the only sign of humanity he exhibits is, as it were, an inhuman one, when he scorns the pleas of daughter, son-in-law, and wife, pushing aside poor Alice with "a ferocious laugh, as though she were a fool." The More of Janus appeals a good deal more to our sensibilities, just as Janus' century, the sixteenth, often seems so much more accessible than the rigidly stylized one that followed.

Balde ends his ode with More ascending the scaffold, "plenus futuri," "full of the future:" the Jesuit takes it for granted that his readers will imagine that More enters into heaven. Janus opens up paradise before us; it is a scene arranged by a humanist's hand. The King of Heaven crowns the hero with a victor's wreath, and the members of the attendant "senate," the angels, look suspiciously like the poet's birds of classical antiquity:

> Like a thousand swans, which fly to the glassy Meander,
> And beat an applause with their wings, and then as they sing at
>   their sweetest,
> Make on the blue of the air a border of snow with their feathers.
> (BB, II, 144:95–97)

It is a quaintly charming place, this humanist's heaven, a shade more Christian, perhaps, than the afterworld to which Janus had brought his father, another Latinist and incorruptible judge.

The poem is by no means over: Margaret, More's gifted and learned daughter, stands sadly beside the Thames. Janus has more compassion for her than Balde would for the martyr's family; he understands well, he says, why she weeps, despite the heroic nature of her father's death. For it has been an unworthy death, too; Janus describes the mutilation and exposure of the corpse, and tells how (for all the heroism in the world) the hero's head will become hideous. Janus is keen to death's ghastliness (on which he dwelt so often in the *Itineraries*); and his description of the ugly remains calls attention again to the bitterness of Thomas' choice. The horrors continue—horrors which Henry's conscience will visit upon its owner as he comes to realize what he has done. But Janus' Henry is not just the typical stage tyrant, driven insane with remorse at his misdeeds; like his victim, Thomas, he is made into a fuller human being, a man who killed a friend he loved and respected. After a prediction of fall and exile for Henry, the poem ends as it had opened, with a summons to mourning for More, "the good bard," the humanist. Almost *en passant,* Janus remarks in his conclusion that More has died "for the sake of his sacred faith"; but he has provided a different statement about More's death earlier in the poem—there the death was caused by More's desire to stay true to himself. And where is More now, in the *coda,* as he receives and judges the quality (the humanist man-of-letters, even in death) of his young colleague's poem?

Hail, you worthy old man, hail now and farewell forever!
Whether you bide in Elysium or in the bright halls of heaven,
Take this endeavor of mine, and do not condemn it too harshly.
(BB, II, 147:161–63)

Janus names two possibilities; but antiquity's Elysium comes first, before Christianity's celestial realm.

IV *The* Silvae

The *naenia* to More is easily the most interesting of the exhibits in the *Funerum liber;* it has the intensity of the erotic poetry, transferred to another realm: "Cet être de feu se livre tout entier dans la nénie," Blanchard says (*Moreana,* p. 30). It shows that Janus was able to go beyond his own self-imposed limitations, rising to a heroic theme and keeping a longish poem alive. It is not the only extended piece by Janus which can be rated an artistic success; a few more are to be found in the miscellaneous poems, the *Silvae.* These are ten in number, or rather nine, since the ninth is Molza's feigned "letter by Catherine of Aragon." The renderings of Lucian's dialogues are early exercises, as is the "Expostulatio cum Neptuno." Other poems lead into the later years of the short career: the *Reginæ pecuniae regia* is from the first months in Spain, the Orpheus eclogue somewhat farther along in the Spanish stay, the *heroide* of Henry VIII probably was written around the time of More's execution, thus in 1535. The song on the changeableness of human fortune, the echo poem, and the epithalamium cannot be dated.

The poem on Queen Money, in 264 hexameters, probably sprang, or so Burmann-Bosscha think, from a Horatian seed; in Epistles I,6, Horace hands out some cynical advice to Numicius: "Of course, Queen Money [*Regina Pecunia*] gives a wife with a dowry, credit, [and] friends, birth, and good looks," and Janus attempts to take a similar tone in his poem. (Queen Money is also mentioned in the second book of More's *Utopia*.) Janus himself had reason to think about money matters; the letter of May 31, 1534, to Everardus tells how much he fears being a burden to others: it is Janus' excuse for having entered the service of Tavera, to whom the present satire makes flattering reference at the outset. For, Janus begins, it may well be that the kingdom of money is beneath the lands of Spain, where Augustus (Charles) reigns, and where sublime Toledo, the city of Tavera, lies. It is not hard to see what Janus is driving at: perhaps he will find his fortune in Spain and although, as the poem develops, he affects a certain philosophical contempt for money, he does not pretend that he could get along without it. Having made these hints for practical necessity's sake, the poet descends into the realm where the sun does not penetrate; the subterranean chambers are lit by shining gold. We are shown the queen straight off, sitting all gilded and regal: what Janus indulges in here is a rhetorical-structural *hysteron-proteron;* having been given a glimpse of the queen herself, the object of man's striving, we are taken back to the labyrinthine ways through which the crowd ("youths, old men, men in their best years") presses, looking for her. The attrition is considerable: found unworthy, many are rejected, others break off the journey, railing against the gods, still others perish, "blocking the narrow path with their bodies." A few survivors, "born under better stars," worm their way into the queen's aula; but, blinded by the sudden brilliance, they grope for baubles, unable to see the countenance of the goddess they have sought. In the throne room again, Janus abandons action (the scene with the clogged path has been very effective) for description; the plastic artist, who had been so fascinated by the tombs at Saint Denis, furnishes the chamber with appropriate groups of statuary: earth itself, done in gold and emeralds, and the waters of earth in a silver flood. Ellinger called the poem a parade piece; certainly, satirical intention is forgotten in an effort to rival the shield of Achilles. But, in a while, Janus gets to more germane *sujets:* Midas frozen in gold, Jason daring the dragon for the fleece, Jupiter pouring himself into the womb of Danaë—"three signs of the queen's triumph." Nearer to the queen there stand allegorical figures, representing other forces subject to her power: Bellona, Peace, Fortune, Pride, Virtue, the Arts, Religion itself—dressed in the regalia of an archbishop. The passage on religion, somewhat longer than its companions, provides some riddles: could Tavera have found it offensive? Or was Janus sure of Tavera's broadmindedness? Or did he exempt Tavera from his implied criticism, just as he must have exempted his father's memory from the members of the corrupt Senate, lying at the great mistress's feet and turning themselves into every shape, besting Proteus, at her bidding? Having set up a venal Religion and a Law more venal still, Janus grows darker in his observations: Rapine laughs at justice, Avarice is surrounded by her ugly brood—Theft, Fraud, and Trickery. Then come Usury and Libitina (the goddess of corpses, and of litigation over wills), and across the golden beams and ceilings the sleepless Cares fly, "beating their noisy wings." The world is at Lady Money's mercy, it has sold out to her. Even the realm of love has been perverted by the great queen. She prefers the embraces of old men to those of handsome boys—the more disgusting the aged lover, the better. Or, it is possible that, on rare occasion, the queen will take a handsome youth into her bed, and shower favors on him. The appearance of the royal favorite would seem to go against the drift of the satire, but does not: however cognizant we are of the queen's evil, we should all like to be in the Sunday child's place.

The poem concludes with the observation that, in the throne room, "scarcely a poet or two can be seen." They are absent not because they scorn the queen, as might at first be thought, but because she has long made a practice of scorning them. Indeed, the poet who writes here ("Ipse ego," "I myself") had been led —or thought, he adds, he had been led—into the queen's realm, and prayed that he not be awakened; but, as soon as she noticed his presence, she told him to leave—and herself, with all her wealth, vanished into thin air. The *Reginae pecuniae regia* can be tedious, but with its continuing ambiguity of attitude toward the queen—whom we all love, although we perceive how she debases us—it is a not wholly unworthy contemporary of humanism's masterpiece of irony, the *Moriae Encomium.*

The poet takes center stage in the eclogue "Orpheus," another poem in hexameters—exactly one hundred lines shorter than the *Reginae pecuniae regia*—in which Janus says something about himself while ostensibly speaking of other matters. The shepherd Lycidas has been made wretched by the "cunning and craft" of urbane Neaera, who "bests the nearby snows of the icy Pyrenees in both her whiteness and her coldness." Sad as he is, he begins to sing; in his song, Orpheus tells the story of Eurydice, twice lost, dividing the narrative with the refrain, "Euridice, miseri Euridice misera uxor amantis" ("Eurydice, Eurydice, unhappy wife of an unhappy lover"). The emotional burden of Orpheus' song is self-reproach: too much love on his part has condemned his wife to the underworld, and himself to unhappiness. At length, the song overwhelms Calliope, Orpheus' mother, who has mistaken Lycidas, thanks to his poetic gifts, for the dead Orpheus; she silences him with her embrace. The meaning is plain: Janus (Lycidas/Orpheus) reproaches himself on the one hand for the blind devotion from which he cannot escape; on the other, he puts himself in the ranks of poetry's immortals. These themes are familiar from the *Monobiblos* and the *Basia:* the poet's excessive affection for Julia and Neaera, his habit of blaming himself for whatever goes wrong, and his awareness, all the same, that his genius gives him an immortality which he, in turn, can bestow upon his beloved. Who would remember Eurydice, if Orpheus had not sung about her?

The Orpheus eclogue gives plenty of opportunities for seeing through the triple role: Janus playing Lycidas playing Orpheus. Goethe says: "Dichter lieben nicht zu schweigen, / Wollen sich der Menge zeigen." It might be presumed, though, that Janus could find little opportunity to say something about himself in the other piece of "Rollendichtung" he wrote, the *heroide* inspired by the words which Molza put into Catherine's mouth (see p. 68). In the "Responding Letter of Henry VIII," he has the chance to paint a monster of lust and ingratitude, if not of cruelty. Yet his Henry is seen objectively, an unhappy man, whose actions Janus can understand. As a matter of fact, the reader is made to feel sorry for Henry at the outset; women are a troublesome lot, and imagine the misery they can cause a monarch, responsible for his kingdom's well-being, especially if they have high connections of their own. Henry tells what went wrong with his marriage: Cupid and Venus had made him burn with incestuous flames, and thus brought "initial ruin to [his] crown." (Catherine had first been married to Henry's older brother, Arthur, although the marriage had not been consummated.) After some Senecan tirades, Henry reveals a painful scene in the royal bedchamber; Arthur's ghost had driven him away from Catherine, saying, "These are my pleasures." The poem could not have been offensive to Charles, for his aunt's sake, if he read it; the blame for the marital failure is put on Henry's unhappy decision to wed his late brother's bride. Just the same, Henry himself is more to be pitied than censured for "seeking out other beds," at least in Janus' interpretation—and Janus was a poet aware, as we know, of the problems arising on the couch of love. The poem, which is about a third the length of Molza's, breaks off suddenly; Henry toys with the thought that Catherine, like Polyxena, might want to "throw her mutilated body down beside Achilles' tomb," in order to bring the promised pleasures to the dead Arthur; then he switches directions and wishes her a long and happy life. Did Janus stop so abruptly because he noted what a human Henry he had created?

Love, unhappy love, is the subject of another of the *Silvae*, too, the virtuoso *Viator et Echo*, where the traveler, in the wilderness, hears Echo mock his Petrarchan cries of passion. The traveler says: "Dic, oro, poterit quid impotenti / Seros ponere limites amori?" and Echo replies: "Mori." In Crane's translation, this goes: "I pray thee, tell, what end, however slow / My destiny for this vain love commandeth?" The answer comes back: "Death." Such artfulness is not characteristic of Janus; the only other poem in his *oeuvre* which indulges in a comparable trick is the sixty-second epigram, a telestichon, in which the final letters of the poem's eight lines of tributes to his father spell out "Everardi." According to Burmann-Bosscha, Janus got the idea from Callimachus' thirtieth epigram, or, according to Crane, more likely from Erasmus' *Echo* colloquy in Latin and Greek prose (1526); whatever the case of the inspiration may have been, Janus, by dint of his great popularity during the sixteenth and seventeenth centuries, encouraged the spread of the echo poem, of which his verse dialogue is "one of the earliest" modern examples.[10] Italy, England, France, and Germany all produced echo poems; from Germany, for example, we have echo verses by Opitz, Zesen, and Harsdörffer, memorable today as illustrative specimens. If Janus was among the first to try the "genre," he was also among the best: the echoes come not mechanically but naturally in the poem, are not overused (eight echoes in fifty-one lines), and enhance the poem's sense.

Many poets of the second or third class imitated Janus' echo poetry; in another case, a great poet, and an avid reader of Janus, was prompted to use a certain meter because of Janus' employment of it in the *Silvae*. At least, this is a claim hinted at by Ellinger and made boldly by Schroeter. The poem in question is the "In vicissitudinem rerum instabilemque Fortunam" ("Concerning the changefulness of things and unstable fortune"), in Scriverius' superscript, and the meter is the Adonic, the fourth line of the Sapphic strophe, composed of a dactyl and a trochee or spondee. The poet who supposedly liked Janus' repetitive use of the lively short line is Goethe, and the places where he uses it are, among others, "Grenzen der Menschheit," and "Gesang der Geister über den Wassern," as well as the *chorus mysticus* in *Faust*. Something can be said for Ellinger's suggestion (III:1:64) and Schroeter's proposal (pp. 219–20): the two poems in question come from the latter part of the 1770s, when Goethe also wrote his tribute to the spirit of Secundus, "Lieber, heiliger, grosser Küsser." [11] What is more important, the Goethe poems have a resemblance in theme to Janus' Adonic verses. The Latin poem's message is that nothing is constant in the life of man:

> That which stands lowest
> Tends ever upward,
> That which stands highest
> Tends ever downward.
>
> (BB, II, 166:6–9)

In Goethe's text, however, a limit of mankind is its impermanence:

> Uns hebt die Welle,
> Verschlingt die Welle,
> Und wir versinken,

while the spirits above the waters end their song thus:

> Seele des Menschen,
> Wie gleichst du dem Wasser!
> Schicksal des Menschen,
> Wie gleichst du dem Wind!

The secret of the Adonic line, as Secundus and Goethe—who made variations upon it—discovered, was its restlessness, its air of constant movement; the poem's dress is perfectly suited to its message. As for the message itself, there is nothing novel about it; Janus had but to look at his Horace (among how many other possible sources) to be reminded of it: Odes I,34, for example, where Jove can "exchange the lowest and the highest," would provide the Neo-Latin poem's theme, or Odes IV,7, would offer the poem's main image, the changing of the seasons as a metaphor of man's fate. Is the poem an exercise, then, a tribute to a standard theme of antiquity (related, of course, to Ecclesiastes' vanity of vanities), or an expression of real fear in the face of growing crisis? We have no way of knowing when it was written, or in what circumstances—whether, in some way, it stems from what Trevor-Roper has called the "spectacular revolutions" of the sixteenth century. Indeed, a reader, unaware of the poem's authorship, might want to put "Nemo beatus" into that subsequent world which we loosely call the "Baroque," assigning it, perhaps, to Bidermann's Belisarius, the triumphant general who ends blinded and a beggar.[12]

The poem on the instability of human existence attracted the attention of one German poet, the *silva* which remains to be discussed was translated by another. Johann Christian Günther had a very high opinion of Janus Secundus' merits, putting him into the best poetic company ("Vergil, Horaz, Petrarch, Secundus, Sannazar"); however, Günther's rendering of the poem called *Epithalamium lascivum* by Scriverius is a fiasco. Where Janus uses the hendecasyllabic line, long ago given a plethora of erotic associations by Catullus, Günther chose galloping amphibrachs for his "Hochzeitscherz: Nach Anleitung des

Lateinischen aus dem Johanne Secundo."[13] Janus breaks his
poem up into eleven strophes of unequal length by the refrains,
"O felix iuvenis, puella felix" ("Oh you fortunate youth, you
happy maiden") and "O noctem ter et amplius beatam" ("Oh
you night blessed thrice and still more blessed"), the second
refrain then intensified by the substitutions, "quater et quater,"
"quater, o quater," "nimis et nimis," "nimis, o nimis" ("fourfold"
and "overmuch"). Strophes 1–5 have the first refrain, 6–10 the
second in its various forms, while the envoy, number 11, returns
to the youth and the girl. Günther makes only rudimentary
attempts at any division; thus, the poem, in German, loses its air
of having separate scenes, or stages of passion, and lacks the
refrain which links Janus' poem to Catullus 61 and 62 and to
the *Pervigilium Veneris*. The epithalamium grows longer in
Günther's hands: the 145 hendecasyllabics of the original become 200 tetrameters in German. What is worst, though, is that
Günther misses the lightness and elegance of Janus altogether.
Janus uses the elementary devices of sound repetition and word
doubling, as he describes the first skirmishes of love's battle:

> Figens mille protervus hic et illic,
> Collo basia multa, multa malis,
> Labris basia plura, plura ocellis.

> Boldly placing a thousand kisses on her,
> Giving her throat and cheeks a good-sized number,
> Giving her lips and eyes the more and better.
>
> (BB, II, 196:76–78)

And, a little later on:

> Tunc per candida colla, tunc per illud,
> Quod certat ebori nitore pectus,
> Tunc per crura tenella, perque ventrem,
> Et quae proxima sunt et huic et illis,
> Saltu volve agili manum salacem.

> Then to that throat of snow and to that bosom,
> Which can strive with ivory in its brightness,
> Then to those lovely legs, then to that belly,
> And to what lies between the one and the other
> Stretch out your lustful hand with sudden movement.
>
> (ll. 88–92)

Günther, merging the two separate passages, manages to be both more prudish and more vulgar than Janus, to the point of comedy:

>   Hier mache das Vorspiel, hier spize die Hand
>   Und bringe das Hauptwerck der Wollust in Stand.
> Erhize die Adern durch sanftes Bewegen
> Und klatsch ihr die Backen mit freundlichen Schlägen
>   Und küss ihr die Augen und nez ihr das Kinn.
>   Bald grüble von weiten, bald wälze dich hin,
> Bald strecke den Vorwitz der listigen Finger,
> Bald kneipe die runden und wallenden Dinger
> Und küsse nach vieler Erfindung und Art
> Und forsche, was Amor am tiefsten verwahrt.

(Now ready your prelude, now fold your hand thin,
And get joy's main action all primed to begin.
  Now start her veins flaming with gentle rotation,
  And grant to her bottom a sweet spanking's ration;
Her eyes—kiss them soundly, her chin—make it damp,
Now moon at a distance, now charge like a scamp,
  Extending your curious fingers by inches,
  And giving those round things that heave hearty pinches,
Inventing new kisses of manifold sort,
And seeking the place that's love's deepest resort.)

(11. 95–104)

The American reader may also be troubled by vague rhythmic associations with *A Visit From Saint Nicholas*.

Part of the difficulty of translating the *Epithalamium lascivum* lies in the very simplicity of Janus' approach: he depends upon a frankness which is not salacious, and an ability to give his work (which, after the opening strophes, becomes an extended development of the *topos*, the battle of the bed) a certain transcendence by the very directness and energy of his verse. The wedding poem, written so frequently in these centuries as a commissioned work, was usually a version of the *hymenaeus*, the song to be sung to the bridal couple, or bride, on the way to the bedchamber. It often engaged in what could be called a kind of preparatory and punning obscenity; for example, in Opitz's poem to Niclas Wasserführer and Fräulein Planch, Niclas is enjoined to plough and wet the field of his bride. (Just so, the "Fescennine jesting" of Catullus had depended not on sexual description but sexual allusion.) The result, since the eroticism of the poem had to be contained in slyness, was often pornography.[14] The poet customarily went into the bedroom only by forecast;[15] he did not describe the stages of the bridal night in fact, one by one: the instruction at the end of Catullus 61 is: "Claudite ostia, virgines" ("Maidens, shut the doors"). The poem of Janus, however, is an epithalamium closer to the word's literal sense—a poem sung at the bridal chamber—and going beyond that sense, entering the room.[16] Janus' hands are practiced, from the *Monobiblos* and the *Basia*, at catching the nuances of physical love between two ideal partners; and here the point is made again and again that the union is splendid because it takes place between the young and the fair. The poem is for a nameless youth and girl; authors of made-to-order wedding poems had to call the bridal couple good-looking, whether or not they were; Janus calls them beautiful because they must be, to meet his poem's requirements.

The poem opens with a preamble saying that the hour now come, "Hora suavicula et voluptuosa," is the best that life has to offer. The second and third sections are given over, respectively, to congratulating the groom on the supreme charms of his bride, and the bride on the supreme longing of the groom; strophes four and five reverse the order, the first of them shows the youth impatient for evening, and the second the nervous bride, whom the young man will have to calm. Thus far the elements are familar enough from the wedding poems of antiquity;[17] as in the *Pervigilium Veneris* or Claudianus' imperial epithalamium, a suggestion is made of a resemblance, and balance, between man and nature. The bridegroom, for example, grows ever more fiery:

> He is set afire by your lips of roses,
> He is set afire by your snowy bosom,
> He is set afire by your hair's sweet shining,
> And has been conquered by your eye's conversing,
> (BB, II, 194:34–37)

while the fires of nature, with some grandeur, have been extinguished:

> Now the Cynthian god has gone to hiding,

> Now he swims in the farthest Spanish waters,
> Making way for his sister, nighttime's courser.
>
> (11. 46–48)

Emulating but outdoing the *Pervigilium,* Janus—it is one of his most effective devices—makes a long crescendo from strophe to strophe, giving the earlier sections a mythological burden (references to Venus, Cupid, Juno, the judgment of Paris) which is shed as the poem grows more intense and moves toward the climax. (Janus' restrained application and prompt abandonment of mythological adornment can be better appreciated after reading the overladen and undramatic epithalamia of Statius or Sidonius or Claudianus.)[18] The natural background and Olympian figures disappear; from the beginning of the fifth strophe, we are aware of the bride and bridegroom alone, as they enter their chamber (11. 54–57); the turns of phrase, to be sure, are still the conventional ones:

> Now the virgin enters the bridal chamber.
> Husband, be sure she does not leave a virgin;
> Now the virgin, stretched on the snowy cover,
> Waits for the bridegroom's coming, waits and trembles.

But these obligations to the genre are quickly and neatly disposed of. In the sixth strophe, the central one of the eleven of which the poem consists, the scene is narrowed to the bed, and the refrain changes from "O felix iuvenis, puella felix" to the numerical praise" ("ter et amplius") of the night on which the two, separately mentioned heretofore in the refrain, will be united. The groom makes his first attempts in the lines, so badly rendered by Günther, quoted above; the bride fights back, offering both mild insult and a plea for mercy: "Satis est!" The imagery has become wholly military; a shower of fighting words, and wordplays,[19] opens the next strophe:

> Pugnet strenua, pugnet illa! pasci
> Pugnando teneri volunt Amores.
> Pugnando tibi duplicatus ardor
> Vires sufficiet novas in arma.
>
> Let her battle, and bravely, for the tender
> Cupids will batten well upon this battling:

> Passion, doubled by battle, mounts within you,
> Calls batallions untried to take their weapons
> (ll. 84–87)

The hand of the lover penetrates the innermost fortifications; at the same time—he has studied the rhetoric of the *Basia*—he bombards the girl with as many kisses "as the skies will have stars of auburn." In the eighth strophe, he essays sweet words; they slow the tempo, by way of contrast, as does the girl's reaction, in the ninth strophe: "She will speak to you ever sweeter love-words, / Trying new finger-games in her fresh passion, / Making wantonness worse by her inventions" (ll. 118–20), before final assault and unconditional surrender (strophe ten). Venus and Cupid issue their last call to arms ("ad arma") to the bridegroom; from the latter part of the fifth strophe—the entrance into the chamber—to this climactic tenth, the poem has been an exhortation and instruction to the man. (He is young and innocent, of course, in the fiction of the poem, and passes the instruction along to his still more innocent mate.) With his weapon, the bridegroom deals those happy wounds—a time-worn metaphor from the language of erotic poetry, but one that gets new life in Janus' fast verses: "Huc, illuc agilis feratur hasta" ("Let the quick lance move back and forth, quite freely"), and

> Nec quies lateri laborioso
> Detur, mobilibus nec ulla coxis.
>
> Leave no chance for repose to loins that labor,
> Nor give respite to hips that swing so swiftly.
> (ll. 129–30)

At strophe's end, as Janus puts it with clinical refinement: "uterque / Sudabit varii liquoris undas" ("The partners / Both will sweat out their waves of varied liquid"). In the concluding strophe, they are urged—now in the plural imperative ("Sudate ut libet")—to continue their damp labors through the long days and nights, and to bring forth the "turba minuta" whose company Janus once enjoyed at Everardus' house. The enjoinder to be fruitful is again a standard epithalamic formula; but again it is made with brevity and even dignity. Laurentius Finkelthus' prediction of the birth of a "Bersmanulus" [20] in his wedding poem for his fellow poet Gregor Bersman is clumsily cute (and strongly reminiscent of Catullus' vision of a "Torquatus . . . parvulus"); Janus, in his rapid move from the pleasure of the lovers to those of parenthood, and then, in the last lines, to old age and death itself, puts his description of physical love into its proper connection with the whole order of nature.

A strong monotony—it has often been remarked—cannot be avoided in the *carmina nuptialia*. It is unavoidable, save when the little genre is practiced and ennobled by a Spenser, or by a Janus Secundus, who could take the commonplaces of Latin erotic verse, and by dint of his semiinnovative boldness (in his description of the deflowering),[21] his sense of balanced and dramatic structure, and the enormously effective use of repetitive devices in his verse, mix the commonplaces into a masterpiece. Perhaps more clearly than any other of his poems, the *Epithalamium lascivum* shows how he could transform the old and the borrowed into something new and characteristically his own. Maybe his final secret lies in the fact that, while dealing with a world of pleasure, he still maintained a shimmer of promise, an air of not being quite fulfilled. In the *Monobiblos* and the *Basia*, he suggests now and again that the best lies in the preparation, and that genuine satisfaction is a dream. In the *Epithalamium*, amid the realities of the bed, he does the same thing, and by the most elementary trick: he is careful—after all, the bridegroom is being instructed—to put a great many of his verbs into the future tense. Yearning stays, even as consummation is described.

CHAPTER 5

Conclusion: Speculations and Surmises

IN 1566, the Netherlands were at the end of a bright era, and on the eve of a bloody one. In this "hunger year," the iconoclast disturbances swept through the country; Philip II, impatient with the independent spirit of his subjects, sent the Duke of Alba and ten thousand troops to Brussels. He had already been distressed by the skill with which, two years before, William of Orange, Egmont, Hoorn, and their supporters had maneuvered Antoine Perrenot de Granvelle—the son of the patron of Janus Secundus—out of his post as chief advisor to Margaret of Parma, regent of the Netherlands, and Philip's half-sister. Alba established the special court of which Hadrianus Marius was a member, and some four thousand Netherlanders fell victim to it. The eighty-year war began by which the northern provinces would establish their freedom, and which would separate them for good and all from their comrades in language and culture to the south. The "Flandria laeta," the "happy Flanders," of Janus (by which he meant the whole of the Lowlands) had vanished; Janus would have thought the world turned upside down had he lived, say, as long as Constantijn Huygens did (1596–1687); at the beginning of the seventeenth century he would have found the Netherlands a place where families moved not from north to south, from The Hague to Mechlin, but in the other direction, under religious duress.

Five years before Janus' birth, Philip the Fair of Hapsburg, the ruling prince of the Netherlands, had become joint ruler of Castile, with his wife Joanna, the daughter of Ferdinand and Isabella; two decades after Janus died, Charles V retired to San Yuste, leaving Philip II on the Spanish throne and as the Netherlands' new master. It was Janus' good fortune that his life lay within this prosperous half-century; he also lived at a favorable time in the history of Netherlandic humanism.[1] The spadework had been done in the latter part of the previous century, by the adoptive Netherlander, Alexander Hegius of Westphalia, the rector of the school of the Brothers of the Common Life at Deventer, by Rudolf Agricola, by Janus Murmellius of Alkmaar, by More's friend Aegidius of Antwerp, and by Erasmus himself. Like the dramatist Macropedius (almost a generation older than Janus but whose works were printed, for the most part, only after Janus' death),[2] Janus found an instrument ready for him, a supple Neo-Latin, amenable to every artistic purpose; he died just as humanism was becoming the tool of warring religious factions and the plaything of learned men. He possessed those qualities which the humanists valued so highly, *elegantia* and *eloquentia* and even *eruditio* (although he made small display of the last); but he used them for aims he chose himself, and which were not pressed on him by the new times' confessional strife or by the demands of scholarly virtuosity—the virtuosity of Lernutius (1545–1619) or Lipsius (1547–1606) or Heinsius (1580–1655) or Janus' editor, Petrus Scriverius (1576–1666). He was born too early to be tempted by the possibility of writing in his own vernacular, a temptation which he might not have been able to resist, inclined as he was to despise learning for learning's sake, and aware as he showed himself to be, in the *Itineraries*, of national differences. Thus he did not feel impelled to struggle, as Jan Dousa, Jan van Hout, and Jan van der Noot did, a generation after his death, with the problems of composition in a tongue that had to be given a new, "Renaissance" literary form. He provided material for the posthumanistic vernacular literature of the Netherlands, of France, of England, of Germany; but he did not have to suffer the pioneer's painful sense of insufficiency.

In many respects, Janus is a typical northern humanist-*littérateur* of his day. Like Erasmus and Celtis and the rest, he was an ardent traveler; like Celtis and Hutten an ardent patriot. He also had the humanist's devotion to the city, celebrating Brussels and Mechlin as others did Erfurt and Ingolstadt. He detested war, like most of the other humanists; yet, again like his colleagues, found it quite possible to plan to sing of the emperor's triumphs. He sought patrons and protectors by flattery, following a humanistic practice that would continue long after Latin had given way to the vernaculars. He liked having friends, and cultivated friendships, thus qualifying as a

Conclusion: Speculations and Surmises 143

member of humanism's mutual-admiration society. His preoccupation with eroticism is typical of humanist verse; however, he was more like Italian humanists of the recent past—Pontanus and others—than Germans of the present and future in his adoration of physical beauty, in his celebration of the "vis superba formae."[3] Even the philogynous Celtis, as he describes Hasilina, Elsula, Ursula, and Barbara, is communicating lessons in German geography and Neoplatonism.

Like every other humanist, Janus was steeped in the Latin classics, and lifted phrases and ideas from them without blushing. He tried his hand at the conventional subdivisions of the Neo-Latin lyric; in the style of his verse, too, he appears to run along the same tracks as his contemporaries. He likes anaphora, *polyptoton, hysteron-proteron,* metonymy, all used with the intent of heightening the emotional force of his verse; he can string *adynata* together with the best, or the worst, of them; he can supply the apt simile in descriptive passages; and, like every humanist poet worth his salt, he has a good store of *loci amoeni* and their terrible opposites. Commonplaces are his: how often he assures the reader that poetry is the only sure bestower of immortality, that love is the cruelest and yet most welcome master, that women are changeable indeed.

If he was not a revolutionary in his art, he was even more conservative in his attitude toward the world around him. Thus he entertained ill feelings toward the French because that was both the imperial and the Flemish thing to do; he had nothing of the political awareness, if that term may be used, of a Hutten or a Lotichius Secundus. As for his religious thoughts—and he surely could not have remained oblivious to the Protestant ferment—he was satisfied with the world the way it long had been; there are hints of impatience with certain Catholic practices, in the *Itineraries,* but that is all. Otherwise, his only pronouncement on the enormous upheaval is the poem against the Anabaptists, for the most part a poem in praise of God. The Anabaptists get a postscript in the last three strophes, as if Janus felt that he did have to mention them, after all, painful as the task might be: they are destructive forces, "under the shadow of new religion," troublemakers, thieves, madmen. The question of a possible conflict in Janus, between Christianity and a literary paganism, has elicited several opinions, a greater burden of commentary than the frail evidence can bear. Van Tieghem says that: "Second ne fait aucune place au christianisme; sa religion, c'est le culte du beau, c'est l'antiquité qui revit en lui." Thierry Sandre implies that he was so secure in his Catholic faith—a faith friendly to beauty—that he was unaware of a discrepancy between his poetry and his church. As for Crane, he speaks of Janus' "pagan and constitutional tolerance," and quotes a passage from Pope, on Janus, to support his opinion.[4] It may have been that Janus lacked the organ for abstract thought of any kind, and so could scarcely be expected to worry about such a conflict, any more than he could express himself on the science or philosophy of his day.

Janus' moderation—his willingness to stay within traditional limits—played him false, it could be argued; there was nothing remarkable about him, one might say, except the romantic aura surrounding the early dead. Here too he had been a Sunday child; fate's best gift to him was his premature passing. The argument could continue thus: sentimentality, coupled with a little prurience, kept his reputation alive until the present; now that sentimentality is out of fashion, and prurience has found much stronger literary food, Janus Secundus can be given the *coup de grâce* by sober scholarship, which will readily discover —again—that he was a skillful maker of pastiches, and nothing more. Such scholarship would have to admit only that he helped to encourage a taste for Catullus, the Roman love elegy, and for the *erotopaignion*, among vernacular poets in France, in Holland, and elsewhere. Thus Janus would fit neatly with what is expected of the run of humanist poets. As K. O. Conrady says: "Die Bedeutung der neulateinischen Literatur und Dichtung liegt in ihrer Vermittlerrolle,"[5] and, to be a transmitter, one does not need to be original; in fact, it is better if one is not. Janus' lucidity, the ease with which he is comprehended, would contribute to his value as a middleman.

Nevertheless: there exists that museum of praise which Janus received over the centuries, and which appears to place him in a class apart from and above his colleagues in Neo-Latin poetry. Dousa gave this feeling the formulation which has been quoted again and again: "Mihi Secundus unus instar omnium est" ("By himself, Secundus stands for me in place of all")—a paraphrase of Cicero on Plato. His poetry mostly lost its direct force as an inspirer of the great during the rococo age (where it was read as rococo poetry), only to receive that great final accolade from

Conclusion: Speculations and Surmises 145

Goethe, who regarded Janus as a living classic, not a charming relic. The nineteenth century, which learned "the Romantic prejudice" [6] against the Neo-Latinists because they did not write in the tongue of their heart, still maintained a nostalgic affection for Janus; [7] but today, there is probably no poet or general reader who would say of Janus what Robert Graves did of Janus' contemporary, John Skelton: "Old John, you do me good!" Until recently, though, scholars of Neo-Latin literature—who should be in the best position to recognize how unoriginal and unremarkable Janus is—have persisted in paying tribute to his singularity: the enthusiastic Schroeter called him "a genius," Ellinger said that he belonged to "den eigentümlichsten Erscheinungen" not only of Neo-Latin literature but of the German and Dutch literature of the sixteenth century taken as a whole, regardless of language, Latin or vernacular. Van Tieghem, Thierry Sandre, the Dutchman Kalff [8] extend his supremacy in Neo-Latin verse well beyond the boundaries set up by Ellinger, including other lands—even Italy, the fountainhead. Van Tieghem makes no bones about it: "le plus illustre représentant de la poésie amoureuse néo-latine" (p. 69). Wright puts him in faster company, the whole of world literature, coming to the conclusion that, "in spite of all the disadvantages of age, country, and profession, [he is] one of the half-dozen greatest love lyrists in world literature" (p. 24). Crane concurs: "From the mass of Neo-Latin writers he stands out as a figure of singular vitality" (p. 37). A quarter of a century afterward, in 1957, Gerard Knuvelder wrote that, for the most part, "Neo-Latin lyrics were a whited sepulchre [een gepleisterd graf]: but even the whiting fails to attract our reverence today," yet Janus—in whose poetry "we sense the heartbeat of his own life" —is the exception proving the rule.[9] Reedijk comes to an equally sweeping conclusion: "He was one of the very few genuine Neolatin poets of the Renaissance; one of the very few that were driven by a purely artistic urge to create beautiful verse in a language which it was in their power to revive without a trace of artificiality." [10] Of late, Harry C. Schnur has rendered the judgment that "der junge Dichter, der aus tiefstem Empfinden heraus schrieb, [verdient,] mit Properz und Catull auf eine Stufe gestellt zu werden" (p. 472).

Praise continues to be heaped on praise, then; we are left wondering, all the same, about the nature of Janus' "genius."

Reedijk asks a pertinent question: "How was it that he alone appears to have found the formula for which the best of his fellow-countrymen groped in vain, while the majority of them felt completely happy about their output of prosodically correct but jejune lines?" He decides that the question, however justified it may be, cannot be answered: "Literary history seems to deny us an answer to these questions. And a solution on the basis of speculations and surmise would hardly be satisfactory." The historical situation of humanism in the Netherlands may have encouraged the appearance of a Janus Secundus, as we have hinted: its Neo-Latin language was ready for original employment, but had not yet become worn out, or succumbed to excessive ornamentation for novelty's sake. The emotional deepening, the urge to observe the inner self, which had been fostered by Netherland's mysticism, "the new devotion," and the Brothers of the Common Life, might conceivably have helped to create the climate in which Janus, with his emotional explorations, could flourish—Erasmus' connections with these currents have often been investigated. But here we wander too far into the morass of Reedijk's speculations and surmises. In short, we cannot say what formed his "genius." We can only try to describe the manner in which he used it.

First of all, he developed the style which was peculiarly his own. As assiduous a borrower from the classics as any of his colleagues, he borrowed not to show how learned he was but for the sake of the poem at hand. Also, he learned, or borrowed, something more important from the Roman lyricists, the idea that the poem was an entity in itself, with a life of its own, a work of art, not primarily a demonstration of skill. Moreover, the poem could be a part of a larger work, the poem cycle, as in the *Monobiblos* or the *Basia*. Thus, he was able to subordinate the Neo-Latinist's besetting urge to exaggerated use of rhetorical device, and mythological detail, to an ideal of proportion: no wonder that Goethe named only him and Jacob Balde, another Neo-Latinist with a keenly developed sense of form, in his tribute to Neo-Latin verse in the *Maximen und Reflexionen,* 1804. Janus is a master of structure: he knows how to build his individual poems in a fashion which will make the maximum effect upon the reader, and he knows how to link them in a series. Coupled with his feeling for moderation and effective structure, there is that "imperative quality" of his verse which

Conclusion: Speculations and Surmises

Ellinger noted—the fact that it is not merely made, but written because it had to be, "poured out," in that favorite word of Janus himself. Today, we are much less inclined than Ellinger was to emphasize the importance of "experience" for Janus; plainly, he reacted in verse to what he saw and felt, but, just as plainly, his reaction was expressed in forms and formulas he had learned, and which he tried to use to maximum effect. Spitzer speaks of the incantatory nature of Pontanus' poetry; in Janus' case it may be justified to take up Ellinger's "imperative" again, if we are cognizant that Janus achieved this quality not because, say, his heart was breaking but because he was extraordinarily skillful at giving his verse an air of intensity—through concentration, through structure, through the use of his favorite and simple reiterative devices. To be sure, such craftsmanship is a kind of genius, especially in a poet with so short a career. Nor, taking that brevity into account, should his quality as an innovator be forgotten: Grotius was right. The coupling, in the *Monobiblos,* of the frankness, and the self-analysis, of the Roman love elegy and Catullus with certain currents of Petrarchism (and Janus often talks like a Petrarchist without being one: he sometimes gets the girl, and the girl has only good looks and strong passions to recommend her); the construction of the cycle of erotic play with the *Basia;* the straightforward sexuality of the Epithalamium—none of these "discoveries" is quite pristine (what literary discovery is?), but Janus gave them all, again, such lucid, simple, and attractive verbal dress that generations were lured into imitating him, hardly ever with success.

The range of his interests is small, his limits are all too obvious. As George Brandes wrote of Emil Aarestrup, the erotic poet *par excellence* of the Danish Golden Age: "He has only one subject . . . and in praising it he is a virtuoso, in painting it a master." Was Janus about to find other realms when he died? Or, had he lived on, would he—the Latin secretary of the Emperor Charles—have tried to repeat the triumphs of the *Monobiblos* and the *Basia,* and perhaps have parodied himself? Speculations and surmises.

Notes and References

Preface

1. F. A. Wright, *The Love Poems of Joannes Secundus*. A Revised Latin Text and an English Verse Translation, together with an Introductory Essay on the Latin Poetry of the Renaissance (New York: E. P. Dutton, 1930). (Hereafter Wright.)

2. Dougall Crane, *Johannes Secundus, His Life, Work, and Influence on English Literature*, Beiträge zur englischen Philologie, XVI (Leipzig: Tauchnitz, and London: Williams and Norgate, 1931). (Hereafter Crane.)

3. Maurice Rat, *Jean Second: Les baisers et l'épithalame, suivis des odes et des élégies*. Traduction nouvelle avec une introduction et des notes (Paris: Garnier, 1938). (Hereafter Rat.)

4. Adalbert Schroeter, *Beiträge zur Geschichte der neulateinischen Poesie Deutschlands und Hollands*, Palaestra, LXXVII (Berlin: Mayer & Müller, 1909), pp. 165–222. (Hereafter Schroeter.)

5. Georg Ellinger, *Geschichte der neulateinischen Literatur Deutschlands, III:1: Geschichte der neulateinischen Lyrik in den Niederlanden vom Ausgang des fünfzehnten bis zum Beginn des siebzehnten Jahrhunderts* (Berlin and Leipzig: de Gruyter, 1933; reprint 1969), pp. 28–78. (Hereafter Ellinger.)

6. Harry C. Schnur, *Lateinische Gedichte deutscher Humanisten* (Stuttgart: Reclam, 1966), pp. 378–93; Fred J. Nichols, *An Anthology of Neo-Latin Poetry* (New Haven: Yale University Press, 1979), pp. 486–523. Schnur translates *Basia* 2, 4, and 8–14, Nichols has *Epigrammata* I, 58 ("To the Grammarians, Why He Writes Wantonly"), *Basia* 1–18, and the *Epithalamium lascivum*.

7. Ellinger (p. 50) thought the Julia-elegies (Book I) were the best work of Janus: "Dieser völlige Einklang von Inhalt und Form weist den Elegien unter den poetischen Bekenntnissen des Secundus die erste Stelle an." Frederick Brittain, *The Penguin Book of Latin Verse* (Harmondsworth and Baltimore, 1962), says that the *Basia* are Janus' "most famous work" but provides a translation only of *Elegies* I, 6.

8. Crane, pp. 42–79; Paul Laumonier, *Ronsard* (Paris: Hachette, 1923), pp. 514–34; Ellinger, ed., *Joannes Nicolai Secundus: Basia, Mit einer Auswahl aus den Vorbildern und Nachahmern*, Latei-

nische Literaturdenkmäler des XV. und XVI. Jahrhunderts, 14 (Berlin: Weidmann, 1899), pp. xv–xlv; Johannes Vorrink, *Het Minnegedicht in de zeventiende Eeuw* (Leiden: A.W. Sijthoff, 1919), pp. 107–30. See also German Joos, "De Nederlandsche vertalingen der werken van Janus Secundus," *Wetenschap in Vlaanderen*, 2 (1936–1937), 137–39; and German Joos, "De Fransche en Duitsche vertalingen der werken van Janus Secundus," *Wetenschap in Vlaanderen*, 3 (1937–1938), 89–94. Some French translations and versions of the *Basia* from the sixteenth and seventeenth centuries are discussed by André Blanchard, "Jean Second (1511–1536) et quelques poètes français," *La muse française*, 18 (1939), 76–84.

9. Ellinger, *Basia*, also lists some of the Neo-Latin imitators of Janus. Hans Pyritz's investigation of the *Basia* in connection with a Neo-Latin erotic cycle of the Baroque, *Paul Flemings Suavia* (Inaug. diss., Berlin; München: Kastner & Callwey, 1931), is of great importance, since it treats the *Basia* as literary structures, not fragments of a confession. Pyritz's call (p. 16) for "eine wirklich eindringende Untersuchung," which would grasp Janus "in seiner stil- und geistesgeschichtlichen Bedeutung," has not yet been answered. Heinz Schlaffer, in *Musa jocosa: Gattungspoetik and Gattungsgeschichte der erotischen Dichtung in Deutschland*, Germanistische Abhandlungen 37 (Stuttgart, 1971), would appear to assign less importance to Janus than Pyritz did, and mentions him only in isolated instances.

10. For a complete listing of the printings of Janus' works, see German Joos, "De uitgaven der lateinsche werken van Janus Secundus," *Revue belgique de philologie et d'histoire*, 18 (1939), 5–18.

11. *Opera omnia*. Emendatius et cum notis adhuc ineditis Petri Burmanni Secundi, denuo edita cura Petri Bosscha (Leiden: S. & J. Luchtmans, 1821). (Hereafter BB.)

12. *Opera*. Nunc primum in lucem edita. Quorum catalogum proxima facies enumerabit (Utrecht: Hermannus Borculous, 1541). A facsimile edition was published in the *Monumenta Humanistica Belgica*, 4 (Nieuwkoop: De Graaf, 1969).

13. *Opera*. Accurate recognita ex museo P. Scriverii (Leiden: Franciscus Hegerus, 1631).

Chapter One

1. The possibility exists that the family had belonged to the nobility; the portrait of Janus in the University Library at Leiden shows a family scutcheon and the name, twice, "Joannes Secundus a Gripskercke," while Janus' sister is called "Isabella a Gripskercke" in cloister records; thus Grijpskerke, in Zeeland, should be taken as the family seat. See W. J. C. van Hasselt, "Het geslacht der Nicolai en de portretten van Joannes Secundus," *De Gids*, 9 (1839), 356–57, L.

Galesloot, "Nicolas Everardi," *Biographie Nationale de Belgique* (hereafter BNB) (Brussels: H. Thiry-van Buggenhoudt, 1878), VI,751: "Smallegange [Mattheus Smallegange, 1620–1709, Netherlandic historian and genealogist] prétend le rattacher à une ancienne famille du nom de Grypskerke, connue en Zélande dès l'année 1250", and A. M. M. Dekker, "Secundeana," *Hermeneus*, 42 (1970–1971), 342–54. However, the family had come down in the world by the time of Nicolaus Everardi's birth, if indeed it had possessed the patent of nobility.

2. Quoted in Scriverius, p. 347: "Everardo patre, de Glycera genitrice creatum, / Valchria Nicoleon me tulit inter acquas." Also in Rhanutius Ghero (Janus Gruterus), *Delitiae C Poetarum Belgicorum huius superiorisque aevi illustrium* (Frankfurt: Typis Nicolai Hoffmanni, sumptibus Iacobi Fischeri, 1614), II:630–31. (Hereafter *DPB*.)

3. See J. van Kuyk, "Everardi," *Nieuw Nederlandsch Biografisch Woordenboek*, III (Leiden, A. W. Sijthoff, 1914), 358–60 (hereafter NNBW); Lambertus Johannes van Apeldoorn, *Nicolaas Everaerts en het recht van zijn tijd* (Amsterdam: Koninklijke Akademie van Wetenschapen, 1936), and René Dekkers, *Het humanisme en de rechtwetenschap in de Nederlanden* (Antwerp: De Sikkel, and The Hague: Belinfantes, 1930), pp. 1–36.

4. P. S. and H. M. Allen, *Opus Epistolarum Des. Erasmi Roterdami*, IV–VI (Oxford: Oxford University Press, 1922–1926).

5. *DPB*, II, 553. According to Janus' letter of May 31, 1534 (BB, II, 277), one of the sisters was named Gulielma.

6. See A. H. L. Hensen, *NNBW*, VI (1924), 1046–51, A. van Dijk, *Cornelius Musius, een Delfste Martelaar van 1572* (Utrecht: Het Spectrum, 1947), Pieter Noordeloos, *Cornelis Musius (Mr. Cornelis Muys) pater van Sint Agatha te Delft: humanist, priester, martelaar* (Utrecht: Spectrum, 1955), and J. Vandervelden, "Cornelius Musius," *La Rinascita*, 2 (1939), 86–95.

7. J. Fruytier, *NNBW*, VI,497–98, notes that the records are silent concerning Petrus' career from 1523 until his death.

8. Janus liked the phrase and used it, as well, in a somewhat different ambiance, predicting fruitful happiness for the young couple at the end of his epithalamium (BB, II, 200:140).

9. L. Galesloot, *BNB*, VI,754–56, and J. van Kuyk, *NNBW*, III,914–15.

10. According to Joos (preface, note 10) a second edition came out at Antwerp in 1530; the translations are included in the *Silvae* (BB, II, 179–92). Robert Burton quoted a distich from the "Polyphemus" dialogue in the *Anatomy of Melancholy* (III,1), calling it "that conceited Dialogue of Lucian, which Joannes Secundus, an elegant Dutch modern poet, hath translated into verse."

11. L. Galesloot, *BNB*, VI,756–59, Eugène de Seyn, *Dictionnaire des écrivains belges* (Bruges: Editions "Excelsior", 1930), I,1790, and D. J. L. ter Horst, *NNBW*, X (1937), 306–7, who says, like Galesloot, that Grudius died in obscurity, in Venice, sometime after 1572.

12. L. Galesloot, *BNB*, VI,760; J. van Kuyk, *NNBW*, III,914.

13. Reprinted in Scriverius, p. 371, and BB, I, xlv.

14. Reprinted in BB, I, lvii–lxviii.

15. Lilius Gregorius Gyraldus, *De poetis nostrorum temporum*, hrsg. von Karl Wotke, Lateinische Literaturdenkmäler des XV. und XVI. Jahrhunderts, 10 (Berlin: Weidmann, 1894). p. 70. As an example of Janus' verse, Gyraldus quotes the first of the two epitaphs for Thomas More (BB, II, 147–48).

16. Constantijn Huygens, *Momenta desultoria: Poematum libri XIV* (The Hague: Comitum, 1655), p. 74. In his autobiography, Huygens seems more interested in Janus as plastic artist than as poet; cf. A. H. Kan, *De jeugd van Constantijn Huygens, door hemzelf beschreven* (Rotterdam and Antwerp: Donker, 1946), pp. 87–88; however, Huygens' letter of April 10, 1609, to his father (who had accused him of aping Janus in his own Latin verse) shows how strong Huygens' literary interest in Janus was (*De Briefwisseling van Constantijn Huygens*, uitgegeven door J. A. Worp [The Hague, 1911], I:3).

17. P. Hofmann Peerlkamp, *Liber de vita, doctrina et facultate nederlandorum qui carmina latine composuerunt*, editio altera emendata et aucta (Haarlem: Vincent Loosjes, 1838), p. 36.

18. Does he mean "Het Haagsche Bosch," the hunting woods of the Counts of Holland? Lodovico Guicciardini describes a grove "near The Hague, . . . of a pleasantness and beauty that it might almost seem to be one of those groves which the poets of antiquity called sacred," *Belgium universum, seu Omnium inferioris Germaniae regionum accurata descriptio* (Amsterdam, 1646), III,55. (First edition, Antwerp, 1567.)

19. H. E. van Gelder, "Twee zestiende-eeuwsche Haagsche kunstenaars," *Die Haghe Jaarboek*, (1938), 14.

20. C. P. Hoynck van Papendrecht, *Analecta belgica* (The Hague: Gerard Block, 1743), II,1:288–89 (Letter CXIX, October 14, 1541). For more information on Viglius, see Dekkers, op. cit., pp. 37–96 and B. H. D. Hermesdorf, *Wigle van Aytta van Zwichem, hoogleraar en rechtsgeleerd schrijver* (Leiden: E. J. Brill, 1949), particularly pp. 44–45, where the author discusses the connections of Viglius' thought with that of Nicolaus Everardi.

21. Henry de Vocht, *History of the Collegium Trilingue Lovaniense, II: The Development*, Humanistica Lovaniensia, 11 (Louvain: Librairie Universitaire, 1953), pp. 434–35, 440–41. D. J. H. ter Horst, in his otherwise authoritative article, "Janus Secundus," *NNWB*,

Notes and References

X (1937), 431–33, avoids the problem, simply saying that Janus went to Bourges "after preparatory education."

22. The tribute to Louvain in the poem to Aegidius Buslidius the Elder (BB, II, 77–78:26–44) is quite impersonal, made to flatter Aegidius.

23. Henry de Vocht, *Monumenta Humanistica Lovaniensia,* Humanistica Lovaniensia, 4 (Louvain: Librairie Universitaire, 1934), p. 505, says that he died before May, 1528; C. Reedijk, *The Poems of Desiderius Erasmus* (Leiden: E. J. Brill, 1956), p. 335, prints Erasmus' four-line epitaph for Volcardus, and conjectures that he died in the autumn of 1526.

24. Scriverius (p. 362) and Bosscha (BB, I,xxvii) call Volcardus the first teacher of Janus and Stenemola the second; they do not mention a Louvain sojourn.

25. As a sign of thanks, Stenemola wrote a dedication to Nicolaus Everardi which was included in the brothers' Lucian translations.

26. See D. S. van Zuiden, "De plundering van den Haag door de Gelderschen, 6–9 Maart 1528," *Die Haghe Jaarboek,* (1911), 130–44 and J. Smit, "Het geldersche gevaar tijdens de regeering van Karel V," *Die Haghe Jaarboek,* (1925–27), pp. 94–186. The idea of a connection between the van Rossem affair and the recall of Nicolaus Everardi to Mechlin was proposed by van Hasselt in *De Gids* 9 (1839), 357–58.

27. Among the many treatments of Margaret's "Burgundian court," that of Josef Strelka, *Der burgundische Renaissancehof Margarethes von Oesterreich und seine literaturhistorische Bedeutung* (Vienna: A. Sexl, 1957), is particularly helpful and factual.

28. Guicciardini was struck by the central location of Mechlin, "in the heart and very middle of Brabant," between Louvain, Brussels, and Antwerp.

29. Victor Tourneur, "Jean Second et les Busleyden," *Revue belge de la numismatique,* 70 (1914), 140–72.

30. Félix Nève, "Le conseiller Jérôme Busleiden, écrivain latin et protecteur des lettres (1470–1517)," *Bulletin de l'Académie royale de Belgique,* 42nd année, 2nd série (1873), 377–431, and Henry de Vocht, *Jerome de Busleyden: Founder of the Louvain Collegium Trilingue,* Humanistica Lovaniensia, 9 (Turnhout: Brepols Press, 1950), p. 19.

31. Alphonse Roersch, "Maximilian Transsylvanus, humanist et secrétaire de Charles Quint," *Académie royale de Belgique: Bulletin de la classe des lettres,* 5e série, 14 (1928), 94–112; "Nouvelles indications concernant Maximilian Transsylvanus," *Revue belge de philologie et d'histoire,* 7 (1928), 871–79 (particularly 876–78, where Roersch discusses the poem of Janus); "Le conseiller de Charles Quint, Maximilian Transsylvanus," in Roersch, *L'humanisme belge à*

l'époque de la Renaissance: Etudes et portraits, Deuxième série, Humanistica Lovaniensia, 3 (Louvain: Librairie Universitaire, 1933), pp. 33–54.

32. Henry de Vocht, *John Dantiscus and His Netherlandish Friends,* Humanistica Lovaniensia, 16 (Louvain: Librairie Universitaire, 1961), pp. 122–23.

33. The first edition came out at Bologna in January, 1530, the second at Cracow in February, and the third at Antwerp. Cf. de Vocht, *History,* II,438, and Joos, "De uitgaven van Janus Secundus," pp. 6–7.

34. In *Monumenta Historica Lovaniensia,* p. 614, de Vocht identifies Ottingerus (Oettinger?) as a teacher and friend of the Portuguese humanist, Damião de Goes.

35. J. F. M. Sterck, "Joannes Scorel en Joannes Secundus," *Het Boek,* 10 (1921), 217–18.

36. J. Bruyn, "Enige gegevens over de chronologie van het werk van Jan Scorel," *Oud-Holland,* 70 (1955), 194–95, realized that Sterck's understanding of "propempticon" was wrong, but mistakenly and unnecessarily emended the word to "proempticon," calling it a personal coinage of Janus, meaning "let go" or "spur on"! Dekker (see chapter 1, note 1) set him to rights (p. 347, note 1).

37. de Vocht, *Dantiscus,* pp. 132–33. The second line to Dantiscus goes: "Phoebeae pie cultor artis," and to Scorel "Divinae renovator artis."

38. See de Bruyn (p. 195) and Dekker (p. 347).

39. Pierre Ronsard, *Oeuvres complètes,* ed. Gustave Cohen (Paris: Gallimard, 1950), I,619 (*Cinquième livre des Odes,* XI,81–88).

40. Jules Simonis, *L'art du médailleur en Belgique* (Brussels: Librairie Numismatique de Ch. Dupriez, 1900), I,39. After reviewing the life of Janus (pp. 35–46), Simonis lists and describes the medallions (pp. 47–92); plates II–V are reproductions. H. E. van Gelder, *Die Haghe Jaarboek,* (1938), 19–27 also describes them, providing reproductions.

41. Both Janus Lucius and his brother, Janus Alexander Brassicanus, professor at Vienna in the afterglow of Celtis and Vadianus, were poetasters. Other distinguished men who got verse, but not medals, were the Mechlin physician Joachim Rolandus, the author of a book on the sweating sickness (Epigrams I,47), the Frisian mathematician Reinerus Gemma (I,68), and the Portuguese humanist Angelus Andreas Resendius (I,67 and 74), who was staying at Louvain.

42. Henry de Vocht, *Literae virorum eruditorum ad Franciscum Craneveldium 1522–28,* Humanistica Lovaniensia, 1 (Louvain: Librairie Universitaire, 1928), pp. liii–lxxxii.

43. Ellinger, III,1:30. André Blanchard, *Itinéraire de Jean Second*

Notes and References 155

(1511–1536) (Saumur: Girouard & Richou, 1940), pp. 23–26, argued that Everardus, the recipient of the verse-epistle (I,1) from Middelburg, is said in the poem to be in Mechlin at the time; he adds that Everardus was transferred from Leeuwarden to Mechlin at the beginning of 1531: thus the "expostulatio" would have been written the same year. Yet neither the text itself (which simply says that Janus wishes *he* were in Mechlin) nor other authorities support Blanchard: both Galesloot and van Kuyk (see note 9) give 1533 as the date of Everardus' return.

44. Scriverius included them in the second (1631) edition of the collected works. A Dutch translation of the itinerary from Mechlin to Bourges, by J. G. La Lau, appeared in *De Gids,* 9 (1839), 397–407. Georges Prévot translated the entire work into French, with commentary, as "Les 'Itinera' de Jean Second," *Revue du Nord,* 9 (1923), 161–92 and 254–74; José López de Toro translated them into Spanish, "Las 'Tres Jornadas' del holandés Juan Segundo," *Boletín de la real Academía de la Historia,* 160 (1967), 157–94. They have been treated essayistically by Alphonse Roersch, "Les 'Itinera' de Jean Second," *Revue belgique de philologie et d'histoire,* 3 (1924), 279–88; and as "Les carnets de route de Jean Second" in Roersch, *L'humanisme belge,* pp. 55–65.

45. In a letter to Nicolaus Grudius, of March 12, 1532, he described his visit with Polites (whose real name was Borger or Burger), but tells us no more than he does in the *Itinerary;* in fact, he appears to have used the letter to compose the Paris passage in his travel book; cf. Georges Prévot, "Jean Second à Paris: Une lettre inédite de 1532," *Revue belgique de philologie et d'histoire,* 9 (1930), 353–58.

46. The *Rime* of Cino were first published in 1559.

47. On June 22, 1532, Viglius Zuichemus, perhaps fearing the worst, wrote to Janus, exhorting him to work hard at his legal studies. Hoynck, *Analecta,* II,77–81 (Letter XXVIII)

48. See Hippolyt Boyer, *Un ménage littéraire en Berry au XVIe siècle* (Bourges: Jollet-Souchois, 1859), pp. 23–28. Her name was rendered in Latin by Janus as Joanna Fontana.

49. Occo (1514–1588) became a wealthy merchant and a distinguished leader of his municipal government, without abandoning his humanistic studies; another Netherlandic friend at Bourges was Petrus Bausanus, a jurist and friend of Viglius. In his ninth ode (BB, II, 17–18), Janus tells Bausanus that they are "companions absorbed in the same studies" (1. 4) and adds (11. 19–20): "With laughter, jests, and games, and loving / Let us endeavor to bear our exile." see J. F. M. Sterck, "Pompejus Occo, mercator sapiens," *Onder Amsterdamsche Humanisten* (Hilversum, 1934), pp. 23–30.

50. Hoynck, *Analecta*, II,1:38–44. (Letter from Zuichemus to Sucquetus, August 26, 1531). See also de Vocht, *History*, II:152–53.

51. According to Janus, Hadrianus also wrote an epitaph for Reinaldus, which is included in the *Itinerary;* this was then printed as a work of Janus himself in the *Funera* (22), and with a different title, "Epitaphium Lucii Tabellarii, in via a latronibus occisi."

52. Was the "Lord of Nassau" Hendrik van Nassau, or his son, the young René de Châlon? According to Karel van Mander, in his *Schilder-boek*, Scorel had done "some works" at the castle of Breda for both of them.

53. Alphonse Roersch has identified "Hilarius the poet" as Hilarius Bertulphus, a friend of Erasmus, Dantiscus, and Rabelais; cf. Roersch, "Ad Joannem Secundum," *La musée belge*, 26 (1922), 55–56. Hilarius, who had gone to Lyons in 1532, died there, of the plague, in the very summer of Janus' visit. The fate of the painter, Cornelius, was much happier; he was named painter to the Dauphin, followed the court on its travels, and settled down in Lyons, where he spent the last thirty years of his life. See Pierre de Nolhac, "Jean Second et Corneille de Lyon," *Mélanges offerts à Paul Laumonier* (Paris: E. Droz, 1935), pp. 109–12.

54. Blanchard, *Itinéraire*, pp. 51 ff. On p. 59, Blanchard establishes the date of Janus' Madrid letter to Everardus (BB, II,279–282): February 28, 1535.

55. de Vocht, *Dantiscus*, pp. 214–16, has a prose letter from Janus to Dantiscus, dated Toledo, April 28, 1534, in which he notes the death of Hilarius the poet, and says that he has been in Spain "for about a year, with the court."

56. He also says that "Tavera himself could become pope. . . . See how much it would add to the glory of our family if the authority of the two brothers [Grudius and himself] could prevail in the vicinity of two such lords of the world [Charles and Tavera]." Evidently, he is aware that his imagination is running away with him, because he adds directly, "Sed hae spes sunt Alchimicorum," which could be translated, "But these are castles in Spain."

57. de Vocht, *History*, II,449–50; Galesloot, *BNB*, VI,762: "On prétend que sa passion pour le sexe ne fut pas étrangère à cette fin prématurée."

58. The first line, "Praecipue, hortorum custos membrose virentum," recalls *Corpus Priapeorum*, 5:1: "Sed rubor hortorum custos, membrosior aequo" ("But the ruddy guardian of gardens, larger-membered than is fitting . . .").

59. José López de Toro, "El poeta Juan Segundo, secretario de Carlos V," *Carlos V (1500–1558): Homenaje de la Universidad de Granada* (Granada, 1958), pp. 233–55, reviews the Spanish acquaintanceships of Janus. A later correspondence between Zurita and Gon-

zalo Pérez took place; cf. Angel Gonzalez Palencia, *Gonzalo Pérez: Secretario de Felipe Segundo* (Madrid: Instituto Jeronimo Zurita, 1946), pp. 198–201. Zurita distinguished himself as an historian *(Anales de la Corona de Aragon)*, and Gonzalo as secretary both to Charles and to Philip.

60. The result was Zárate's classic *Historia del descubrimiento y conquista de las provincias del Perú.*

61. Thierry Sandre, *Jean Second: Le livre des baisers* (Amiens: Edgar Malfère, 1922), p. 21, took the passage literally: "Jérôme Surita . . . obtenait tout de Néère, et Jean Second rien."

62. P. A. Budik, *Leben und Wirken der vorzüglichsten lateinischen Dichter des 15. bis 18. Jahrhunderts* (Vienna: J. B. Wallishausser, 1827–28), I,245, advances the notion that Hurtado Mendoza arranged for the post.

63. J. F. Foppens, *Bibliotheca belgica* (Brussels: Petrus Foppens, 1739), II,726; Valerius Andreas, *Bibliotheca belgica* (Louvain: Henricus Hastenius, 1623), p. 530. Both authors refer to Paul III as Paul IV. Scriverius (p. 363) mentions a trip to Italy preceding that to Spain, but leaves out the papal secretaryship; here, he follows the letter which Cripius wrote to the surviving brothers in 1561 (BB, I, lxvi).

64. de Vocht, *Dantiscus*, p. 248; Hoynck, *Analecta*, II,1:212 (Letter LXXVIII). Like Crane (p. 24: "He left in the spring of 1536") and de Vocht (see note 65), Blanchard once held the idea of a return in 1536 *(Itinéraire*, pp. 63–64: "vers avril [1536]"), but has lately abandoned it: cf. Blanchard, "Jean Second et ses poèmes sur l'exécution de Thomas More," *Moreana*, 36 (December, 1972),6.

65. de Vocht, *History*, II,198 and 446, and Hensen, *NNBW*, III,1047. De Vocht also gives "the spring of 1536" here, which is contradicted by the evidence of the de Schepper letter in his own *Dantiscus* book (it appeared eight years after his *History*, II).

66. Although de Vocht does not mention it, the distinguished French Neo-Latin poet, Jean Salmon Macrin (1490–1557), the "French Horace," resided in Poitiers at this time, and was a friend of Musius; cf. J. D. McFarlane, "Jean Salmon Macrin," *Bibliothèque d'humanisme et renaissance*, 21 (1959), 325.

67. Blanchard, *Moreana*, gives the complete story of the poem's various printings, together with a French translation of it and the associated epitaphs and epigram.

68. André Jolles, "Een oude vergissing," *Neophilologus*, 13 (1928), 60–65, 132–36.

69. Thus the old suggestion by Bosscha (BB, I, 306)—that the epigram on the departure from Spain is probably the last of Janus' poems—cannot hold water.

70. Scholarship has not noted the likelihood that it was Scorel who

arranged for the post with van Egmond; Scorel had made a portrait of van Egmond in 1532 (reproduced, as plate 18, in G. J. Hoogewerff, *Jan van Scorel: Peintre de la renaissance hollandaise* [The Hague: M. Nijhoff, 1923]). See also Hoogewerff, "Jan van Scorel: zijn leven en persoonlijkheid, II," *Onze Eeuw,* 15 (1915), 399.

71. This is what Hadrianus Marius says at the beginning of his *naenia* (Scriverius, p. 374); the material about Tavera, Perrenot de Granvelle, and Charles is from near the end (p. 378).

72. Dekker, *Hermeneus,* vol. 42 (1970–71), has reproductions of the portraits in the Gemeentemuseum at The Hague (Il1.2), and the University Library, Leiden Il1.4), as well as the engraving in Scriverius (Il1.3); G. J. Hoogewerff, *De Noord-Nederlandsche Schilderkunst* (The Hague: M. Nijhoff, 1941–42), IV,110 (Il1.48) has the portrait in the University Museum at Amsterdam; H. E. van Gelder, *Die Haghe Jaarboek,* (1938), has the Gemeentemuseum version (Il1.2) and the engraving from Scriverius (Il1:16).

73. Dekker points out that this date is now generally accepted by Scorel scholars.

74. Two other "portraits," the one "with a Spanish cap" which served as a basis for the frontispiece to the Burmann-Bosscha edition, and the one of a "sick" Janus, by the seventeenth-century Dutch artist, Pieter Rottermondt (reproduced in H. E. van Gelder [Il1.15] and recently used as a cover illustration for *Moreana* vol. 36 and described there by the editor as looking like a "fastuous hippie"), still have not been thoroughly investigated. The first, according to Bosscha, is based upon a Scorel painting which once belonged to Constantijn Huygens. The second has been called a product of the painter's fantasy, by Van Gelder and Dekker; a copy of it is in the Rijksmuseum at Amsterdam.

Chapter Two

1. Prévot, "Les 'Itinera,' " p. 171.
2. These listings are made in imitation of Ovid's catalog of the Roman elegists in the *Tristia* (IV, 10:53–54): Tibullus, Gallus, Propertius, and Ovid himself.
3. In a symposium on Janus Secundus, held at the Neo-Latin Seminar of the Modern Language Association of America on December 28, 1968, Father Walter J. Ong characterized Janus as an "Ovidianizer of Catullus." Cf. *Neo-Latin News,* 18 (1969),39 (Entry N–31).
4. It is the Ovidian attitude in the *Amores* which is of more importance for Janus than any verbal borrowing; Georg Luck, in his invaluable book, *The Latin Love Elegy,* 2nd ed. (London: Methuen,

1969), repeatedly calls attention to Ovid's "elegant" self-deception and self-analysis.

5. Ellinger, *Deutsche Lyriker des sechzehnten Jahrhunderts, Lateinische Literaturdenkmäler des XV. und XVI. Jahrhunderts,* 7 (Berlin: Weidmann, 1893), p. xxviii. Ellinger's statement, of course, does not apply to German Neo-Latinists alone.

6. Paul van Tieghem, *La littérature latine de la Renaissance: Etude d'histoire littéraire européenne* (Paris: E. Droz, 1944, Geneva: Slatine Reprints, 1966), pp. 16–19.

7. Hoverius (Francis de Houwers) was a teacher from Mechlin. Alphonse Roersch, *Correspondance de Nicolas Clénard* (Brussels: Palais des Académies, 1949), II,17, says that Hoverius appears to have left Mechlin in 1531, for a stay in France and Italy which lasted at least until 1536. This would indicate, then, that Janus had read Marullus fairly early, some time before Hoverius' departure—and, of course, before the composition of the Julia-elegies.

8. Michael Marullus, *Carmina,* ed. Alessandro Perosa (Zürich: Thesaurus Mundi [Artemis Verlag], 1951), p. 4 (Epigrams I, 3:1–4).

9. Judging by Janus' medallion (see Simonis, Plate IV, 6), Julia showed the beginnings of a double chin; as for her coloring, the fifth elegy says that she had black eyes, and the second "solemn elegy" that she had black hair as well. In a lush passage, Schroeter extrapolates from the evidence of the medallion: "die freundlichen Züge einer jener in üppiger Jugendkraft schwellenden, mehr frauen- als mädchenhaft Schönen, deren vollendete Typen die Rubensche Kunst unerschöpflich und immer stolzer darstellt" (p. 185). She left other writers on Janus with the impression that she was not a little bovine, or, as Wright says, "placid," or, in de Vocht's term, "irresponsive."

10. Ellinger, "Goethe und Johannes Secundus," *Goethe-Jahrbuch,* 13 (1892), 204; Einar Löfstedt, "Ur den romerska kärleksdiktens historia," *Romare* (Stockholm: Norstedt, 1956), pp. 44–58, translated by P. M. Fraser as *Roman Literary Portraits* (Oxford and New York: Oxford University Press, 1958).

11. P. C. Molhuysen, "Julia," *Handelingen en medcdeelingen van de maatschappij der nederlandsche letterkunde* (1911), pp. 107–9.

12. Pseudo-Petronius, "Ad Juliam" ("Me nive candenti petiit modo Julia"), and *Anthologia Graeca,* V, 281 (280). (The references supplied by BB, I, 112, and Rat, p. 262, are both incorrect). The conceit itself is neatly summed up in the title of Leonard Forster's essays on Petrarchistic poetry, *The Icy Fire* (see below, chapter 4, note 21).

13. It has been translated into English by Wright (p. 29).

Chapter Three

1. Quoted in BB, I, xxxvii.

2. Janus Dousa the elder (Jan van der Does, 1545–1609), Janus Lernutius (Jean Lernaut, 1545–1619), Janus Bonefonius (Jean Bonnefons, 1554–1614): Dousa and Lernutius wrote *Basia* in imitation of Janus, while Bonefonius called the separate poems of his cycle *Pancharis* by the name which Janus had made popular.

3. Hoynck, *Analecta*, II,1, 212. (March 12, 1536, Letter LXXVIII)

4. P.-F. Tissot, *Baisers et élégies de Jean Second* (Paris: Fain & Cie., 1806), xix–xxii.

5. See preface, note 8: Ellinger's description of the predecessors and imitators of the *Basia* remains a standard work, as does his edition of the text. An edition based on the 1561 printing was made by N. J. Beversen, *Joannis Secundi Hagiensis, Poetae Elegantissimi, Basiorum Liber* (Utrecht: Alexander Stols, 1928); this was not known to Karl Jacoby when he put together his "Die Küsse des Johannes Secundus: Ein bibliographischer Versuch," *Philobiblon*, 8 (1935):7–14, reissued in English (mimeographed) as "The Kisses of Johannes Secundus: a biobibliographical essay," by the University of Kentucky Library (Lexington, 1949).

6. German Joos, "Eenige grieksch-latijnsche en italiaansch-renaissance invloeden op de 'Basia' van Janus Secundus," *Revue belgique de philologie et d'histoire*, 20 (1941),5–14.

7. Harry E. Wedeck, "A Medieval Catullus: Joannes Secundus," *Philological Quarterly*, 19 (1940), 400–404, gives a brief summary of Catullan echoes in Janus' language; see also A. Ramminger, "Aus dem Nachleben der Catullischen Basiagedichte," *Motivgeschichtliche Studien zu Catullus Basiagedichten* (Würzburg, 1937), pp. 76–119, and Mary Morrison, "Catullus and the Poetry of the Renaissance in France," *Bibliothèque d'humanisme et renaissance*, 25 (1963), 25–26; p. 26: "Marullus and Secundus are 'Catullan' poets with a predilection for the hendecasyllable, who parody the extremely personal style of Catullus."

8. Ellinger reprints the poems in question in his edition of the *Basia* (pp. 17–23); pp. 23–38 consist of selections from the *imitatores*, Buchanan, Lernutius, Dousa, Eufrenius, Bonefonius, Muretus, and Barth.

9. Paul van de Woestijne, "Joannes Secundus en Vergilius," *Gedenkboek August Vermeylen* (The Hague: M. Nijhoff, 1932), pp. 463–68. Woestijne seems critical of Janus' "copying" of Vergil: "It may be called strange that this *eroticus*, in an introductory poem, puts himself under the lofty protection of Vergil." However, part of the attraction of the cycle is the self-irony which Janus, in one way and another, exercises throughout.

10. Also, Horace, *Epodes*, 15:5–6, and Claudianus' Fescennine verses IV (XIV): 18–20, for the marriage of the Emperor Honorius

to Maria, the daughter of the Vandal Stilicho. J. P. Guepin, "De beroemdste nederlandse dichter," *In een moeilijke houding geschreven: opstellen* (The Hague: Bert Bakker/Daamen, 1969), p. 125, gives still other possible sources; see, in addition, Peter Demetz, "Elm and Vine: Notes toward a History of a Marriage Topos," *PMLA*, 73 (1958), 521–32.

11. Georg Rudolf Weckherlin has the opening lines in "Kuss": "Gleichwie das Epheu, grün den baum jung oder alt, / Gleichwie die liebend-gaile Reben, Den Pfal und auch sich selbst umgeben . . ." and Gottfried August Bürger in "Die Umarmung": "Wie um ihren Stab die Rebe/Brünstig ihre Ranke strickt,/Wie der Efeu sein Gewebe/ An der Ulme Busen drückt. . . ."

12. *Oeuvres complètes*, I:295, *Les amours diverses*, Chanson III.

13. Buchanan (1506–1582) in his *Hendecasyllabi*, VI ("Ad Neaeram"), Dousa in his first *Basium* (11. 17–18) and in his fifth (both to "Rosilla"), and Hadrianus Relandus (1676–1718) in his *Galatea*, III:25–26. (The reference in BB, I, 252, note to verse 1, is not accurate.)

14. *Anthologia Graeca*, V, 305 (304), and Sannazaro, "Ad Ninam."

15. Which Goethe, rather forgetfully, quoted without the "O" (*Maximen und Reflexionen*, 755).

16. The diminutive in Janus has been studied by L Van der Elst in an unpublished Louvain dissertation, *Het latijnse diminutief en zijn aanwending door Janus Secundus* (1969).

17. Wright, p. 85; *Johannes Secundus, Die Küsse und die feierlichen Elegien*, deutsch von Franz Blei (Leipzig: Insel, 1906), p. 25; *Johannes Secundus, Küsse*, hrsg. von Felix M. Wiesner (Zürich: Verlag Die Waage, 1958), p. 45. See also the interpretation of the poem by Guepin, op. cit., pp. 119–23.

18. Jean Second, *Les baisers*, traduction nouvelle de Georges Prévot (Saint Raphael, 1920), p. 29; Wright, p. 87.

19. BB (I, 277) notes that the line is based on the *Corpus Priapeorum*, 54 (not 55, as in BB): "Quidam mollior anseris medulla" ("Someone, softer than a goose's marrow"). Catullus (25,2) also has "anseris medulla" to denote an effeminate man. Gaston Vorberg, *Glossarium eroticum* (Hanau: Müller & Kiepenheuer, 1965), p. 338, adduces Propertius' use of the word (I, 12:17, "medullae siccae") as an indication of sexual exhaustion. These three passages could be used to support still another interpretation of the last two lines. Janus—speaking in jest, of course—says that Neaera has nothing to fear from him, since the tumescence has subsided.

20. Janus Dousa translated the poem into Dutch as a sonnet; see P. C. Molhuysen, "Jan van der Does, Nederduitsche Gedichten," *De Navorscher*, 51 (1901), 260–68, 384–99, 461–71; here, p. 393. However, it must be added that he also used the sonnet form for

numbers 4, 11, and 15 (which again is a fourteen-line poem in the original). The early translations by Dousa, Jan van Hout, and a third unnamed person, were reprinted in book form, *Het Boeck der Kuskens van Joannes Secundus* (Maastricht: A. A. M. Stols, 1930).

21. Theodore de Bèze (1519–1605), in his epigrams to "Candida."
22. Albertus Eufrenius Georgiades, (Albert Joriszoon Goedhart, 1581–1626), whose girl was "Isabella."
23. Marcus Antonius Muretus (Marc Antoine Muret, 1526–1585); the imitations are the elegies, in his *Juvenilia*, to "Margaris."
24. Concluding his fine analysis of the *Basia*, Fred J. Nichols writes: "The ease with which Secundus manipulates . . . different facets of the classical tradition, and the skill with which he persuades the reader of the authenticity of the passion he describes, shows how thoroughly the Neo-Latin poetic tradition had domesticated itself by the early sixteenth century, even in Northern Europe." See Nichols, "The Renewal of Latin Poetry in the Renaissance: Rhetoric and Experience," in Michel Cadet, Milan V. Dimić, David Malone, and Miklós Szabolcsi, eds., *Actes du VIe Congrès de l'Association Internationale de Littérature Comparée/Proceedings of the 6th Congress of the International Comparative Literature Association* (Stuttgart: Bieber, 1975), pp. 89–98.

Chapter Four

1. Maurice Rat, "Un grand poète latin du xvi siècle, Jean Second," *Mercure de France*, 289 (Jan.-Feb., 1939), 589.
2. Damning with faint praise, Bosscha said that they did not attain "Horatian sublimity, but were pure, nonetheless." However, W. Leonard Grant, *Neo-Latin Literature and the Pastoral* (Chapel Hill: U. of North Carolina Press, 1965) finds that they have been unjustly ignored, an opinion he shares with Rat.
3. See chapter 1, note 49.
4. Ellinger, III, 1:74: *"effundere, ein Lieblingswort des Secundus."*
5. Another example, much earlier than Buchanan's, is the *Psalterium Davidis carmine redditum* (1537) of Helius Eobanus Hessus.
6. James Hutton, *The Greek Anthology in France and in the Latin Writers of the Netherlands until the Year 1800*. Cornell Studies in Classical Philology, 28 (Ithaca: Cornell University Press, 1946), pp. 220–23, notes that Janus, instead of being attracted to the amatory epigrams, did the "sententious and satirical pieces . . . the epigrams that he translates are among those inevitably chosen by the schoolmaster, so that we may suspect that these versions are exercises from his schooldays." Hutton takes issue with Ellinger (and Bosscha) con-

cerning the importance of the *Anthology* for Janus' original poetry, being much less inclined to see connections.

7. The meter is the Second Asclepiadean, which Horace (III, 15) used for shaming the wife of the "impecunious Ibycus,' who tried to act younger than her years.

8. Even to Clericus (BB, II, 64–71), the conventions of the epistle-form triumph. After assuring Petrus of his affection at great length, Janus tells the story of Julia, Petrus, and himself once again: the stilted account suffers by comparison with the *Monobiblos*, and with Janus' elegy to Petrus and his prose letter to him.

9. Jacob Balde, *Carmina lyrica*, ed. Benno Müller (Munich, 1844), pp. 6–7 (Odes I, 3:21–24). Balde's odes were first published in 1643.

10. Eldridge Colby, *The Echo-Device in Literature* (New York: New York Public Library, 1920), does not mention Janus' poem. An earlier example in the vernacular is Poliziano's "Pan ed Echo" (1498), and, in Italy's Neo-Latin verse, some epigrams of Antonius Tebaldeus (1460–1537).

11. "An den Geist des Johannes Secundus" is dated November 2, 1777, and, in turn, inspired Herder's clumsier epigram to Goethe (*Goethe-Jahrbuch*, 8 [1887], 26) about "Johannes Secundus Evangelista" and "Bruder, Tertie."

12. Karl Otto Conrady, "Die Erforschung der neulateinischen Literatur: Probleme und Aufgaben," *Euphorion* 49 (1955), 443–44, argues: "[Das] Gefühl des Verfalls, der Vergänglichkeit ist nicht so 'barock' wie man gerne meint. Die Zeiterfahrung der Neulateiner ist bisweilen von einem bestürzenden Wissen um Nichtigkeit und Eitelkeit alles menschlichen Tuns durchwoben." Conrady returns to the matter in his major work, *Lateinische Dichtungstradition und deutsche Lyrik des 17ten Jahrhunderts* (Bonn: Bouvier, 1962), p. 290: "Hier ist noch ein weites Feld für Einzeluntersuchungen, die zeigen könnten, wie eng die beiden Jahrhunderte in ihrem Erleben und Denken verbunden sind." Certainly, expressions of despair and confusion can be found in the Neo-Latin poets of the sixteenth century, especially as the century wears on; however, they are relatively rare among the humanists of Germany and the Netherlands during the last decades of the fifteenth and first decades of the sixteenth century. As Dieter Wuttke remarks, "[Conrady] erweckt den Eindruck, als besitze die neulateinische Literatur des 16. Jahrhunderts nur insoweit Wert, als sie der Erhellung des Barockphänomens dienlich ist," *Deutsche Germanistik und Renaissance-Forschung*, Respublica litteraria 3 (Bad Homburg v. d. Höhe and Zürich: Gehlen, 1968), p. 15.

13. *Sämtliche Werke* (Darmstadt, 1964), I, 313–18.

14. Scaliger, in the *Poetics*, III, 6 (1561), allowed that "wantonness and trifling" could be mentioned, and, at the poem's end, "more

licentious jokes" could be mixed in, like the "Fescennine songs" of antiquity.

15. Ausonius does so, in the "Imminutio" ("Deflowering") of his *Cento nuptualis;* the verse, of course, made up of half-lines from Vergil, is as dead as that of Janus is alive. Robert H. Case, *English Epithalamies* (London: John Lane and Chicago: A. C. McClurg & Co., 1896), pp. xvii–xx, said that it was Joannes Pontanus who gave Janus the idea for his penetration of the bedroom: "His Epithalamium, taking, as I think, the cue from Pontanus, ventures on a liberty of plan and expression in which it may be as well that he has seldom been followed." The poem where Pontanus most obviously presages the *epithalamium lascivum* is not one of Pontanus' formal epithalamia (collected in *De amore conjugali*), but the brief—indeed, the fragmentary—"De nuptiis Ioannis Brancati et Maritellae" (*Hendecasyllabi* XVIII, in *Carmina,* a cura di Johannes Oeschger, Scrittori d'Italia, 198 [Bari: Gius. Laterza, 1948], pp. 297–98), which has more the air of "Fescennine" verse, written for a bachelor's dinner.

16. Robert Muth, *"Hymenaios* und *Epithalamium,"* Wiener Studien: Zeitschrift für klassische Philologie, 67 (1954), 5–45, discusses the age-old confusion in the usage of "epithalamium."

17. "Epithalamic" conventions have been listed, among others, by Arthur L. Wheeler, "Tradition in the Epithalamium," *American Journal of Philology,* 51 (1930), 205–223, and Thomas L. Greene, "Spenser and the Epithalamic Convention," *Comparative Literature,* 9 (1957), 215–28, and Professor Greene's unpublished doctoral dissertation (Yale, 1954). Professor Greene rightly calls the epithalamium of Janus "atypical."

18. In his colloquy, "Epithalamium Petri Aegidii" (published 1524), written for the marriage in 1514 of Aegidius Buslidianus the elder, Erasmus made mild fun of the learned epithalamium.

19. It could be advanced that, in his language, Janus imitated the Fescennine verses of Claudianus for the wedding of Honorius and Maria, particularly in his use of sound-repetition (alliteration, semi-rhymes), word repetition (anaphora, *epizeuxis*), and other elementary *colores rhetorici.* Here, attention could also be called to Pontanus and what Leo Spitzer describes as the "musical effects" of his verse; cf. "The Problem of Latin Renaissance Poetry," *Studies in the Renaissance,* 2 (1955), 134–35 and *Romanische Literaturstudien* (Tübingen: M. Niemeyer, 1959), p. 941. (Spitzer adds the detail that it was Pontanus himself who coined the word "alliteration.")

20. Schnur, pp. 148–53 and pp. 434–45: "Das Gedicht ist typisch für alle [Heiratsgedichte] und besser als viele dieses Genres."

21. Leonard Forster, "Conventional Safety Valves: Alba, Pastourelle and Epithalamium," *Lebende Antike: Symposion für Rudolf Sühnel,* herausgegeben von Horst Meller und Hans-Joachim Zimmermann

(Berlin: Erich Schmidt, 1967), pp. 120–37; also in Leonard Forster, *The Icy Fire: Five Studies in European Petrarchism* (Cambridge: Cambridge University Press, 1969), pp. 84–121. Forster also calls attention to the flourishing of "lubricious and detailed description of the joys of the marriage bed" in "the latter half of the [sixteenth] century," adducing, as an example, a French epithalamium of Bonefonius-Bonnefons, the imitator of Janus' *Basia*. Forster's argument—where he agrees with Case's proposal of Janus' imitation of Pontanus, but obviously disagrees with Case's Victorian sigh of relief that the frank Janus had "seldom been followed"—is that Janus began a trend (as he had, of course, with the *Basia*): "Secundus . . . is following Pontanus in this characteristic passage [ll. 66–95], which set the tone for much sixteenth and seventeenth century work all over Europe." Both Forster and Case are right, each in his way: the popular example of Janus' "lasciviousness" made possible, and fashionable, the ever broader sexual hints and instruction of epithalamia to come, but few poets grasped—or, because of the special situation, were able to grasp—the candor of Janus, or its aesthetic purpose. (It could be added that Bonefonius closes his *Pancharis* with a "Pervigilium Veneris" [XXXVIII], obviously imitated from Janus' epithalamium, but less "bold," because Bonefonius hides his sexual details in so much verbal ornamentation.)

Chapter Five

1. P. N. M. Bot, *Humanisme en Onderwijs in Nederland* (Utrecht and Antwerp: Het Spectrum, 1955), p. 42, observes that old Erasmus, "albeit inclined to pessimism," could only conclude that his own efforts—"I have written my works not for Italians but for Hollanders, Brabanders, Flemings"—and those of devoted Netherlandic schoolmen had not been in vain.

2. Thomas W. Best, *Macropedius*, Twayne's World Authors Series, 218 (New York: Twayne, 1972).

3. In *Paul Flemings deutsche Liebeslyrik*, Palaestra 180 (Leipzig: Mayer & Müller, 1932), pp. 193–94, Hans Pyritz remarked that Fleming, in his first Latin cycle, *Rubella*, "bei aller Hingabe an das Vorbild des Secundus doch dessen reinem Schönheitskult nicht folgen konnte"; he pursued instead the *forma-virtus* ideal of the Petrarchistic lyric (while, of course, Janus' "ideal" was that of Roman erotic verse): in the opinion of Fleming, and other Petrarchists, "Mehr als durch ihre leibliche Schönheit wirkt die Frau durch ihre Tugend auf den Dichter."

4. Van Tieghem, p. 71, Thierry Sandre, p. 22, Crane, pp. 40–41.

5. Conrady, "Erforschung," p. 419, and Conrady, *Lateinische Dichtungstradition*, passim.

6. Paul Kristeller, "Studies on Renaissance Humanism," *Studies in the Renaissance*, 9 (1962), 11. Cf. Leonard Forster, *The Poet's Tongues: Multilingualism in Literature* (Cambridge: Cambridge University Press, 1970), p. 19: "It is clear that people in earlier centuries have a much less developed sense of what linguists have come to call 'language loyalty' than most of us have today."

7. Expressed, for example, by Pierre Louys in his poem, "Subscriptum tumulo Ioannis Secundis," where the cult of beauty ("La Beauté lui fit croire à la douceur de vivre"), the erotomania ("Et l'odeur de la femme enchante encore ses livres"), and the early death are chief points.

8. G. Kalff, *Geschiedenis der nederlandsche Letterkunde* (Groningen: J. B. Wolters, 1917), III, 84–85.

9. Gerald Knuvelder, *Handboek tot de geschiedenis der nederlandse Letterkunde* ('s Hertogenbosch: L. C. G. Malmberg, 1957), I, 341.

10. C. Reedijk, *The Poems of Desiderius Erasmus*, p. 33.

Selected Bibliography

BIBLIOGRAPHICAL NOTES

No new printing of any of the works of Janus Secundus in Latin has appeared since the publication of the listings by Joos, "De uitgaven der lateinsche werken van Janus Secundus," *Revue belgique de philologie et d'histoire*, 18 (1939), 5–18, save the facsimile reproduction of the 1541 Borculo. Because of the problems of text criticism which Janus Secundus' works entail—a field which the present book has not dared to enter—a critical edition of the *Opera omnia* might well be called for, also incorporating much of the commentary from Burmann-Bosscha with, it is hoped, necessary corrections of the citations of classical and other authors in BB.

In order to make Janus Secundus accessible to a general public, however, a prose translation of the whole of the elegies, and a large selection from the odes, the epigrams, the *funera* and the *silvae* is necessary. The translations by Nichols of the *Basia*, together with an epigram and the *Epithalamium*, could well be followed by a larger selection from Nichols' hand, in the style of Rat's admirable French collection. Despite the many English translations of the *Basia* and the *Epithalamium* (see the bibliography compiled by Crane, pp. 95–93), the remainder of Janus' work has been neglected. Wright's lively collection contains the *Basia*, eleven of the elegies, four of the odes, nineteen of the epigrams, and the *Epithalamium*, all in Wright's rhymed stanzas, with their advantages (they are colorful) and disadvantages (they are often at a great remove from the Latin text). The *Itineraries*, sadly, have never been turned into English, although they are available in French, Spanish, and, partially, in Dutch.

For readers who know French or German the Rat translation is recommended, as are the selections by Schaur and the Wiesner translation of the *Basia*.

The easiest means to an orientation in the huge field of Neo-Latin studies has been provided in the essay of Jozef IJsewijn, "De studie van de neolatijnse letterkunde; resultaten en opgaven," *Handelingen der Koninklijke Zuidnederlandse Maatschappij voor Taal- en Letterkunde en Geschiednis,* 17 (1963), 292–318, and

IJsewijn, "De studie van der neolatijnse letterkunde: bibliografisch supplement," *Handelingen der Koninklijke Zuidnederlandse Maatschappij,* 19 (1965), 350–62. IJsewijn has subsumed the essays into his *Companion to Neo-Latin Studies* (Amsterdam-New York-Oxford: North Holland Publishing Company, 1977). See also the continuing bibliographies in *Neo-Latin News,* edited by Paul Blackford, Lawrence V. Ryan, Jozef IJsewijn, and Gilbert Tournoy, and the annual "Instrumentum Bibliographicum" in *Humanistica Lovaniensia.* Other useful tools are Alois Gerlo and Emile Lauf, *Bibliographie de l'humanisme belge, précédée d'une bibliographie générale concernant l'humanisme européen,* Instrumenta Humanistica I (Brussels, 1965), and Alois Gerlo and Hendrik D. L. Vervliet, *Bibliographie de l'humanisme des anciens pays-bas,* Instrumenta Humanistica III (Brussels, 1972).

PRIMARY SOURCES

1. Collected Editions

Opera omnia. Emendatius et cum notis adhuc ineditis Petri Burmanni Secundi, denuo edita cura Petri Bosscha. Leiden: S. & J. Luchtmans, 1821.

Opera. Nunc primum in lucem edita. Quorum catalogum proxima facies enumerabit. Utrecht: Hermannus Borculous, 1541. A facsimile edition was published in the *Monumenta Humanistica Belgica,* 4. Nieuwkoop: De Graaf, 1969.

Opera. Accurate recognita ex museo P. Scriverii. Leiden: Franciscus Hegerus, 1631.

2. Translations

a. English

Nichols, Fred J. *An Anthology of Neo-Latin Poetry.* New Haven: Yale University Press, 1979.

Wright, F. A. *The Love Poems of Joannes Secundus.* A Revised Latin Text and an English Verse Translation, together with an Introductory Essay on the Latin Poetry of the Renaissance. New York: E. P. Dutton, 1930.

b. French

Rat, Maurice. *Jean Second: Les baisers et l'épithalame, suivis des odes et des élégies.* Traduction nouvelle avec une introduction et des notes. Paris: Garnier, 1938.

c. German

Schnur, Harry C. *Lateinische Gedichte deutscher Humanisten.* Stuttgart: Reclam, 1966.

Wiesner, Felix M., trans. *Johannes Secundus, Küsse.* Zürich: Verlag Die Waage, 1958.

Selected Bibliography

SECONDARY SOURCES

A listing of the longer works on Janus Secundus, together with a brief evaluation, follows.

BLANCHARD, ANDRÉ. *Itinéraire de Jean Second (1511–1536)*. Saumur: Girouard & Richou, 1940. Helpful but ignores other secondary literature.

CRANE, DOUGALL. *Johannes Secundus: His Life, Work and Influence on English Literature*, Beiträge zur englischen Philologie, XVI. Leipzig: Tauchnitz, and London: Williams and Norgate, 1931. Biographical chapter neglects Netherlandic sources; chapter on the influence in England valuable.

ELLINGER, GEORG, ED. *Ioannes Nicolai Secundus: Basia, Mit einer Auswahl aus den Vorbildern und Nachahmern*, Lateinische Literaturdenkmäler des XV. und XVI. Jahrhunderts, 14. Berlin: Weidmann, 1899. Discussion of the *Basia*'s sources and influences, with extensive examples.

ELLINGER, GEORG. *Geschichte der neulateinischen Literatur Deutschlands im sechzehnten Jahrhundert, III, 1: Geschichte der neulateinischen Lyrik in den Niederlanden von Ausgang des fünfzehnten bis zum Beginn des siebzehnten Jahrhunderts*. Berlin and Leipzig: de Gruyter, 1933, 1969 Pp. 28–85. Learned and informative; critical judgments unsure.

SCHROETER, ADALBERT. "Johannes Secundus," *Beiträge zur Geschichte der neulateinischen Poesie Deutschlands und Hollands*, Palaestra LXXVII. Berlin: Mayer & Müller, 1909. Pp. 165–222. Written with enthusiasm and abandon.

VAN TIEGHEM, PAUL. *La littérature latine de la Renaissance: Etude d'histoire littéraire européenne*. Paris: E. Droz, 1944, Geneva: Slatkine Reprints, 1966. Pp. 69–78. Depends heavily on Ellinger; gives account of Janus' imitators.

Index

Aarestrup, Emil, 147
Aegidius of Antwerp (Gillius Aegidius, Pierre Gillis), 142
Agricola, Alexander, 27
Agricola, Rudolf, 142
Agrippa von Nettesheim, 27
Alba, Duke of (Fernando Alvarez de Toledo), 20, 141
Albrecht of Prussia, 31
Albrecht of Wittelsbach, 23
Alciatus, Andreas, 42–51, 76, 95, 99, 120, 121
Anabaptists, 120, 143
Andreas, Valerius, 66, 166n63
Angerianus, Hieronymus, 21, 71
Arduenna, Remaclus, 27, 31
Arnold, Matthew, 27
Arthur (Tudor), 132
Aurelius, Julianus (Julien d'Avré), 68
Ausonius, 43, 163n15

Baïf, Antoine de, 105
Balde, Jakob, 127, 146, 162n9
Baldus de Ubaldis, 48
Barbey d' Aurevilly, Jules Amédée, 44
Barth, Caspar, 116, 117, 159n8
Bausanus, Petrus, 118, 119, 154n49
Baverius, Andreas, 48, 123
Beaugrant, Guot de, 27
Bembo, Pietro, 75–76
Beroaldus, Phillippus, the Elder, 77, 102, 103
Bersmann, Gregor, 139, 140
Best, Thomas W., 164n2
Beughem, Louis van, 27
Beza, Theodorus (Théodore de Béze), 116, 161n21
Bidermann, Jakob, 134; *Belisarius*, 134

Blanchard, André, 56, 67, 125, 128, 148n8, 153n43, 155n54, 156n64, 156n67, 168
Blei, Franz, 111, 160n17
Blioul, Elisabeth van (van Bladel), 14, 15, 53, 70
Boccaccio, Giovanni, 117; *Decameron*, 117
Boisot, Charles, 53–54
Boisset, Claude de, 54
Boleyn, Anne, 27
Bonefonius, Janus (Jean Bonnefons), 101, 116, 159n2, 159n8, 163n19; *Pancharis*, 159n2, 163n19
Borculo, Hermann, 71, 149n12, 166, 167
Bosscha, Pieter, 26, 41, 66, 78, 101, 129, 132, 149n11, 152n24, 156n69, 157n74, 161n2, 161n6, 167
Boswell, James, 93
Bot, P.N.M., 164n1
Brandes, Georg, 147
Brassicanus, Alexander, 153n41
Brassicanus, Janus Lucius, 37, 153n41
Brittain, Frederick, 148n7
Bronchorst, Theodoricus, 45
Bruyn, J., 153n36, 153n38
Buchanan, George, 45, 105, 116, 120, 159n8, 160n13, 161n5; *Hendecasyllabi*, 160n13; *Paraphrasis in Librum Psalmorum*, 120
Bucho ab Aytta, Bernard, 23
Budick, P.A., 66, 156n62
Bürger, Gottfried August, 104, 160n11
Burmann, Peter, 78, 101, 129, 132, 149n11, 157n74, 167
Burton, Robert, *Anatomy of Melancholy*, 150n10

Index

Buslidius, Aegidius, the Elder, 29, 123, 152n22, 152n29, 163n18
Buslidius, Aegidius, the Younger, 28–29, 37, 118, 152n29
Buslidius, Hieronymous, 27, 29, 49, 152n29–30
Buslidius, Nicolaus, 29, 37, 118, 152n29

Caimus, Marcus Antonius, 42, 48, 123
Callimachus, 73, 102, 132
Camerarius, Joachim, the Elder, 31
Cano, Sebastian del, 30
carmina nuptialia, 140
Carondelet, Jean de, 36, 37, 54
Case, Robert H., 163n15, 163n19
Catherine of Aragon, 65, 68, 69, 125–26, 128, 131–32
Cats, Jakob, 19–20
Catullus, 73–74, 84, 102, 106–107, 110, 112, 114, 134–37, 140, 144–45, 147, 159n7
Catzius, Carolus, 39–40, 53–54, 93, 99
Catzius, Franciscus, 39, 118
Cellini, Benvenuto, 37
Celtis, Conrad, 33, 123, 142, 153n41
Charles the Bold, 23, 54
Charles V, 14, 18–19, 23–24, 26–28, 31–32, 34, 39, 45, 54–57, 60, 62–67, 70, 99, 118, 121, 125, 126, 129, 132, 141, 147, 155n56, 155n59, 157n71
Charles VIII, 44
Charles the Mad, 44
Cicero, 72, 144
Cino da Pistoja (Cynus), 48, 154n46
Claudianus, 72, 137, 138, 159n10, 163n19; *Rape of Proserpine,* 72
Clement VII, Pope, 31, 34, 63–64
Clénard, Nicolas, 158n7
Clericus, Petrus, 32, 39–41, 53, 57, 84–86, 162n8
Cobella (Coebels), Anna, 52, 55–56, 66–67
Conrady, K.O., 144, 162n12, 164n5
Copernicus, 31
Corinna, 73, 83, 92
Cornelius of the Hague (Corneille de Lyon), 55, 155n53

Corpus Priapeorum, 155n58, 160n19
Crane, Dougall, 33, 41, 53, 61, 67, 70, 78, 132, 144–45, 148n2, 148n8, 156n64, 164n4, 166–68
Craneveldius (Craneveld), Franciscus, 37–38, 40, 53, 153n42
Crinitus, Petrus, 102
Cripius, Gulielmus, 21, 156n63
Cynthia, 73–74, 77, 83, 87, 92, 97

Dantiscus, Johannes, 31–35, 37, 64, 67, 82, 99, 153n32, 155n53, 155n55; *De nostrorum temporum calamitatibus silva,* 32, 153n33
Dekker, Alfred M.M., 70, 149n1, 153n36, 153n38, 157n72–74
Delia, 73, 83
Demetz, Peter, 159n10
Domitilla, 85, 87
Dousa, Janus, the Elder (Jan van der Does), 20, 101, 105, 116, 142, 144, 159n2, 159n8, 160n13, 160n20; *Basia,* 160n13
Dürer, Albrecht, 27, 34

Egmond, Georges (Joris) van, 69–70, 156n70
Egmont, Lamoral, Count of, 20, 141
Ellinger, Georg, 19, 25, 41–42, 74, 78, 84–85, 94, 101–103, 116, 123, 130, 133, 145, 147, 148n5, 148n7, 149n9, 153n43, 158n5, 159n5, 159n8, 161n4, 161n6, 168
Elst, L. Van der, 160n16
Erasmus, Desiderius, 14, 27, 30, 36, 38, 49, 69, 99, 100, 126, 131–32, 142, 145, 150n4, 152n23, 155n53, 163n18; *Echo*-colloquy, 132–33, 164n1; "Epithalamium Petri Aegidii," 163n18
Ercole II d'Este, 46
erotopaignion, 21, 117, 144
Estienne, Henri, 107; *Pseudo-Anacreontica,* 107
Eufrenius, Georgiades Albertus (Albert Joriszoon Goedhart), 116, 159n8, 161n22
Everardi, Nicolaus, 13–16, 20–27, 34, 37–38, 42, 50–52, 63, 124–25, 132, 149n1, 150n2–3, 151n20, 152n25–26; *Topicorum seu de*

locis legalibus liber, 14; *Consilia sive responsa juris*, 14
Everardus, the sailor, 13

Fabri, Felix, 43
Ferdinand V, 141
Ferdinand, King of Bohemia and Hungary, 19
Finkelthus, Laurentius, 139, 140
Fleming, Paul, 149n9, 164n3; *Rubella*, 164n3
Florenas, Dr., 55–56
Font, Jeanne de la, 48, 99, 100, 124, 154n48; *Theseus*, 99
Foppenus, J.F., 66, 156n63
Forster, Leonard, 158n12, 163n21, 165n6
Francesco Sforza, Duke of Milan, 46
Francis I, 28, 45, 55, 121
Francois of Valois (the Dauphin), 45, 69, 124, 155n53
Fugger, Johann Jakob, 24

Galesloot, L., 149n1, 150n9, 151n11, 151n12, 153n43, 155n57
Gallus, 83, 157n2
Gattinara, Mercurino, 64, 124
Gebweiler, Hieronymous, 69
Gelder, H.E. van, 22–23, 70, 151n19, 153n40, 157n72, 157n74
Gemma, Reinerus, 153n41
Gnaphaeus, Gulielmus (Willem Claeszoon de Volder), 24, 31
Goes, Damião de, 153n34
Goes, Genoveva van der, 17
Goesius, Hadrianus (Adriaan van der Goes), 38–39, 118
Goethe, 77–78, 84, 103, 108, 131, 133, *144–46*, 158n10, 160n15, 162n11; "An den Geist des Johannes Secundus," 133, 162n11; *Faust*, 133, 137; "Gesang der Geister über den Wassern," 133; "Grenzen der Menschheit," 133, 134; *Maximen und Reflexionen*, 146, 160n15; *Werther*, 77
Gossaert van Mabuse, Jan, 27, 34
Grant, W. Leonard, 161n2
Granvelle, Antoine Perrenot de, 141

Granvelle, Nicholas Perrenot de, 54, 70, 141, 157n71
Grattius Faliscus, 43
Graves, Robert, 145
Greek Anthology, 46, 47, 94, 102, 103, 120, 124, 158n12, 160n14, 161n6
Greene, Thomas L., 163n17
Grotius, Hugo, 101, 147
Gruterus, Janus; *Delitiae C Poetarum Belgicorum*, 15, 19, 20, 67, 150n2, 150n5
Günther, Johann Christian, *134–36*, 138; "Hochzeitscherz: Nach Anleitung des Lateinischen aus dem Johanne Secundo," 134–36
Guepin, J.P., 159n10, 160n17
Guicciardini, Ludovico, 151n18, 152n28
Gyraldus, Lilius Gregorius; *De poetis nostrorum temporum*, 21, 151n15

Hadrian VI, Pope, 35
Hardy, Thomas, 125
Harius, Joannes (Jan Dirckszoon van der Haer), 24
Haro, Francesca de, 30
Harsdörffer, Georg Philipp, 137
Hasselt, W.L.C. van, 70, 149n1, 152n26
Hawkins, Nicholas, 65
Heduus, 64
Hegius, Alexander, 142
Heinsius, Daniel, 43, 142
Hendrik of Nassau, 23, 155n52
Henry VIII, 14, 65, 68, *126–28*, 129, 131-32
Herder, 162n11
Hesiod, 93
Hessus, Helius Eobanus, 31, 33, 161n5; *Psalterium Davidis carmine redditum*, 161n5
"Hilarius the Poet" (Hilarius Bertulphus), 55, 155n53, 155n55
Hoen, Cornelius, 24
Hogenberg, Nicolaus, 34
Hoogewerf, G.J., 156n70, 157n72
Homer, 93
Hoorn, Philip de Montmorency, Count of, 141

Index

Horace, 35, 48, 64, 74, 82-83, 89, 102–104, 106, 108–109, 113–14, 120, 123, 129, 134, 159n10, 161n2, 162n7
Hout, Jan van, 142, 160n20
Hoverius, Franciscus (Francis de Houwers), 76, 158n7
Hoynck van Papendrecht, C.P.; *Analecta belgica*, 151n20, 154n47, 155n50, 159n3
Hurtado de Mendoza, Diego, 60, 74, 123, 156n62
Hutten, Ulrich von, 27, 142, 143
Hutton, James, 161n6
Huygens, Constantijn, 21, 141, 151n16, 157n74
hymenaeus, 136, 163n16

IJsewijn, Jozef, 166–67
Isabeau of Bavaria, 44
Isabella of Castile and Leon, 141

Jacoba of Wittelsbach, 23
Joanna the Mad, 141
John the Fearless, 54
John Albert, King of Poland, 31
Jolles, André, 69, 125, 156n68
Joos, German, 102, 148n8, 153n33, 159n6, 166
Julia, 33–34, 36, 37, 41–42, 61, 73–74, 77–94, 131, 158n9, 158n11
Julius Caesar, 18, 45
Jurisics, Nicholas, 57
Juvenal, 122

Kalff, G., 145, 165n8
Karel van Gelre, 26
Keldermans, Rombout, 27
Khaid-ed-din Barbarossa, 63
Kieveringen, Balthasar a (von Künring), 45
Knuvelder, Gerard, 145, 165n9
Kristeller, Paul, 165n6
Kuyk, J. van, 150n3, 150n9, 153n43

Lang, Matthias, 30
Lascaris, Janus, 46
Latomus, Bartholomaeus, 45
Laumonier, Paul, 148n8
Lemaire des Belges, Jean, 27

Lernutius, Janus (Jean Lernaut), 101, 116, 142, 159n2, 159n8
Lesbia, 73, 92, 106
Lipsius, Justus, 142
Löfstedt, Einar, 84, 158n10
Logau, Georg von, 33
"Lord of Nassau," 52, 155n52
Lorrain, Claude, 22
Lotichius Secundus, Petrus, 22, 33, 73, 143
Louis XI, 54
Louis XII, 44–45
Louise of Savoy, 28
Louys, Pierre, 165n7
Loyola, Ignatius, 45
Lucan, 72
Lucian, 18, 121, 128, 152n25
Luck, Georg, 157n4
Lucretius, 74, 83, 123
Lumey, Count, 15
Luther, Martin, 19, 24, 31
Lycoris, 57, 60, 83
Lydia, 60, 94
Lysippus, 82

Macrin, Jean Salmon, 156n66
Macropedius, Georg, 142, 164n2
Magellan, Ferdinand, 30
Mander, Karel van; *Schilder-boek*, 155n52
Margaret of Austria, 26–28, 30, 31, 34, 37, 64, 91, 152n27
Margaret of Parma, 141
Martial, 57, 102, 112, 122
Marullus, Michael, 21, 71, 75, 76, 102, 113, 158n7-8, 159n7; *Epigrammata et Hymni*, 76; *Epigrammaton liber*, 113
Mary of Burgundy, 26
Mary of Hungary, 18, 30
Maximilian I, 26, 30, 31
Medices, Ansovinus, 49
Meit, Konrad, 27
Melanchthon, Philip, 19, 31
Meleager, 102
Mentor, 82
Milton, John, 108
Molhuysen, C.P., 91–92, 158n11, 160n20
Molinet, Jean, 27

Molza, Francesco Mario, 68, 128, 131–32
Montaigne, Michel, 117
Monti, Hieronymus, 49, 75–77, 83, 99
Moore, Clement, 136; *A Visit from Saint Nicholas*, 136
More, Margaret, 127
More, Thomas, 27, 38, 68, 69, *124–28*, 129, 142, 156n64, 156n67–68; *Utopia*, 129
Moresinus, Hieronymus, 49
Moysia, Joanna, 67
Mulardus, Gerardus (Gerard Mullaert), 38, 40, 53
Muretus, Marcus Antonius (Marc Antoine Muret), 116, 161n23
Marmellius, Janus, 142
Musius, Cornelius, 15, 68, 150n6, 156n66
Muth, Robert, 163n16

Neaera, 57, 60–62, 76, 91, 94–95, 97–99, *102–16*, 131, 160n19
Nemesianus, 43
Nemesis, 73, 83
Nerius, Michael, 71
Nero, 64
Nichols, Fred S., 148n6, 161n24, 166, 167
Nicolai, Arnoldus, 20
Nicolai, Everardus, *16–17*, 20, 54, 58, 62–63, 65, 67, 70, 74, 139, 153n43, 155n54
Nicolai, Franciscus, 16
Nicolai, Gulielma, 150, 150n5
Nicolai, Hadrianus Marius, 15–17, *19–20*, 21, 24, 43, 45, 47, 50–51, 53, 58, 63, 65, 66–71, 78, 91, 93, 101, 118, 141, 155n51, 157n71; *Cymba amoris*, 20, 93
Nicolai, Isabella, 15, 68, 70, 149n1
Nicolai, Janus Secundus.

WORKS—POETRY:
Amores, 93, 99
Basia, 21, 24, 47, 61, 68, 71, 74, 78, 91, *101–17*, 118, 131, 137, 139, 140, 146–47, 148n6, 148n7, 148n8, 148n9, 159n5–8,

Basia—continued
160n17–18, 160n24, 163n19, 166n67
Elegies, 19, 20, 22, 28, 30, 32, 41, 44, 47, 49, 52, 53, 57–62, 64, 67, 68, *72–100*, 148n7, 166, 167
Epigrams, 14–15, 18, 22, 24, 25, 30, 34, 37–39, 44–46,47–52, 57, 60, 64, 69, 76, 110, 111, 118, *120–23*, 148n6
Epistolae, 15–17, 23, 28, 29, 32, 33–35, 40, 42, 43, 48–50, 57, 60, 74, 118, *123–24*
Epithalamium Lascivum, *134–40*, 147, 148n6, 162n14, 163n15–21, 166–67
"Expostulatio cum Neptuno," 41–42, 128, 153n43
Funera, 14, 16, 25, 28, 51–52, 64–65, 68–69, 91, 118, *124–28*, 155n51
In laudem utriusque Cupidinis, 25–26, 74
"In vicissitudinem rerum instabilemque Fortunam," 133–34
Joannis Secundi Hagiensis opera, nunc primum in lucem edita, 17
Julia Monobiblos, 41, 77–78, 82, *88–93*, 97, 104, 131, 137, 140, 146, 147, 158n7, 162n8
Luciani libellus de non credendo calumniae . . . dialogorum, 18, 128, 150n10, 152n25
Naenia in mortem . . . Thomas Mori, 68, 69, 124, *126–128*, 156n64, 156n67
Odes, 29, 32–33, 39, 64, 74, *118–20*
"Orpheus" Eclogue, 61, 131
Poetae tres elegantissimi emendati et aucti: Michael Marullus, Hieronymus Angerianus, Joannes Secundus, 21, 71
Reginae pecuniae regia, 40, 56, 63, *129–31*
"Responding Letter of Henry VIII," 131–32
Silvae, 41–42, *128–40*, 150n10
Solemn Elegies, 61, 89–91
Viator et Echo, 132–33

Index

WORKS—PROSE:
Itineraries, 43–56, 57, 66, 72, 91, 119, 123, 127, 142–43, 154n44, 155n51, 157n1, 166

Nicolai, Nicolaus Grudius, 13, 16, 17–19, 20–21, 24, 52, 56, 64, 66–68, 70, 71, 76, 92–93, 118, 151n11, 154n45, 155n56; *Negotia sive poemata sacra*, 19; *Piorum poematum libri duo*, 19
Nicolai, Petrus Hieronymus, 15–16, 150n7
Nolhac Pierre de, 155n53
Noot, Jan van der, 142

Occo, Sibrandus Pompeius, 49, 153n49
Ong, Walter J., 157n3
Opitz, Martin, 133, 136
Orley, Barend van, 27
Ottingerus, Joannes, 33, 100, 153n34
Ovid, 43, 53, 73–74, 78–79, 81, 83, 102, 112, 157n2–4; *Amores*, 78–79, 112; *Ars amatoria*, 79; *Heroides*, 104

Par, Charles de, 70
Parrhasius, Janus, 46
Paul III, Pope (Alexander Farnese), 62–63, 66, 156n63
Peerlkamp, P. Hofmann, 151n17
Paul the Silentiary, 94, 102, 103
Pérez, Antonio, 96
Pérez, Gonzalo, 57, 60, 96–97, 155n59
Perrenin, Jean, 54
Pervigilium Veneris, 135, 137–38
Petrarch, 48, 134
Petrarchism, 96, 132, 134, 147, 158n12, 163n19, 164n3
Phidias, 82
Philibert of Savoy, 27–28
Philip the Bold, 54
Philip the Fair, 13, 26, 141
Philip the Good, 23, 54
Philip II, 16, 141, 155n59
Piccolomini, Enea Sylvio (Pius II); *Euryalus et Lucretia*, 83
Pindar, 72
Pizzaro, 60

Planudes, Maximos, 46
Planudean Anthology, 46
Plato, 26, 144; *Symposium*, 26
Platpays Morinus, Jacobus, 65
Platter, Felix, 52
Platter, Thomas, 43, 52
Pliny the Younger, 72
Polites, Joachim, 45, 51–53, 68, 154n45
Poliziano, Angelo, 162n10
Pontanus, Joannes, 75, 102, 143, 147, 163n15, 163n19
Poussin, Nicolas, 22
Praxiteles, 82
Prévot, Georges, 56, 113, 154n44–45, 157n1, 160n18
propempticon, 22, 35, 153n36
Propertius, 17, 73, 78, 81, 83–84, 87, 89, 93, 97, 102, 121, 145, 157n2, 160n19
Pseudo–Petronius, 94, 158n12
Pseudo–Plato, 102
Pseudo–Tibullus, 70
Pyritz, Hans, 149n9, 164n3

Rabelais, 117, 155n53
Rat, Maurice, 41, 36, 118, 148n3, 158n12, 161n1, 166, 167
Reedijk, C., 145, 146, 152n23, 165n10
René de Chalon, 155n52
Reinaldus of Ypres, 51, 125, 155n51
Relandus, Hadrianus, 105, 160n13
Resendius, Angelus Andreas, 153n41
Rhenanus, Beatus, 70
Rilke, Rainer Maria, 84, 96, 99; *Die Aufzeichnungen des Malte Laurids Brigge*, 84
Roersch, Alphonse, 152n31, 154n44, 155n53, 158n7
Rolandus, Joachim, 153n41
Rolin, Nicholas, 54
Ronsard, Pierre de, 36, 81, 104–105, 148n8, 153n39, 160n12
Rossem, Maarten van, 26, 152n26
Rue, Pierre de la, 27
Rutilius Namatianus, Claudius, 43

Sabinus, Georg, 31, 33
Sandre, Thierry, 145, 156n61, 164n4

Sannazaro, Jacopo, 76, 102, 134, 160n14; *Arcadia*, 76; *Piscatoriae*, 76
Scaliger, Julius Caesar, 162n14
Schepper, Cornelius de, 32, 67, 156n65
Schlaffer, Heinz, 149n9
Schnur, Harry, C., 145, 148n6, 163n20, 166–67
Schroeter, Adalbert, 41, 61, 82, 112, 115, 116, 133, 145, 148n4, 158n9, 168
Scorel, Jan van, 34–36, 70, 82, 124, 153n35–37, 156n70, 157n73–74
Scriverius, Petrus, 57, 59, 71, 93, 98, 133, 134, 142, 149n13, 150n2, 151n13, 152n24, 154n44, 156n63, 157n71, 157n72, 167
Seneca, 48, 72, 132
Sidonius, Apollinaris, 138
Sigismund I of Poland, 31–32
Simonis, Jules, 36–38, 153n40
Skelton, John, 145
Smallegange, Mattheus, 149n1
Spenser, Edmund, 140, 163n17
Spitzer, Leo, 163n19
Statius, 72, 138; *Silvae*, 72; *Thebais*, 72
Stendhal, 82; *De L'Amour*, 82
Stenemola, Rumoldus, 22, 24–25, 152n24–25
Sterck, J.L.M., 35, 70, 153n35–36, 154n49
Sterck von Ringelberg, Joachim, 37
Stigel, Johannes, 19
Stratius, Joannes (Jan Strass), 59, 99
Strelka, Josef, 152n27
Strozzi, Hercules, 75
Strozzi, Titus Vespasianus, 75
Sucquetus, Carolus, 49–50, 124
Swerts, Jan, 45

Tavera, Juan Pardo de, Cardinal, 22, 58, 62, 63, 69, 70, 99, 129, 130, 155n56, 157n71
Tebaldeus, Antonius, 162n10
Tennyson, Alfred, 108
ter Horst, D.L.H., 151n11, 151n21
Tibullus, 73–74, 79, 82–83, 90, 102, 157n2

Tieghem, Paul van, 74–75, 143, 144–45, 158n6, 164n4, 168
Tissot, P.F., 101, 112, 116, 159n4
Transsylvanus, Maximilianus, 30, 152–53n31
Trevor-Roper, Hugh, 134
Trissino, Giangiorgio, 72

Vadianus, Joachim (von Wadt), 153n41
Velius, Gaspardus Ursinus, 19, 33
Venerilla, 59, 60, 93, 94, 98–99
Vergil, 15, 42–43, 48, 62–63, 65, 72, 74, 93, 94, 102, 103, 134, 159n9, 163n15; *Aeneid*, 16, 72, 102, 103; *Eclogues*, 84
Vergoes, Adriaan, 21
Vermeyen, Jan Cornelis, 27
Vida, Marcus Hieronymus, 18–19, 76; *Christias*, 19, 76
Villers, Denis de, 70
Vinci, Leonardo de, 37
Vives, Juan, 27, 38
Vocht, Henry de, 24–25, 32, 34, 36–37, 68, 70, 151n21, 152n23, 152n30, 153n32–34, 153n37, 153n42, 155n50, 155n55, 155n57, 156n64–66
Volcardus, Jacobus, 24, 25, 124, 152n23–24
Vorberg, Gaston, 160n19
Vorrink, Johannes, 148n8
Vulcanius (de Smet), Bonaventura; *Poemata et effigies trium fratrum Belgarum*, 20, 71

Wagner, Richard, 112
Weckherlin, Georg Rudolf, 104, 160n11
Wheeler, Arthur L., 163n17
Wiesner, F.M., III, 160n17, 166–67
William, Count of Holland, 23
William of Orange, 141
Winghe, Jerome de, 70
Woestijne, Paul van der, 159n9
Wright, F.A., 93, 100, 111, 113, 119, 123, 145, 148n1, 158n9, 158n13, 160n17, 166–67
Wuttke, Dieter, 162n12

Xavier, Francis, 45

Index

Xenophon, 28, 72

Zarate, Augustin de, 60, 156n60
Zassenus, Servatius, 69
Zesen, Phillip von, 133

Zuichemus, Viglius ab Aytta, 23–25, 49, 50–51, 67, 101, 151n20, 154n47, 155n49–50
Zurita, Jerónimo de, 60–62, 72, 99, 155n59, 155n61